IMAGES
of America

AVON

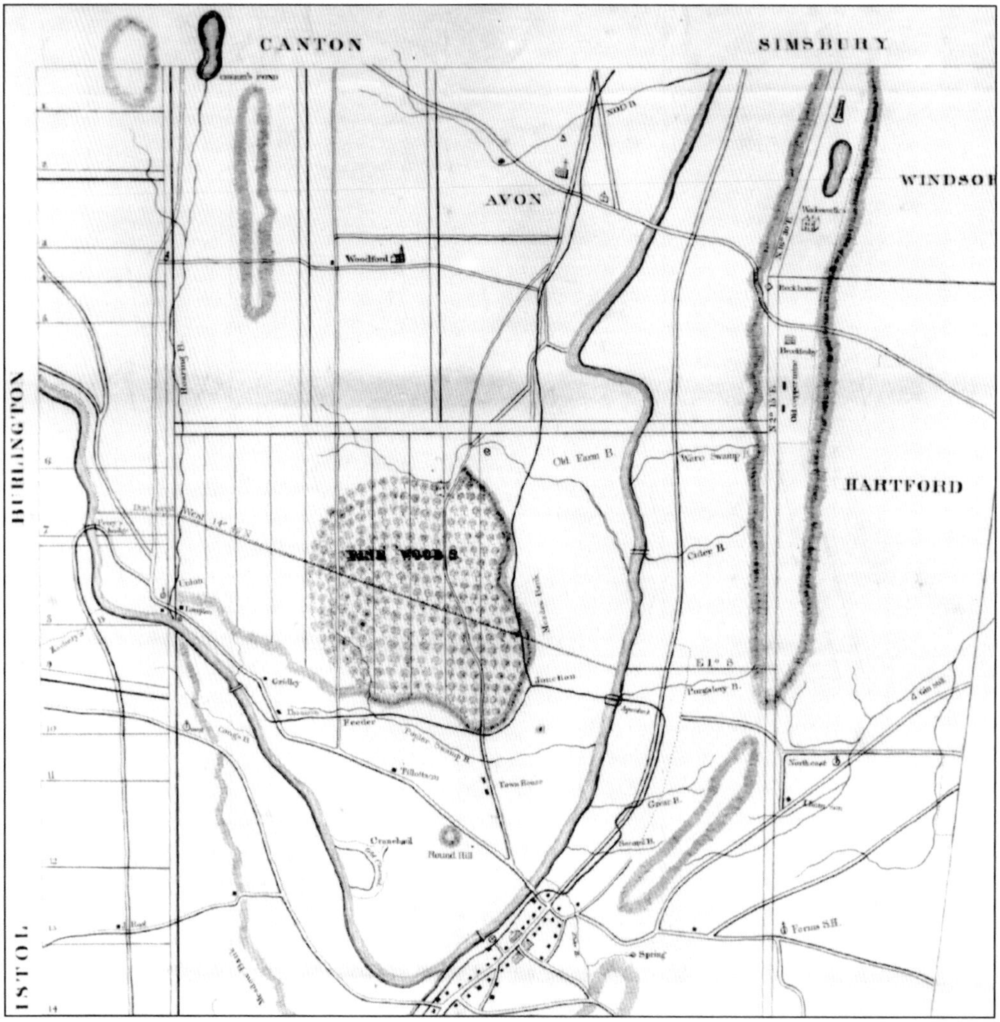

Map of Farmington and Avon, 1835. Incorporated in 1830, Avon appears near the Avon Congregational Church (at top) at the crossroads of the Albany Turnpike and Old Farms Road. The Farmington Canal is the thin dark line running through Avon, crossing the Farmington River at the aqueduct. Other features are the West Avon Congregational Church near the Woodford House, Roaring Brook, and Lovely Street, Pine Woods, and the Wadsworth Home atop Talcott Mountain. The map was published by Stodart & Currier, New York. (The Connecticut Historical Society, Hartford, Connecticut.)

On the cover: **Pine Grove Schoolhouse, 1946–47.** School No. 7 was built in 1865, closed in 1949, and is now operated by the Avon Historical Society Inc. The restored schoolhouse is on the National Register of Historic Places and is open to the public. In the background is Albert and Vesta Thompson's Cold Spring Farm. Pictured with teacher Hilda Mutch are (clockwise from the boy in the striped shirt) Tommy Burnham, George Thompson, Douglas Thompson, Edward Thompson, Dianne Scoville, Jackie Nelson, Judy Burnham, Eleanor LaMonica, Judy Horton, Grace Garrett, Elda Garrett, Nadeen Arnold, Shirley Lettre, Marie LaMonica, Carter Lee, Ray Garrett, Philip Bourque, Ronald Nelson, and Russell Mehl. (Josef Scaylea photograph, Sunrise Farm Collection.)

IMAGES
of America

AVON

Nora O. Howard

ARCADIA
PUBLISHING

ISBN 978-0-7385-0446-9

Published by Arcadia Publishing
Charleston, South Carolina

Printed in the United States of America

Library of Congress Catalog Card Number: 00104077

For all general information contact Arcadia Publishing at:
Telephone 843-853-2070
Fax 843-853-0044
E-mail sales@arcadiapublishing.com
For customer service and orders:
Toll-Free 1-888-313-2665

Visit us on the Internet at www.arcadiapublishing.com

Dedicated to Anthony O'Neill,
grandson of an Avon blacksmith, collector of Avon history, gentleman.

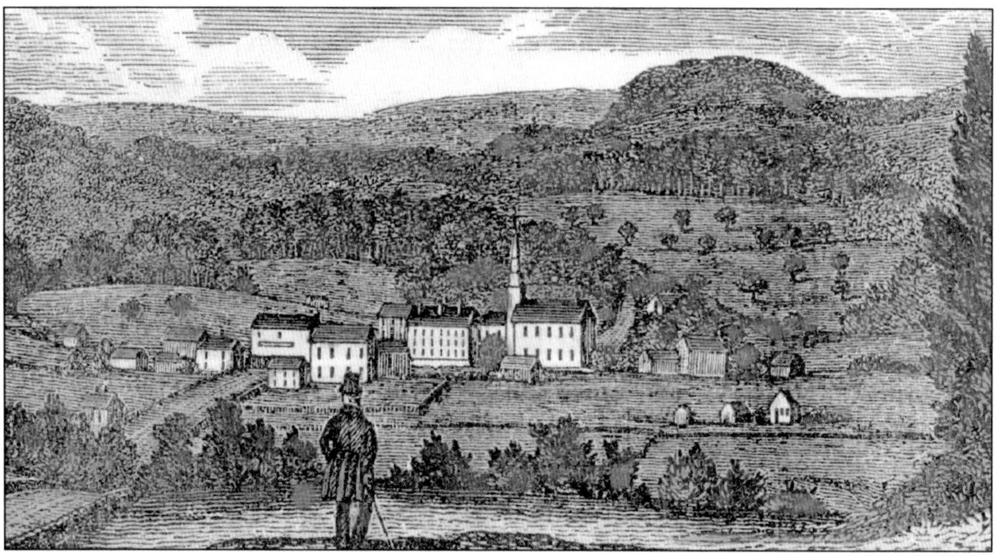

EASTERN VIEW OF AVON. John Warner Barber (1798–1885) sketched this illustration, standing atop Talcott Mountain on October 7, 1834, for *Connecticut Historical Collections*. This view looks west along Albany Turnpike (Route 44). The four largest buildings are (left to right) the Canal Warehouse, the Baptist church, the Canal Administration Building, and the Avon Congregational Church. An observer wrote that Barber's book "came upon the people like a work of magic. Few had ever seen pictures of places with which they were acquainted . . . . Never had any book been published . . . that so fed the fires of patriotism." (Nora Howard Collection.)

Contents

ACKNOWLEDGMENTS

Avon has many generous and enthusiastic people who came forward to help produce this book. I sincerely thank them all, and three in particular. Virginia Vocelli, director of the Avon Free Public Library, put hundreds of photographs and research files at my disposal. She put me in touch with people who lent photographs, coordinated the "great photographic search" that resulted in images coming to light from residents past and present, and was a guiding spirit. Photographs in the book that are attributed to the Avon Collection are from the joint collection of the Avon Free Public Library and the Avon Historical Society Inc. and are located in the Marian M. Hunter History Room at the library. A portion of the book's proceeds will be for the preservation of this superb collection. John Anthony O'Neill graciously lent me his photographs, no matter how many times I returned for more. He took them off the walls and cut them out of his displays. No request fazed him. He looked at every photograph in the book, told me caption details that only he knew, and proofread each one. Anthony's grandfather was blacksmith Patrick O'Neil, and by the time the name got to Anthony, the family had added another "l" to their last name. John Salerni, Avon Free Public Library board member and Avon High School teacher, patiently scanned the photographs onto a disk. His willingness to help was wonderful.

I also thank the Avon Historical Society, especially Peg Carnduff, Dennis Dix, Sally Garvin, Sharon Genovese, Mary Harrop, Ed Pfeiffer, Stephanie Pratt, Olive Russell, Bill Stokesbury, Len Tolisano, Terri Wilson, and Ruth Woodford. Also appreciated is encouragement from Philip K. Schenck Jr., Avon's town manager.

Many other people kindly lent photographs: Jane Hunter Bates, Robert J. Campbell, Dr. Lothar Candels, Janet Carville, Florence Lacy Cellini, the Cider Brook Miller and Bishop families courtesy of Jennifer Vazquez, Peg Curtin, Marian Dawson, Dorothy Southey Dodge, Marilyn Dumas, Martha Fitzgerald, Doris Bonesio Gaioni, James H. Hardy, Eleanor Prowe Johnson, Thomas E. MacDonald, James A. Martino Jr. (chief of police), Regina Pilitowski, Douglas Ross, Jeanette St. Peter, Barbara Plude Thomas, Audrey Thompson, Betsy Hunter Tyne, Patricia Parker Vibert, and Doris Kubik Zumbrowski.

Special collections came from Doris Miller and Seth Stewart, who donated photographs by Clinton and Frank Hadsell. Douglas Thompson and Jeannie Thompson Parker lent Sunrise Farm's collection. Carl Candels shared laughs and photographs from his lifelong collection. Kelley Lanahan donated prints from glass plate negatives that she purchased on E-Bay.

Additional contributors were the Connecticut Historical Society, the Avon Congregational Church courtesy of Rev. Edward Falsey, the West Avon Congregational Church courtesy of Rev. Don Ketcham and historian Jeannie Parker, the Friends of Heublein Tower courtesy of Kathryn Hoidge and Ed Adajian, and Avon Old Farms School courtesy of Carol Ketcham.

Of key importance were three remarkable photographers whose work resides in the Avon Collection: Marvin Deming, Dwight Douglas, and Lewis Mills.

For research assistance I thank Robert and Gladys August, Michael Brighenti, Silvio Brighenti, Stephen Brighenti, the Connecticut Department of Motor Vehicles, the Connecticut State Library, Shirley Corso, Dwight and Betty Douglas, Caroline B. LaMonica, Wick Mallory, Arthur Neriani, Gordon Clark Ramsey, Abbott and Jessica Rhodes, Thomas Rotondo, Rose Bussolini Wollman, and Raymond Zacchera. Mary-Frances MacKie's book *Avon, Connecticut* and Bill Goralski's series of books on Avon were invaluable.

Finally, I gratefully acknowledge others who helped with *Avon*: my editor, Pam O'Neil; my mother, Elinor Oakes; Kathy Iacovazzi; Jean Martin; Ed Mitchell; and Jan Owens. My husband, Roger Howard, and our children, Jackson and Samuel Howard, receive a very special thank you.

—Nora O. Howard, June 2000

INTRODUCTION

Avon was incorporated in 1830, a blink of time away. There is a story worth knowing before then. Some 200 million years ago, dinosaurs with daunting names walked here: Coelophysis, Anchisaurus, Eubrontes. Some 4 million years ago, a shallow sea covered Connecticut, and mountains as grand as the Alps rose up. Time blew the mountains away bit by bit, and rivers carried their pieces to places such as Avon, located low and central. Over eons, this sediment hardened into sandstone and shale. Then came fiery lava and grinding earth, which twisted itself into the steep cliffs of Talcott Mountain.

For the next 2 million years, glaciers came and went. Thick ice buried Avon at least four times, rubbing the rocks raw and leaving boulders from Vermont, New Hampshire, and Massachusetts. It was enough to make a river go crazy. The Farmington River, which once flowed south, cranked into reverse and burst into the Connecticut River at Tariffville Gorge.

And then, that part of the show was over. Some 25,000 years ago, after the ice left, mastodons moved in. About 10,000 years ago, the area was settled by the River Indians. This confederation of local tribes sold land to the English, and the Town of Farmington was established in 1645.

Out from Farmington came Stephen Hart, the first settler to own land in what is today called Avon, called then the "land att Nod." In 1750, the land of Nod broke off from Farmington, when the General Assembly established it as the separate parish of Northington. With this, Northington took control of its religious affairs, called its first pastor in 1751, and built its very own meetinghouse.

These were fine improvements to life in Northington. At the time, there were about 160 residents, who wrote that they had "reason to hope, with the blessing of God on our labors, [that] we shall be well able to support the Gospel among ourselves for the future . . . ."

The location of the new meetinghouse, however, split the parish in two. Most homes of that day were located east of the Farmington River in the Waterville Road vicinity. Accordingly, the Hartford County Court said that the meetinghouse must be there. However, 22 inhabitants living west of the river signed a petition claiming hardship at crossing the river to attend church. The court did not budge, and the first meetinghouse went up in 1754.

Northington's population in the west grew, and there was no bridge to get to church until 1763. Even then, ice and floods destroyed the 1763 bridge; at least five others over the next few decades.

Time and population growth and a suspicious meetinghouse fire in 1817 resolved the issue. With the development of Lovely Street and Whortleberry Hill to the west, power shifted in that direction. Every voice counted for the vote to build a new meetinghouse in what is today West Avon. The new building went up in 1818 (today, the West Avon Congregational Church on Country Club Road). The Northington Society from east of the river built its own new meetinghouse the following year (now the Avon Congregational Church on West Main Street).

With the meetinghouse issue at rest—if not exactly at peace—it was time to make the parish into a town. The business outlook appeared rosy with the completion in 1828 of the Farmington Canal, a 36-foot-wide highway of water linking Avon to Northampton, Long Island Sound, and New York City.

In 1830, the General Assembly approved the vote making Northington Parish the Town of Avon. The town had 1,205 residents, two Congregational meetinghouses, a Baptist church, the Farmington Canal, a bustling Canal Warehouse, Francis Woodford's three-story hotel across the road from Obadiah Gillet's Tally Ho Tavern and Inn, and the Talcott Mountain Turnpike running through town from Hartford and then on to New Hartford and Albany, New York. With the turnpike and the busy canal, Avon was at a dynamic crossroads.

Six years later, in 1836, Avon was among the towns included in *Connecticut Historical Collections*, John Barber's sumptuous book on the history of the state. Barber described Avon as "for the most part a level and fertile tract of land in the valley of the Farmington river, between two mountainous ridges on the east and west."

John Barber got that one right. Avon was fertile. Families thrived on dairy, poultry, and tobacco farms, notably the Alsop, Buckland, Colton, Delbon, Distin, Stone, Strong, Thompson, Watson, Westerman, and Viti farms.

Avon agonized through the Civil War, sending off a heartbreaking sum of 98 men to fight when the whole population of the town was only 1,059. Of those who went to war, 25 did not return. For World War I, Avon contributed 77 men, thankfully losing none of them. For the World War II, 300 Avon men and women served, with losses numbering 13.

Avon blossomed with the coming of energetic and talented men and women from Italy, Ireland, Eastern Europe, and Germany. These new residents worked at the impressive yet volatile fuse factory, farmed, and operated shops. Education advanced even within the constraints of one-room schoolhouses. Pleasures and problems brought on by the automobile continue today.

Avon's past is present. The 1778 First Company Horse Guards still operates. The Town converted the former Ensign-Bickford Company fuse factory buildings into offices and workshops. Early Avon is frozen in the remarkable diaries of Rev. Rufus Hawley, covering the period from 1767 to 1812, and the journals and notebooks of Frank Hadsell, covering the years from 1845 to 1942. Frank and his brother Clinton Hadsell, both photographers, left behind hundreds of glass plate negatives taken *c.* 1889 to 1919, when Avon's population was just over 1,000.

People and places of special interest include the Heublein Tower overlooking Avon, a familiar landmark. It was there that the Republicans asked Gen. Dwight David Eisenhower to run for president. The innovative Avon Old Farms School for boys opened in 1927, planned and financed by Theodate Pope Riddle, an architect with personal flair and firm convictions about design. She first employed stonemasons from the English Cotswolds and later, skilled Italian immigrants, who had built Ensign-Bickford's stone buildings.

In Avon's landscape are reminders of the Farmington Canal, the railroad, and the Albany Turnpike (Route 44). The Avon Historical Society operates the restored Pine Grove Schoolhouse, the Living Museum, and the Derrin House, an 18th-century farmhouse.

This photographic history of Avon stops in 1950. In those years, Avon's population was projected to soon pass 5,000. Thus, town officials adopted a development plan in 1954 and began a new era in local history.

Avon today has 15,500 residents. The Hadsell brothers would hardly recognize the place. With this book, though, we better recognize theirs.

One

Avon Grows

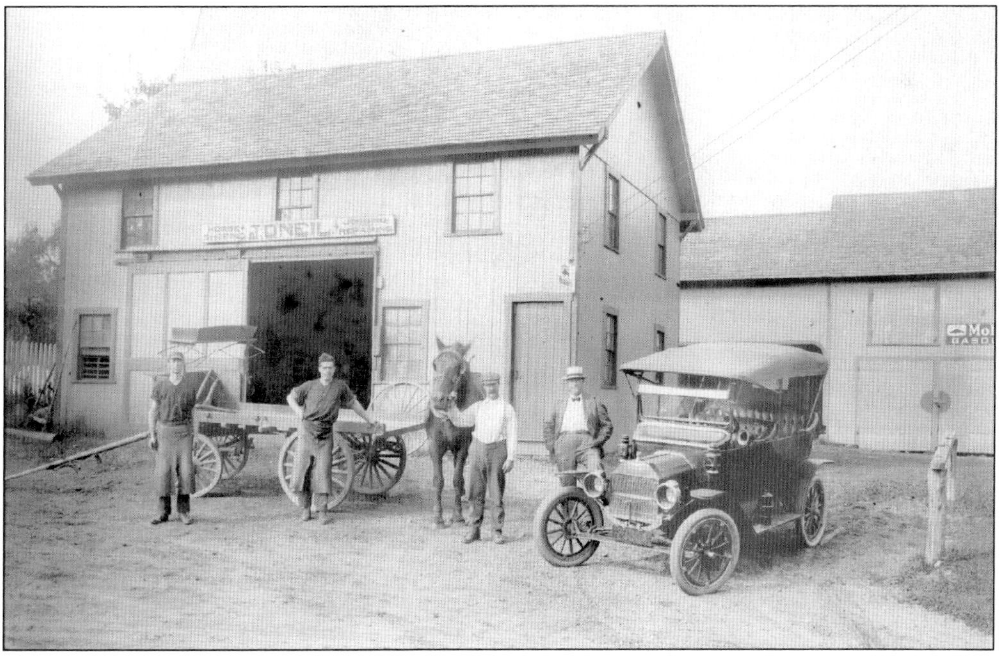

O'Neil's, 1915. The O'Neil blacksmith and transportation business began in 1886 and is today O'Neill's Chevrolet-Buick Inc. The company is Avon's oldest continuously run business with employees. Pictured from left to right are Tom O'Neil, John H. O'Neill (1892–1957), Fred Read, and Ben Miller. The sign reads, "horse shoeing, jobbing, repairing." John O'Neill continued his father's business, installing a gasoline pump *c.* 1912 and selling Mobil gas. Beside the hitching post is a 1913 Ford. The electrical lines were probably installed soon after June 1908, when Unionville's Union Electwric Light & Power Company advertised low-cost electrical installation and fixtures to Avon customers. "Has it occurred to you," said the advertisement in the Farmington Valley Herald, "what a nice Christmas present an installation of this sort would be to your family?" (Anthony O'Neill Collection.)

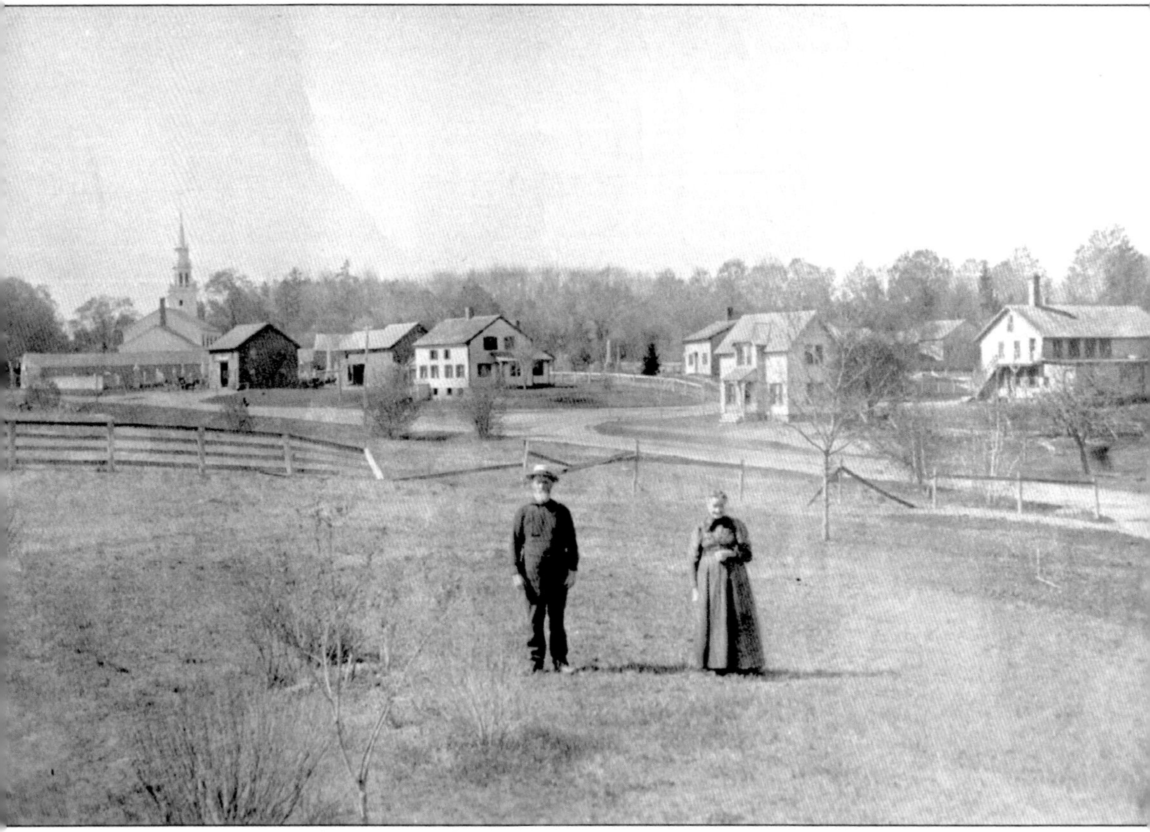

AVON, C. 1910. This view looks south into town. Pictured are the Avon Congregational Church with its long and low carriage barn, Patrick O'Neil's blacksmith shop and home (to the right of the carriage barn), a house at 27 Simsbury Road, still standing and built *c.* 1883, and the Creamery (still standing, far right). (Anthony O'Neill Collection.)

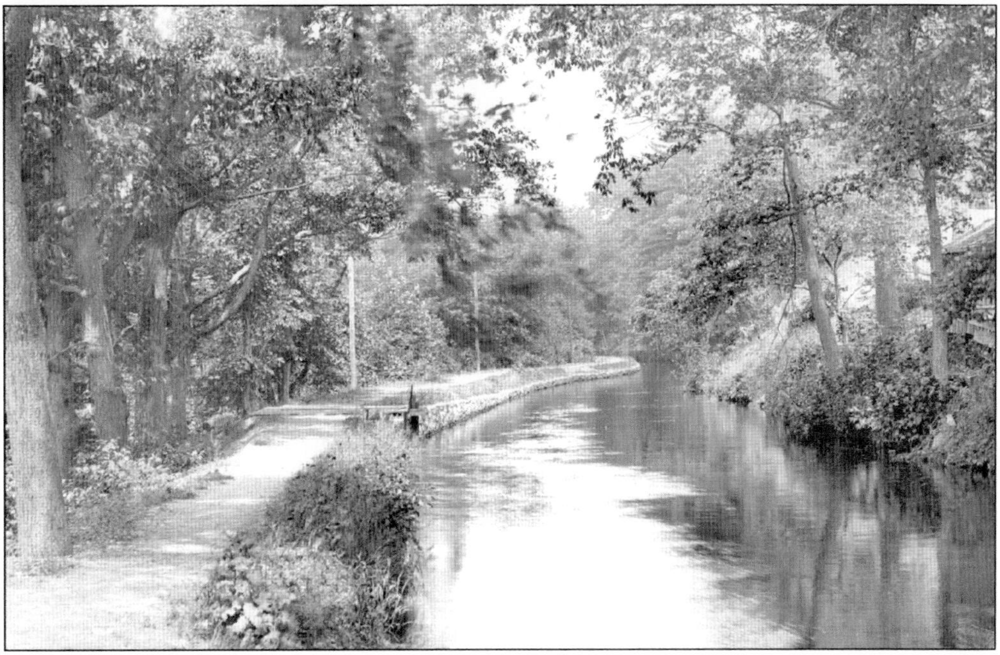

THE FARMINGTON CANAL. The Farmington Canal Company was formed in 1822. In 1828, the canal opened from New Haven to Simsbury, winding through Avon. Seven years later, the canal went to Northampton. It operated for almost 20 years, ceasing in 1847 with the coming of the railroad. Mules pulled freight and passenger boats along the canal. The ten-hour trip from Avon to New Haven cost $1.75. (Avon Collection.)

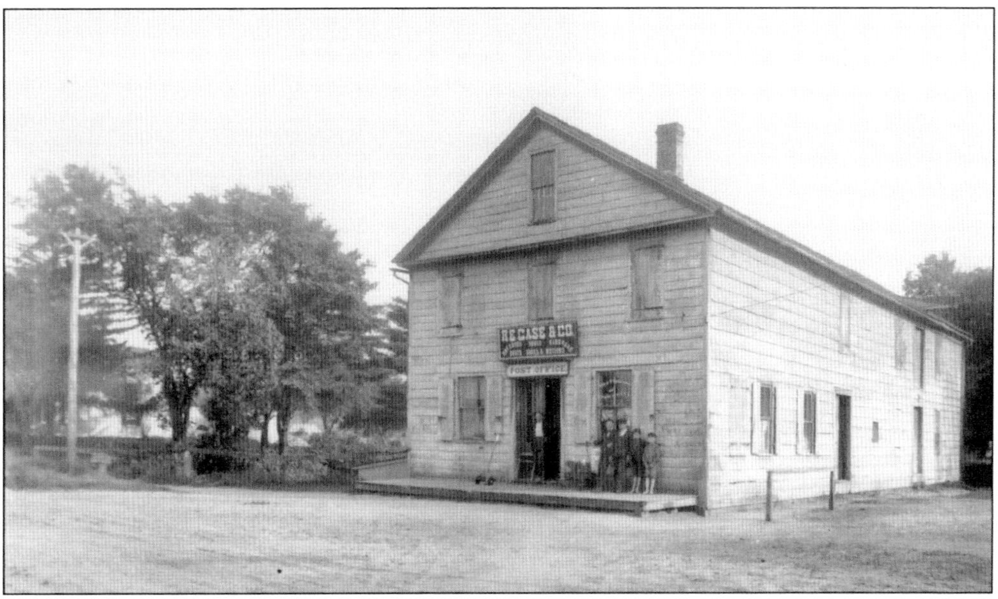

CASE & COMPANY AND POST OFFICE, C. 1907. Boys stand outside Case's (located later across the street). The sign over the door reads, "R.E. Case & Company, Dry Goods Drugs Hardware Boots Shoes & Notions Post Office." When this was the Canal Warehouse, the Farmington Canal ran along the left of the building, under the road. (H.P. Foote photograph, Avon Collection.)

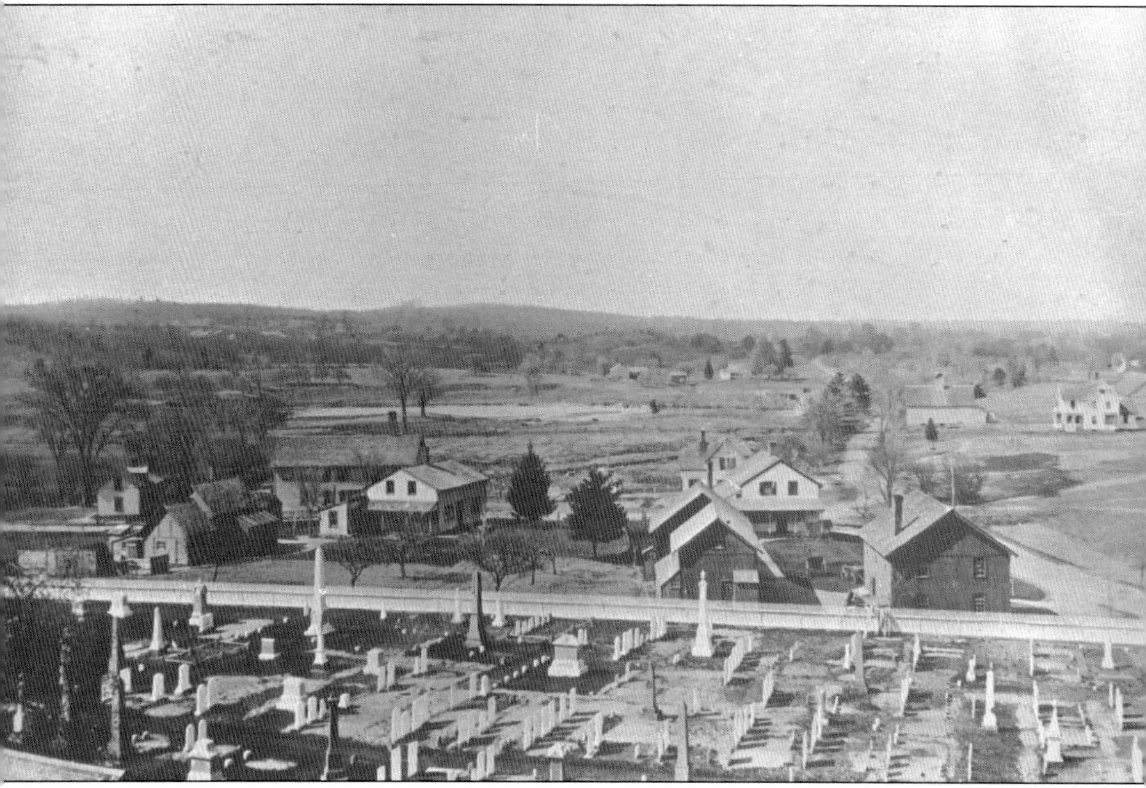

NORTH FROM THE AVON CONGREGATIONAL CHURCH STEEPLE, EARLY 1900S. Patrick O'Neil's blacksmith shop is at the center, to the left of Simsbury Road. Beside the tracks is the train

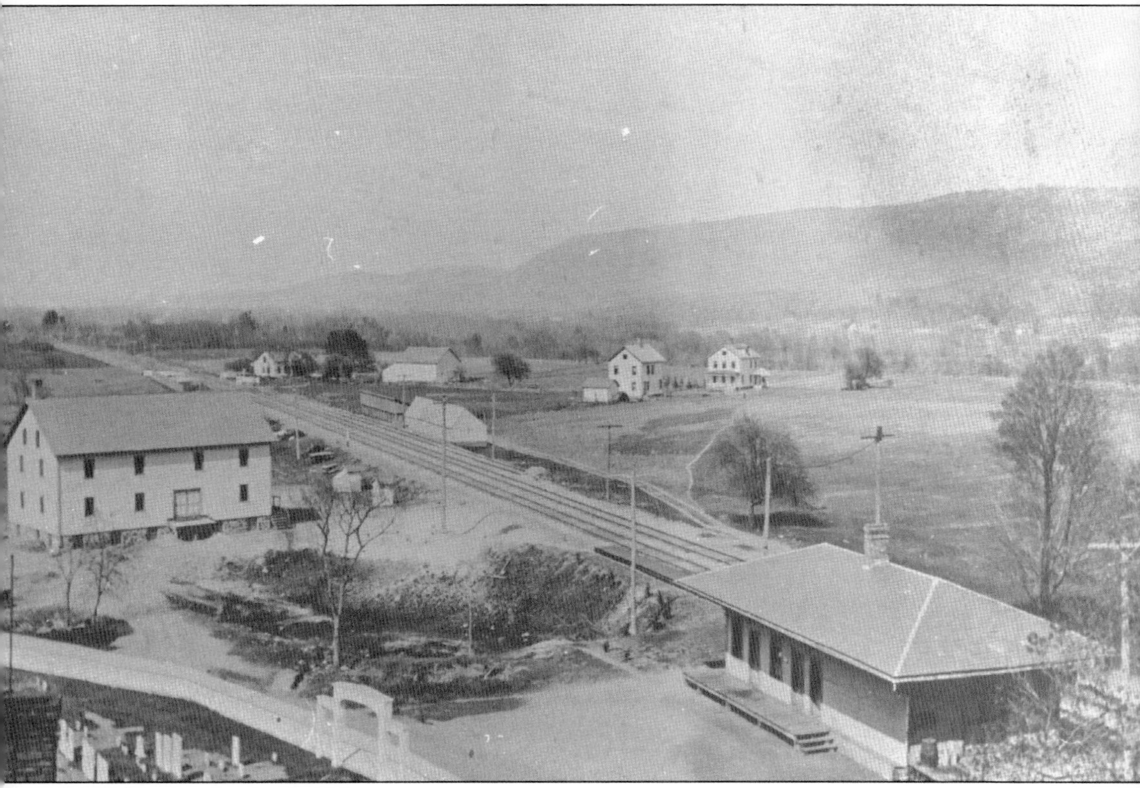

station. The Tobacco Warehouse is the four-story building to the right. (Avon Collection.)

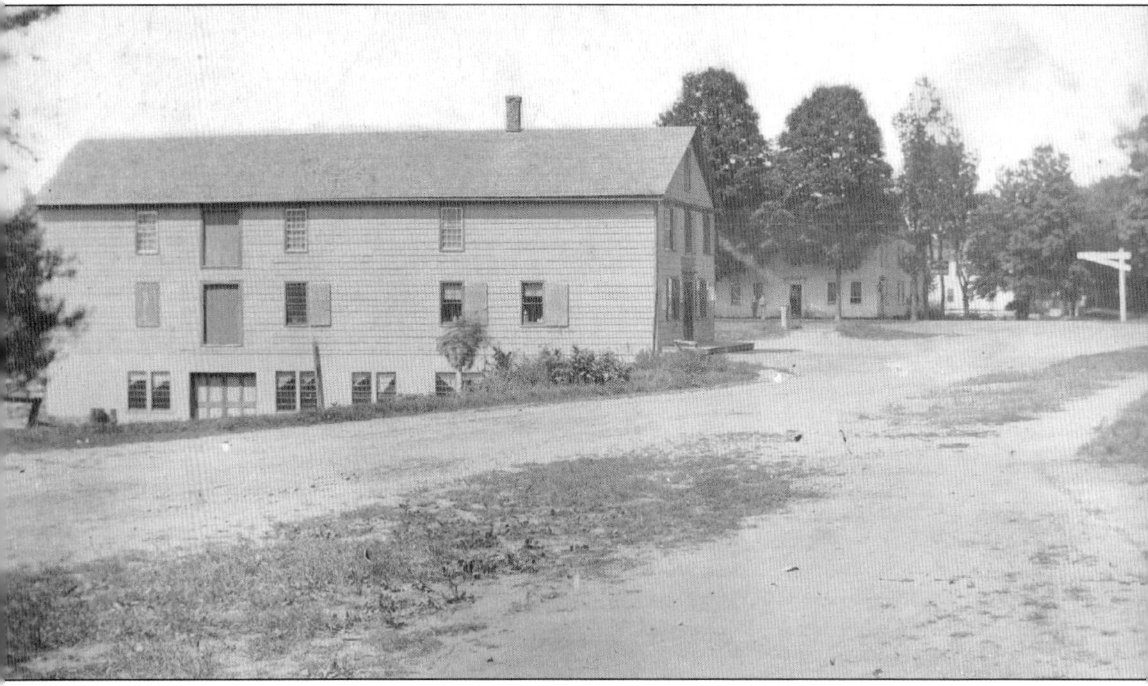

THE CANAL WAREHOUSE, POSSIBLY 1889. The Canal Warehouse was built in 1828, the same year that the canal opened. It was located at the southeast corner of Old Farms Road and Albany Turnpike. Using the canal, Avon exported lumber, tobacco, cheese, cider, produce, iron, and wood items, such as wheel spokes. In 1830, the post office moved here from the Marshall Tavern. After the canal closed in 1847, the building served as a Tobacco Warehouse and a general store. The store was owned by R.E. Case and then, from 1923 to 1932, by Henry Kopp. The building burned down on March 5, 1932. This photograph is possibly by Frank Hadsell, who after the fire wrote that in 1889, he had taken "a fine photo of this old Building before any alterations had been made, and very glad I am now that I did so." (Frank Hadsell photograph? Anthony O'Neill Collection.)

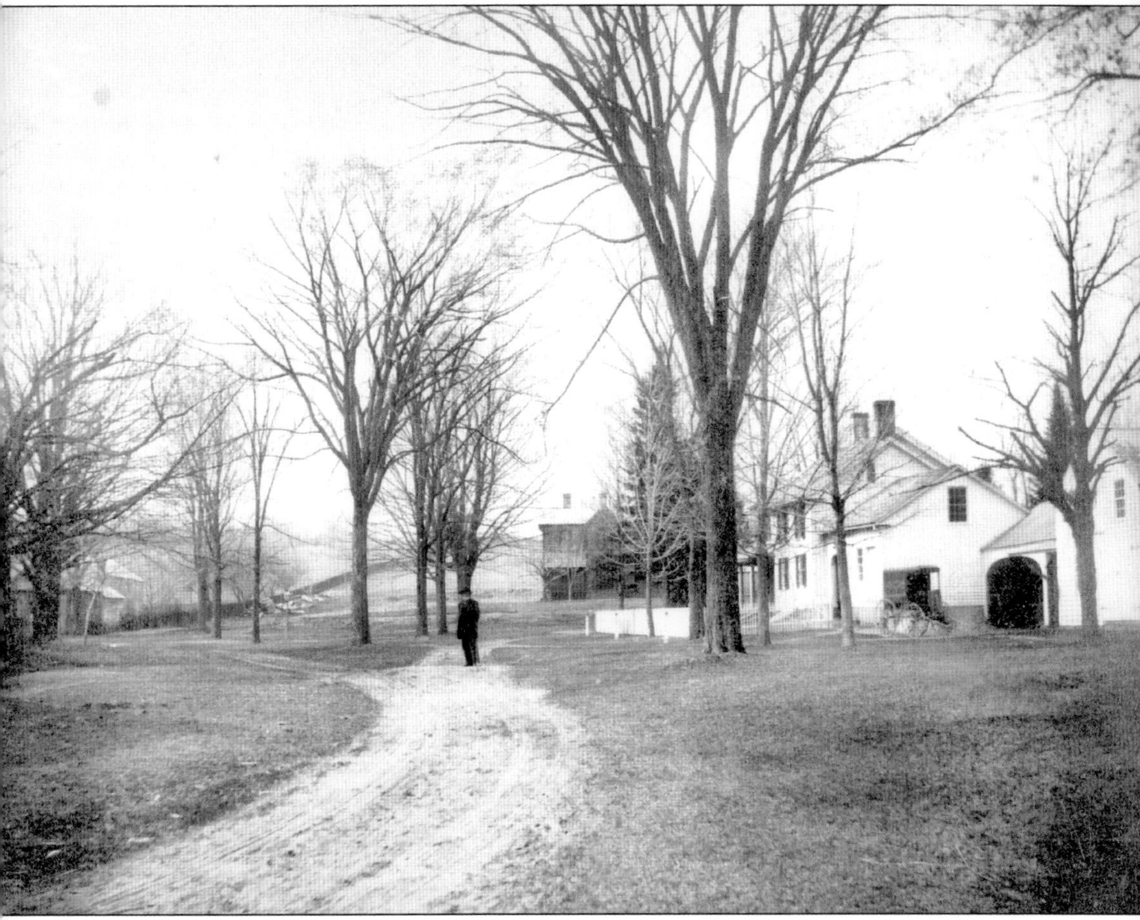

WOODFORD AVENUE, 1890. This view looks south from Woodford Avenue toward West Main Street. At right is the residence of Walter Stowe. Using the wagon pictured, Stowe delivered sewing machines for decades to valley residents. The wagon is now in the collection of Anthony O'Neill. (Anthony O'Neill Collection.)

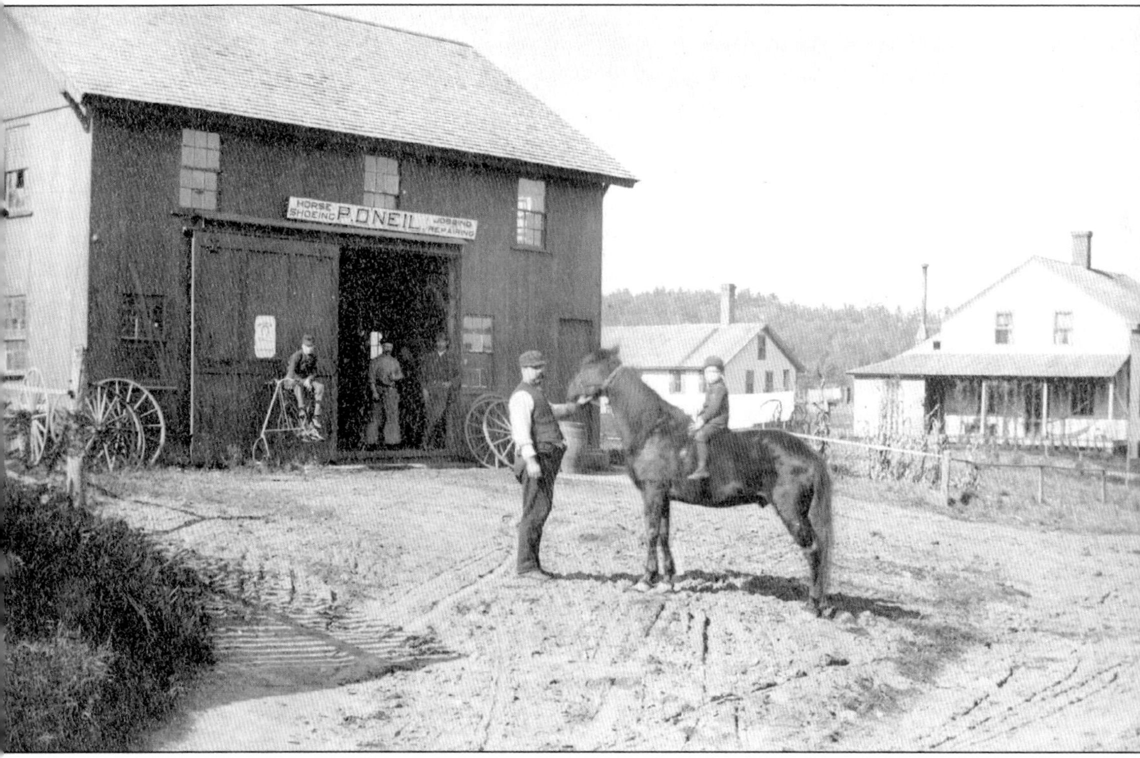

O'NEIL'S BLACKSMITH SHOP, 1894. Patrick O'Neil's second blacksmith shop, built in 1889, stands beside 25 Simsbury Road. On the right is Avon's Creamery and Patrick and Bridget O'Neil's home. Pictured is Patrick O'Neil, holding a horse with his son Thomas P. O'Neil (1885–1935). Patrick O'Neil died in 1909 after a horse kick to the head. His wife, Bridget O'Neil, known for her compassion in dressing the dead, died in 1939. (Anthony O'Neill Collection.)

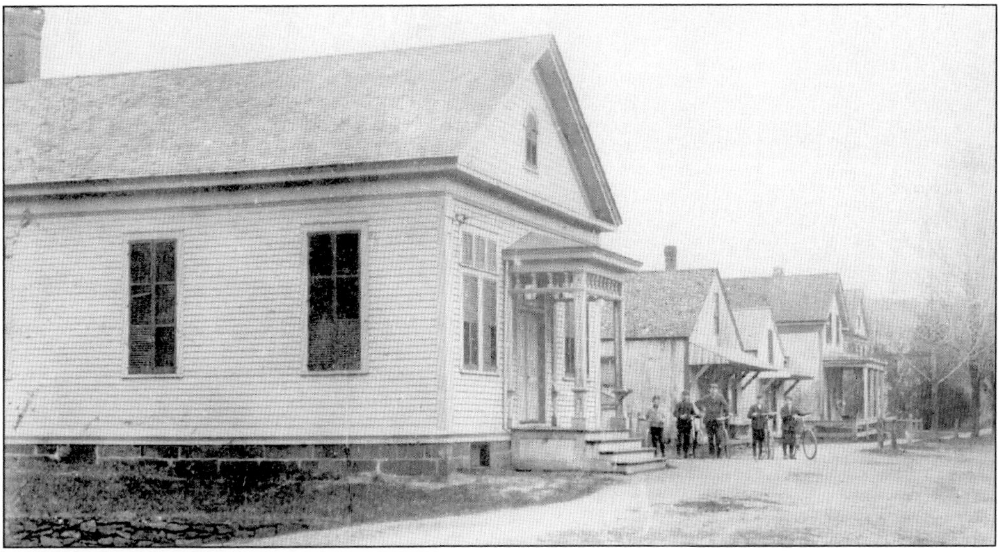

AVON TOWN HALL, C. 1906. Boys gather beside the Avon Town Hall in this postcard view, sold by Frank Hadsell in his shop (third building from left). Located on the present site of the Living Museum, the town hall was used for meetings, socials, dances, basketball, and movies. Built in 1891, it burned down and was demolished in 1967. Talcott Mountain appears in the distance. (Frank Hadsell photograph, Anthony O'Neill Collection.)

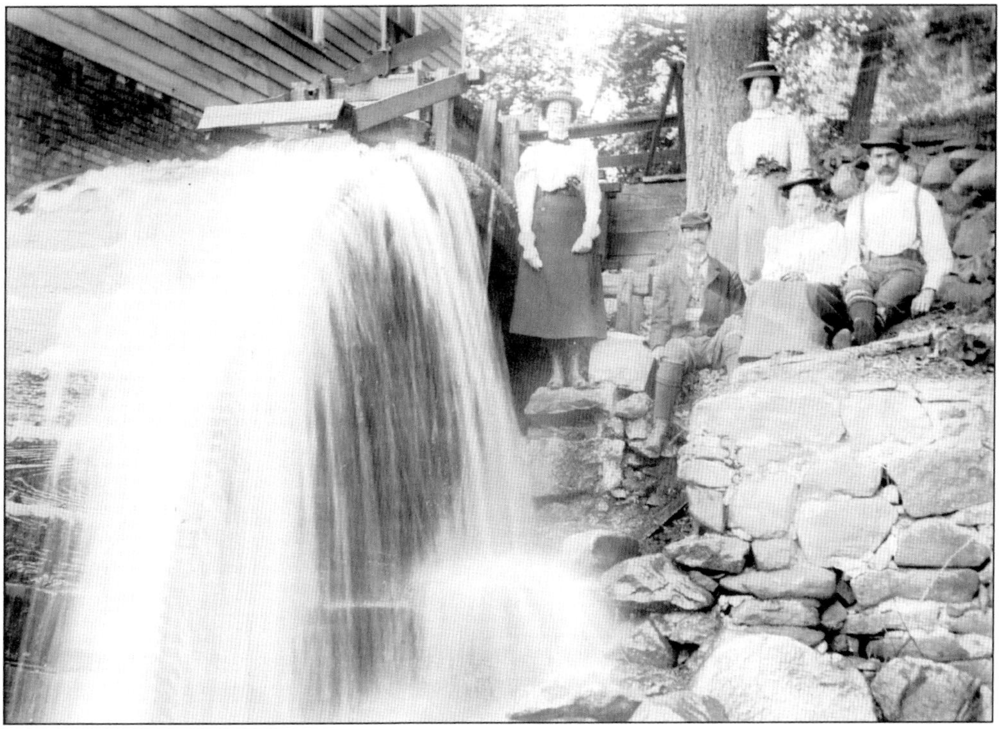

LUTHER WHEELER'S MILL, JUNE 4, 1899. Mary O'Neil (1884–1950), left, is shown at Wheeler's Mill on Woodford Avenue. Luther Wheeler and his son George Wheeler ordered corn, wheat, and oats through a broker in Chicago. The grain arrived on freight cars and was ground up at the mill for people and animals. (Anthony O'Neill Collection.)

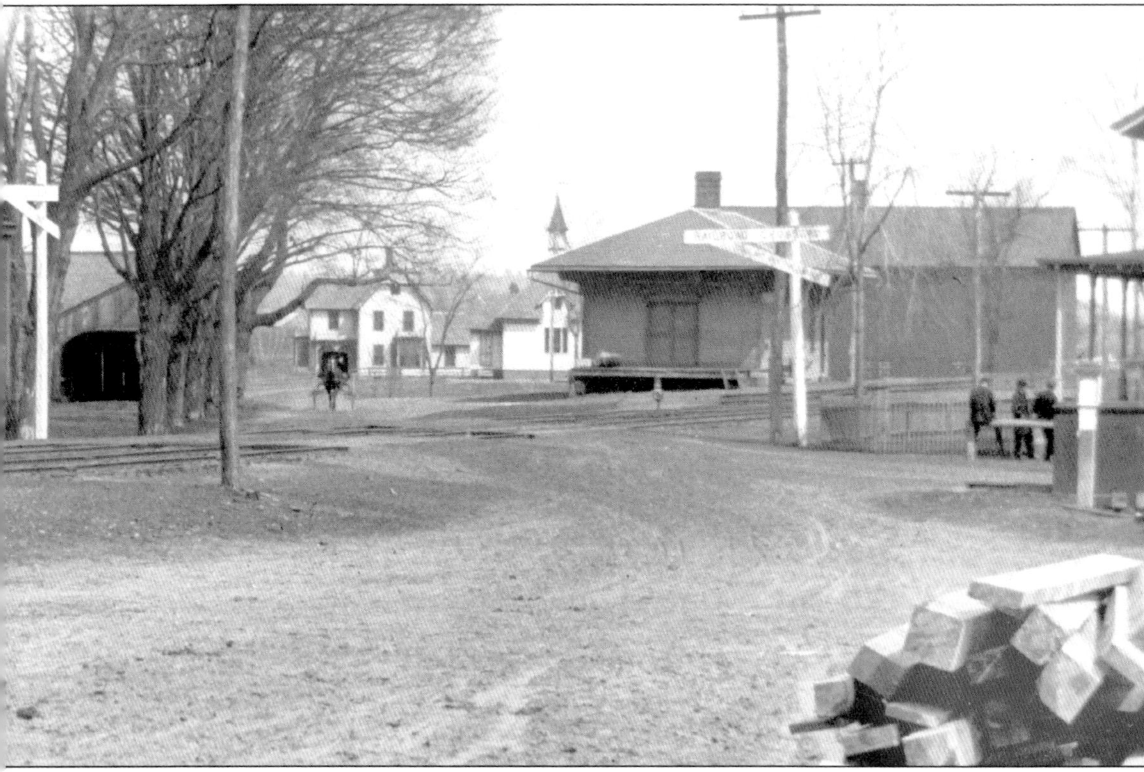

AVON CENTER, C. 1906. This view of Route 44 at Old Farms Road looks northwest. The horse and carriage are on Simsbury Road. Clockwise from the left are the Avon Congregational Church horse shed, the Neville House, Towpath School, the railroad station, the Avon Tobacco Warehouse, and part of Gabriel's store. (Frank Hadsell photograph, Avon Collection, courtesy of Seth Stewart.)

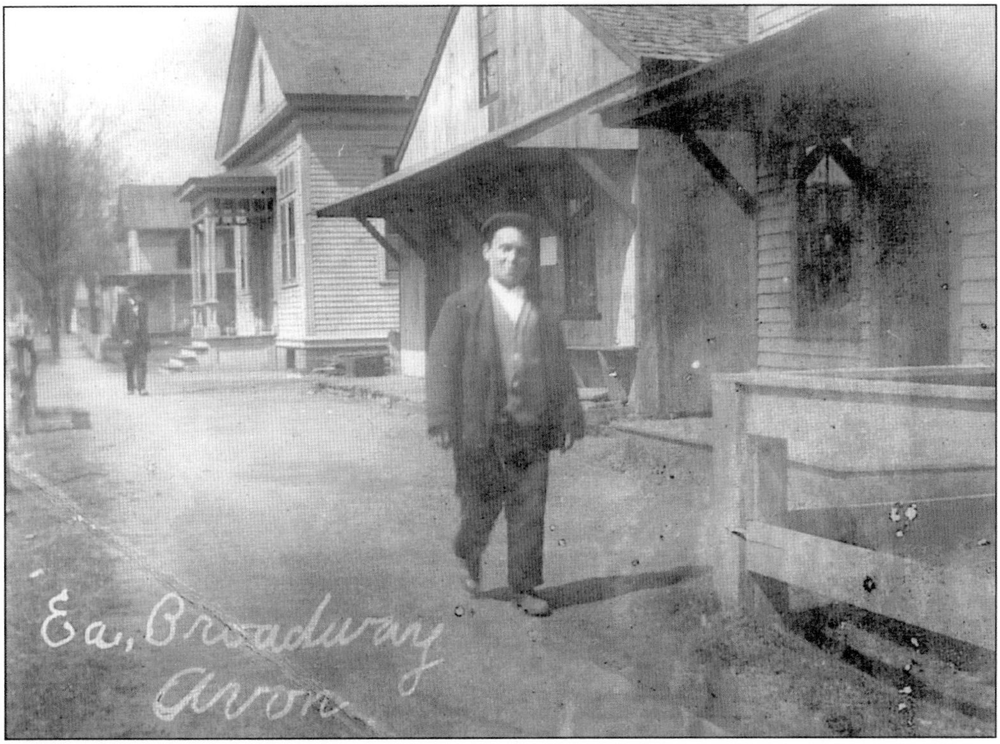

EAST MAIN STREET, C. 1906. This photograph looks west and shows, from left to right, Oliver Gabriel's store, the Avon Town Hall with the front steps, a shop that burned in 1925 and later became the site of Kulpik's Restaurant, and Frank Hadsell's variety store. The fence on the right belonged to the Hadsell home. (Avon Collection.)

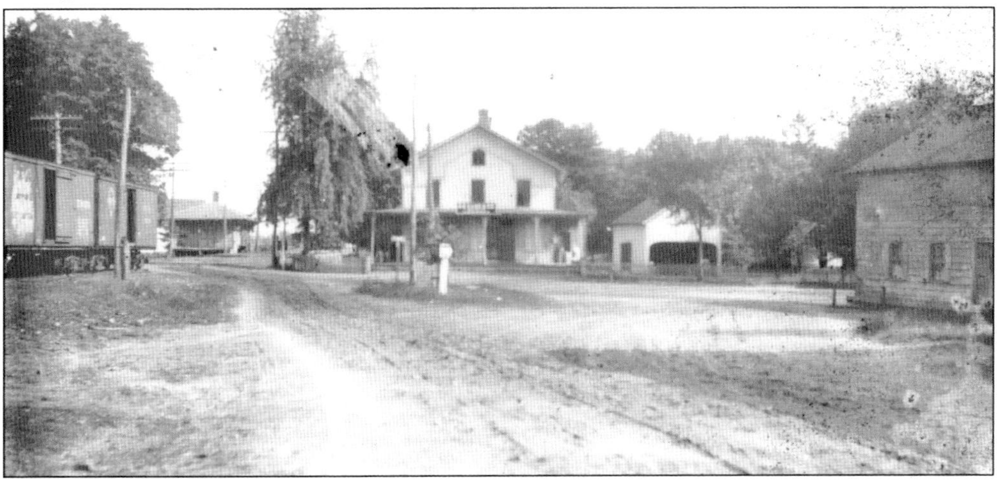

"STREET LOOKING NORTH FROM OLD SCHOOLHOUSE, OCTOBER 1907." This view looks north from Old Farms Road with, from left to right, freight cars, the railroad station, Case & Company, and the former Canal Warehouse. The building housing Case's had been built nearby in 1817 as the Baptist church. From 1870 to 1932, different stores were here—sometimes the post office was too. In the 1930s, Jack Brighenti moved the building to 6 Old Farms Road and rebuilt it for the Avon Appliance & Electrical Company. (Clinton Hadsell photograph, Avon Collection, courtesy of Doris Miller.)

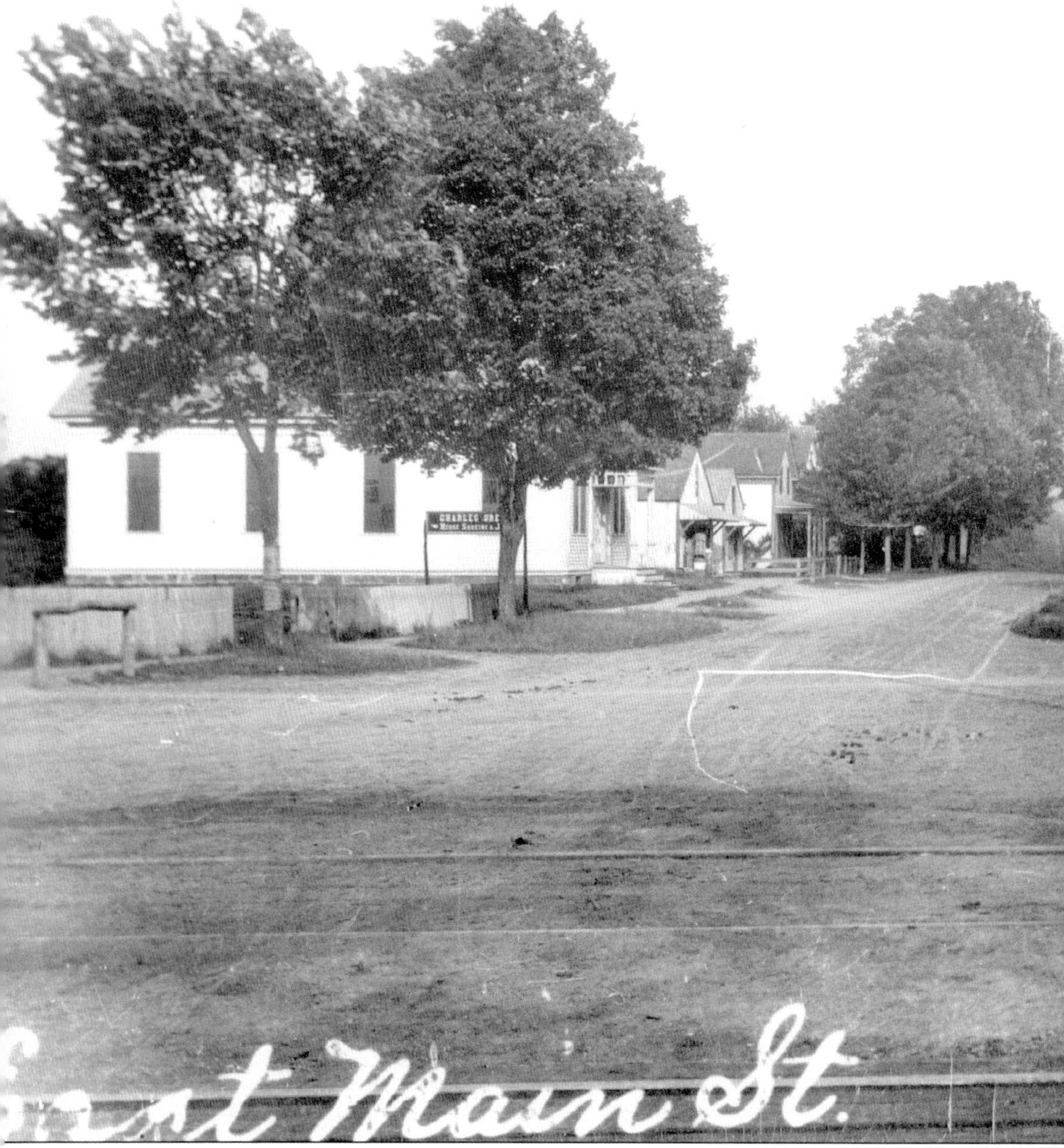

EAST MAIN STREET, C. 1910. This view shows, from left to right, the Avon Town Hall, the LeGeyt store and post office at 10 East Main that burned in 1925, Frank Hadsell's variety store, and the home of Frank Hadsell and his mother, Jane Hadsell. At the right is the former Canal Warehouse, which housed at this time the general store of Case & Company. In the foreground

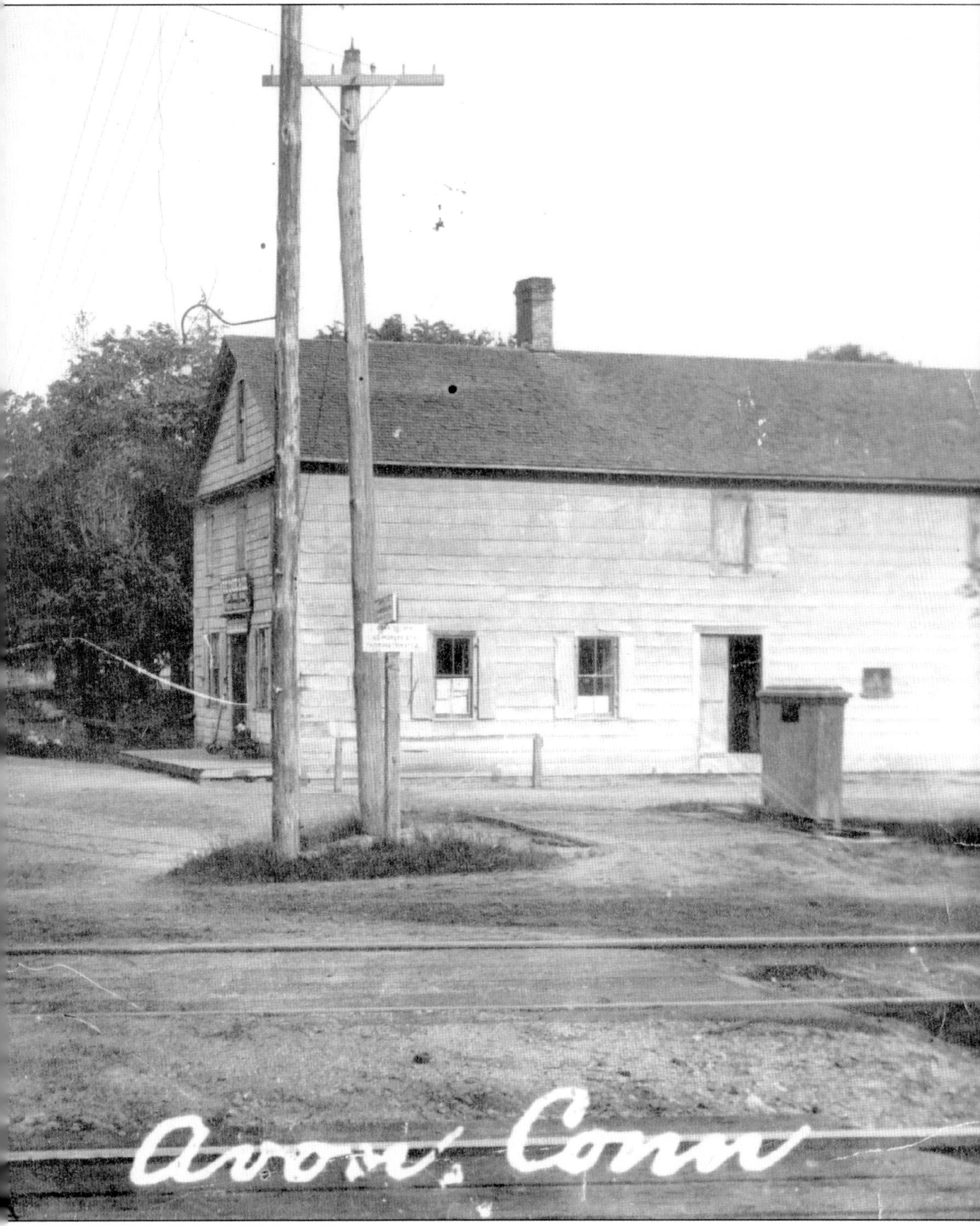

are railroad tracks and hitching posts. At the left is a sign for horseshoeing. On the electric pole is a sign with mileage to Farmington and Simsbury. Talcott Mountain is in the distance. (H.P. Foote photograph? Avon Collection.)

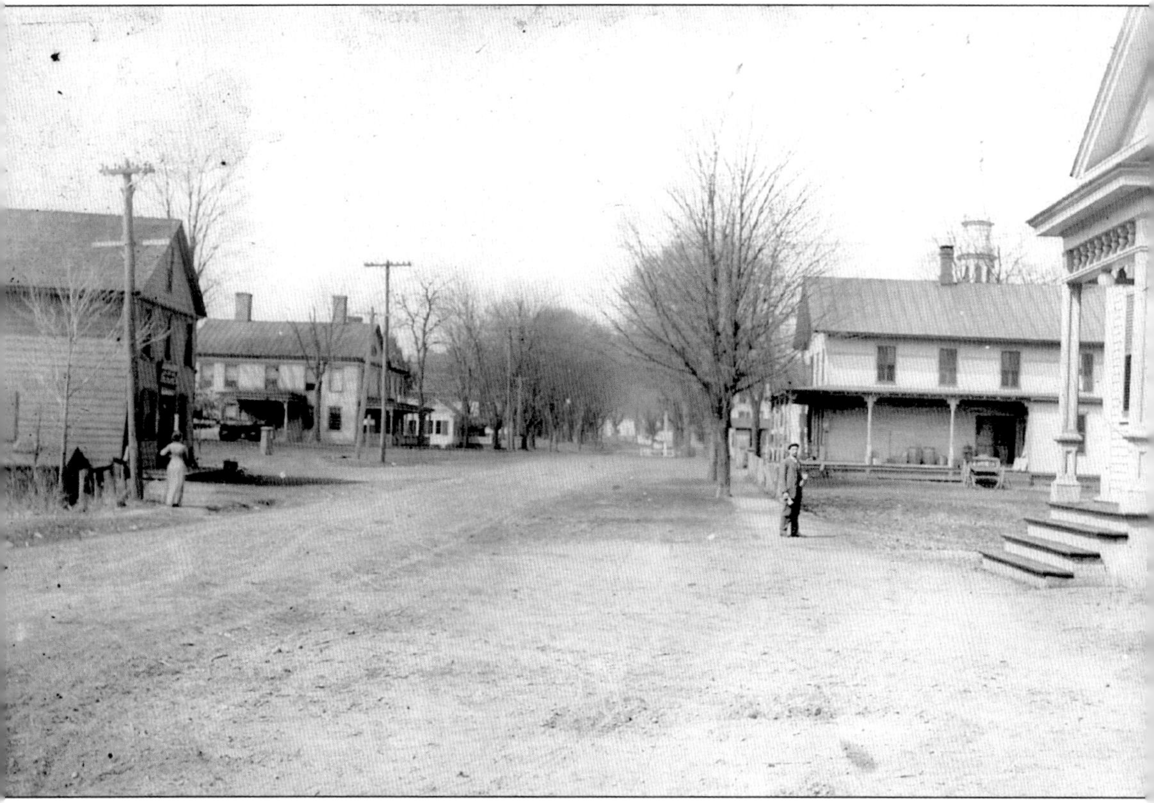

East Main Street, c. 1906. At left is the Tobacco Warehouse, the former Canal Warehouse. Across the street is Gabriel's store, and at the far right is the Avon Town Hall. In 1911, Frank Hadsell had "1,000 cards made from one of my photographs of the street looking west from my store. This card sold well as it included a view of the town hall, Gabriel's store, the old warehouse, R.R. crossing and the old Franklin Woodford House." (Frank Hadsell photograph, Avon Collection.)

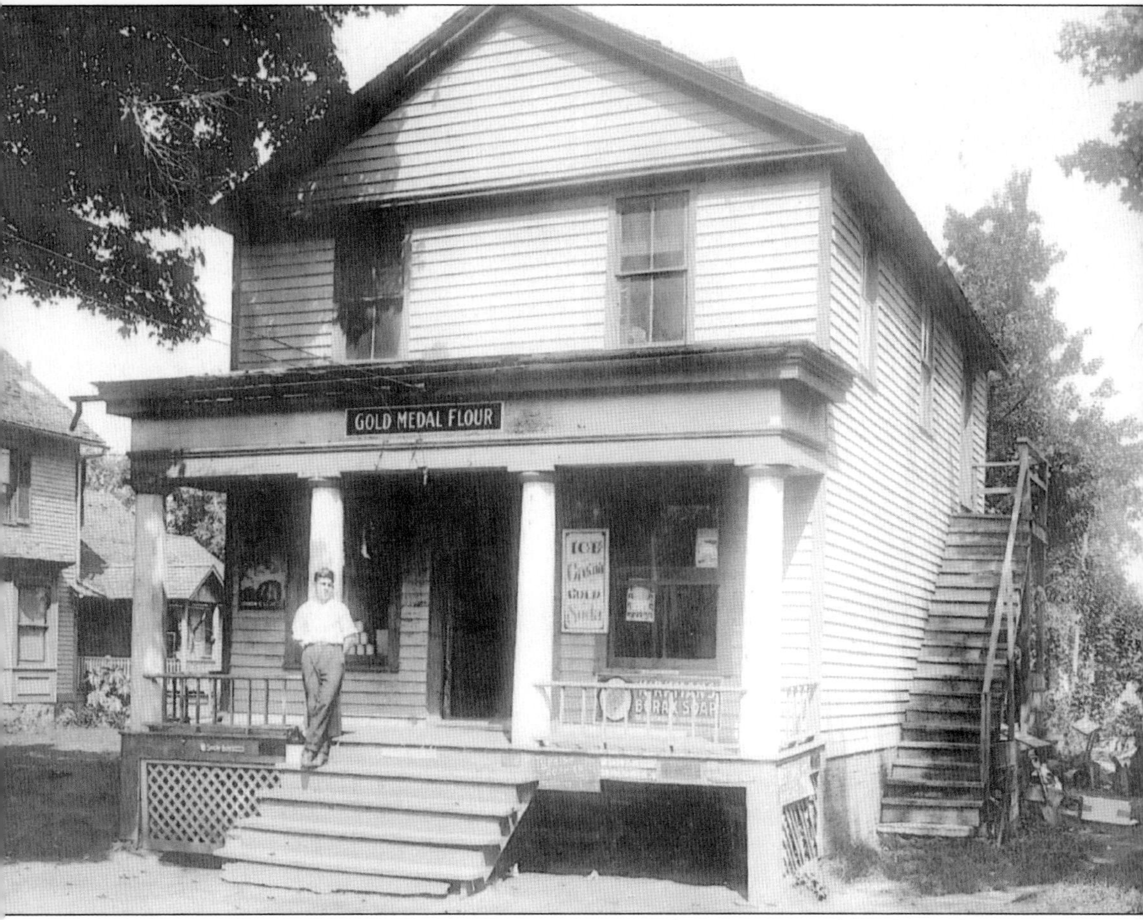

HUNTER'S STORE, 14 WEST MAIN STREET, C. 1910. The store opened in the early 1900s and closed *c.* 1929 because it could not compete with the new Atlantic & Pacific Tea Company store (A & P), which delivered groceries to customers. Owner Walter Hunter sold groceries, meat, soda, candy, grape julep, ice-cream floats, and mugs of cocoa. It closed only on Thanksgiving Day. Hunter was an Avon Water Company director for 33 years. (Betsy Hunter Tyne and Jane Hunter Bates Collection.)

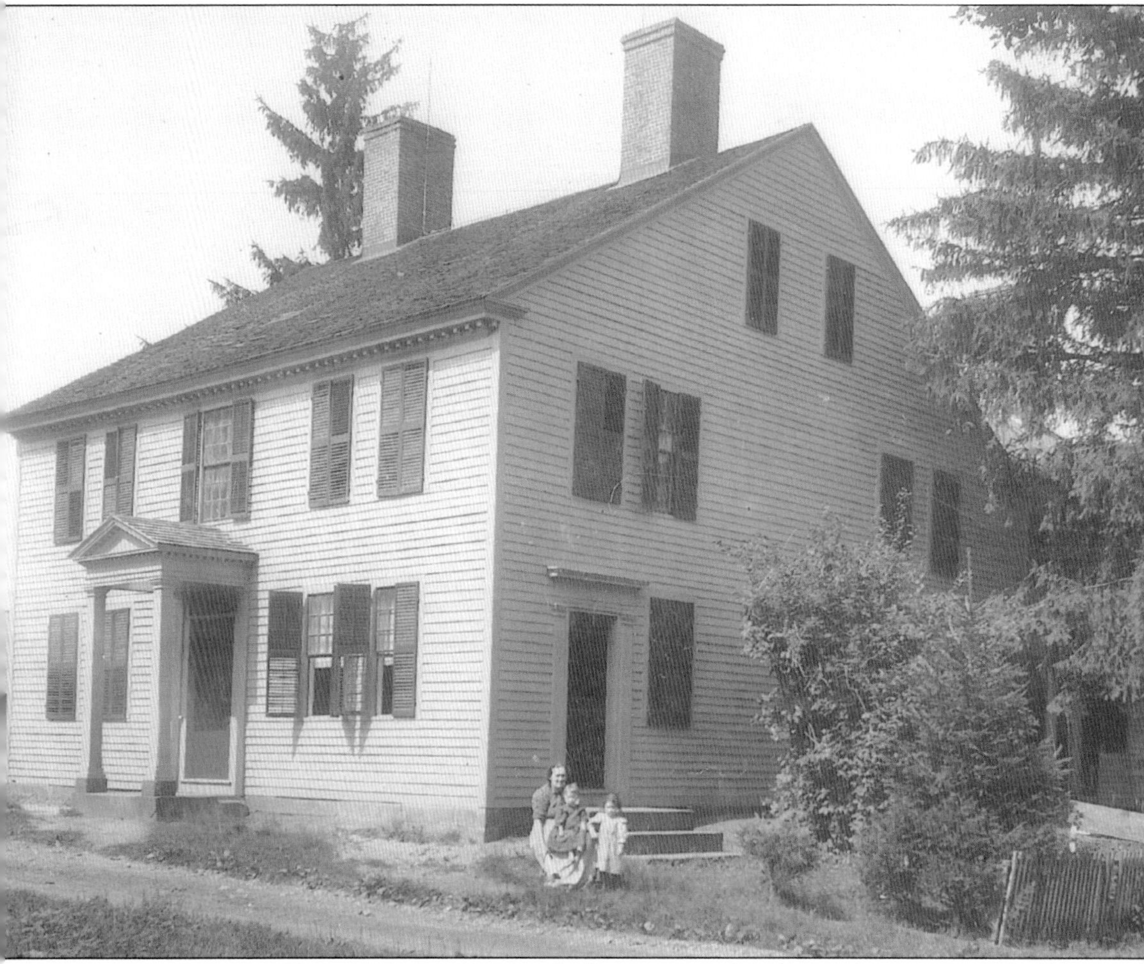

The Marshall Tavern, 1902. The Marshall Tavern stood at the southwest corner of Albany Turnpike (Route 44) and Waterville Road. Preserved Marshall operated the tavern from 1796 until his death in 1843. It was a popular stagecoach stop, with accommodations, refreshments, liquor, a ballroom, stables and a barn for resting and switching horses, and the Nod District Post Office (until 1830). Marshall was also the postmaster. In 1841, Mrs. Marshall sold the house to Nathan Case (1809–93), and later it was sold to Joseph Alsop. In 1933, the State of Connecticut demolished the house to improve traffic safety and sight lines at the intersection. The State sold the house's contents: the circular tavern bar, nine fireplaces with fixtures, and wainscoting. The photograph is by brothers Alvah and George Howe, traveling photographers from Ashfield, Massachusetts, who took more than 23,000 pictures of New England. (Howes Brothers photograph, Avon Collection.)

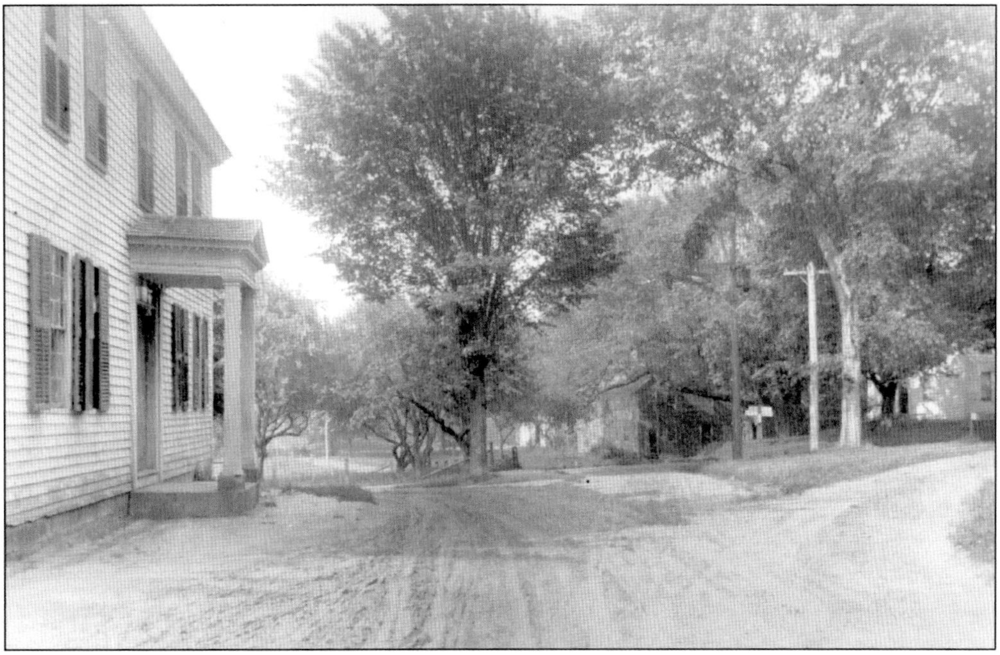

NOD FOUR CORNERS, C. 1907. In this view looking north on Waterville Road toward Albany Turnpike, the former Marshall Tavern is at the left. Across the road is the location of the Avon Old Farms Inn today. (H.P. Foote photograph, Avon Collection.)

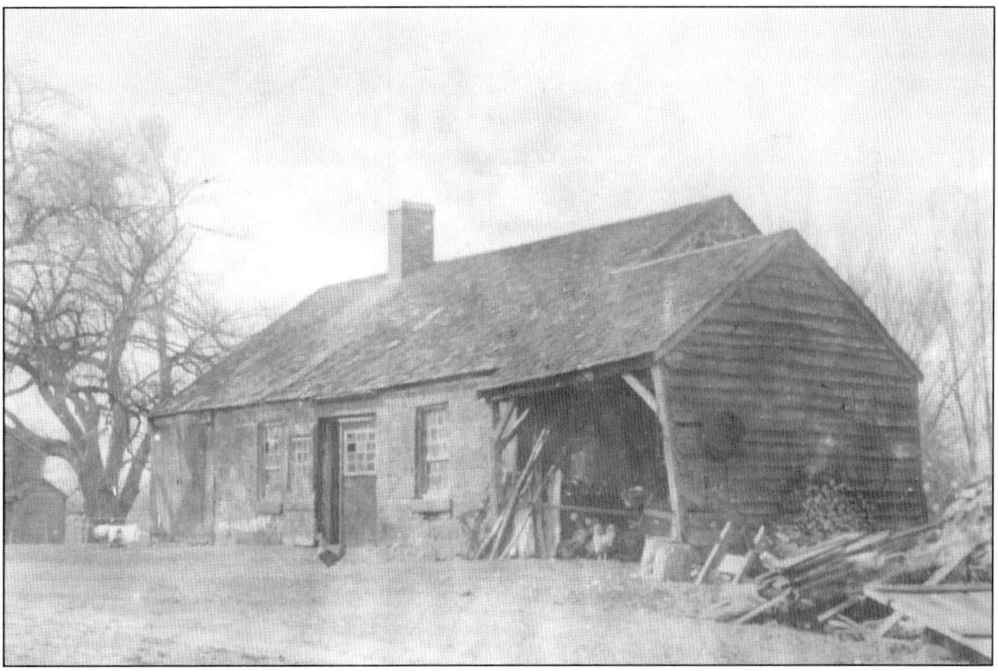

"NORTH'S BLACKSMITH SHOP, 1911." Built in 1832 by Joseph North, this building still stands as the Forge Room of the Avon Old Farms Inn. Blacksmiths made shoes for horses and oxen, repaired and sharpened farm implements, put iron on wagon wheels, and did other work. (Clinton Hadsell photograph, Avon Collection, courtesy of Doris Miller.)

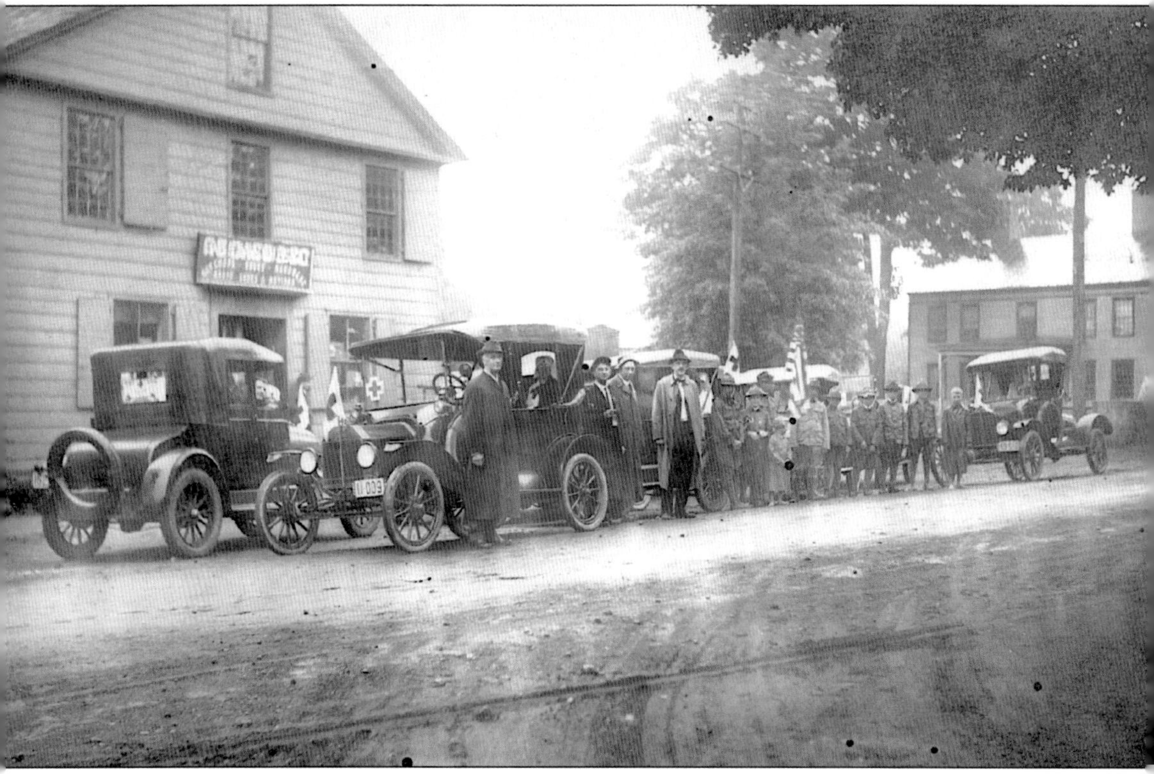

THE PARADE CELEBRATING THE END OF WORLD WAR I, 1918. Gathering outside of Case's store are Avon men and Boy Scouts, with Red Cross flags nearby. A total of 77 Avon men served in the war, and all returned safely. Volunteering for the Red Cross was once part of the school curriculum. Frank Hadsell wrote "[The surrender] was the signal for manifestations of joy and relief all over the country, and even in Avon something had to be done. An impromptu parade was hastily organized and Mother and I stood in the door way that cool November day and watched it pass by." (Avon Collection.)

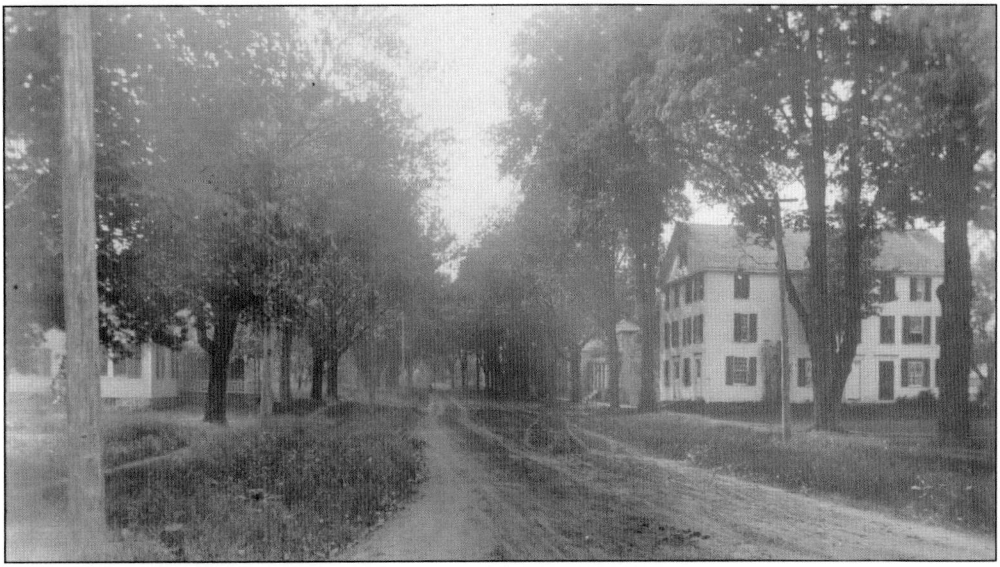

West Main Street, c. 1907. This view is of the former Farmington Canal Administration building at 12 West Main, right, just past the Albany Turnpike and Simsbury Road intersection. The post office was located here from 1947 to 1967. (H.P. Foote photograph, Avon Collection.)

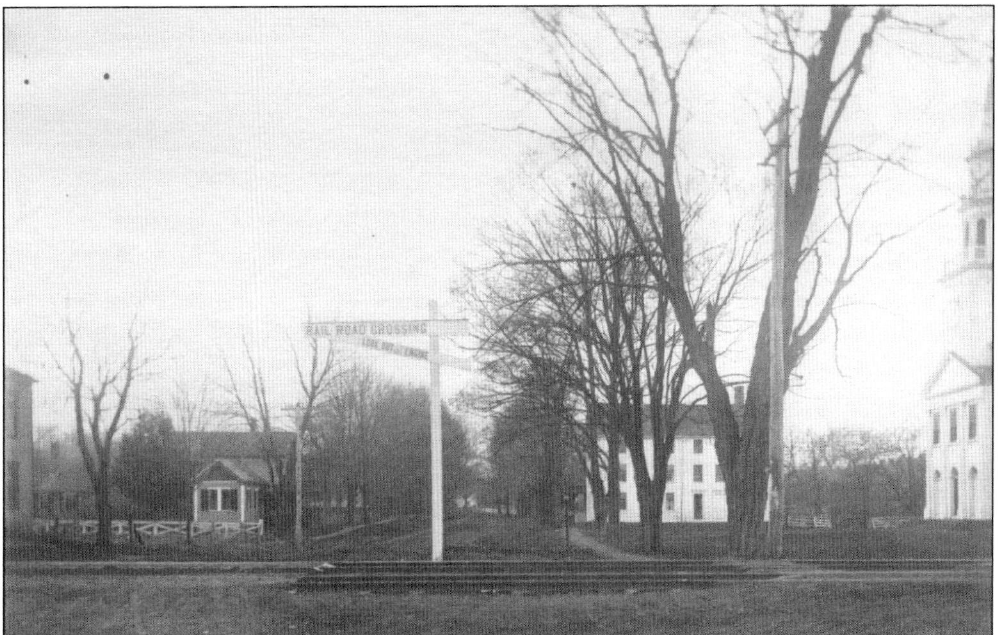

West Main Street, Early 1900s. Tracks mark the unpaved streets, and the sign reads, "Rail Road Crossing, Look Out for Engine." At the right is the Avon Congregational Church. (Avon Collection.)

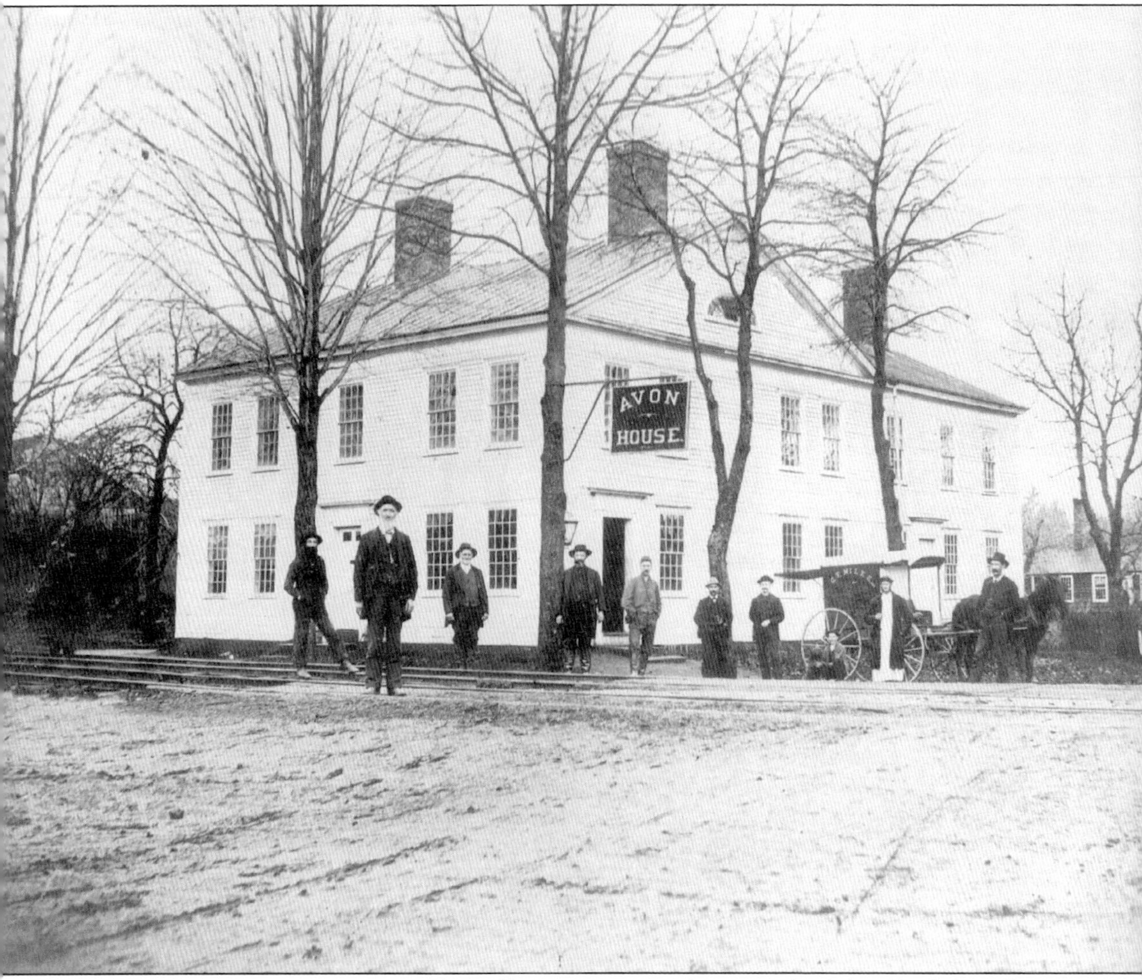

THE AVON HOUSE, C. 1900. The Tally Ho Tavern and Inn was built by Obadiah Gillet soon after the Talcott Mountain Turnpike was completed in 1799. Francis Woodford bought it c. 1840 and renamed it the Avon Hotel. It was also called the Avon House. Later converted to stores, it burned on June 26, 1946, and was demolished. The site is today home to O'Neill's Chevrolet-Buick. (Avon Collection.)

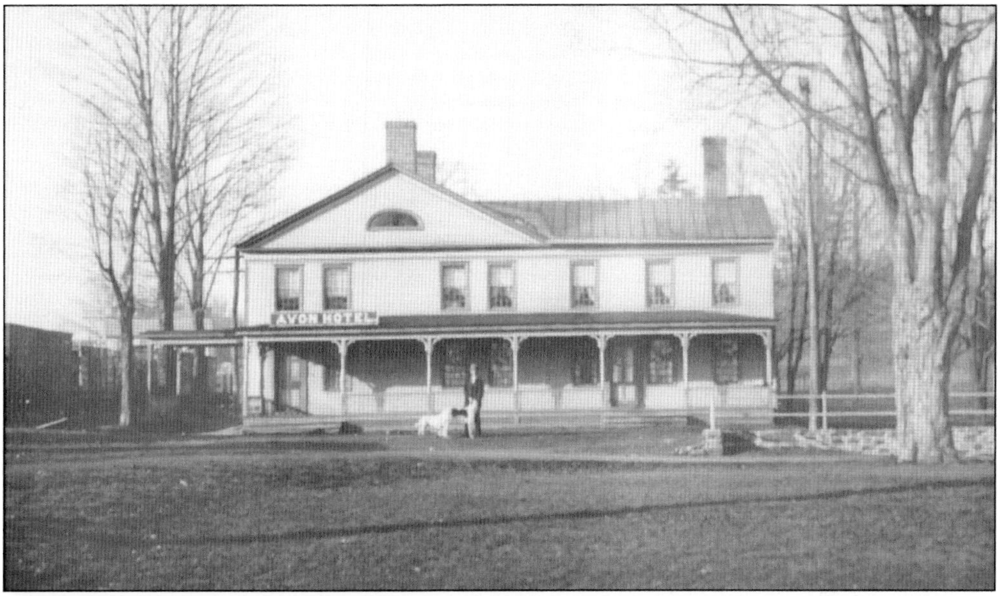

"THE AVON HOTEL, MAY 1912." A man stands with two dogs in front of the Avon Hotel. The stone wall remains in place, located very near the much wider Albany Turnpike (Route 44). (Clinton Hadsell photograph, Avon Collection, courtesy of Doris Miller.)

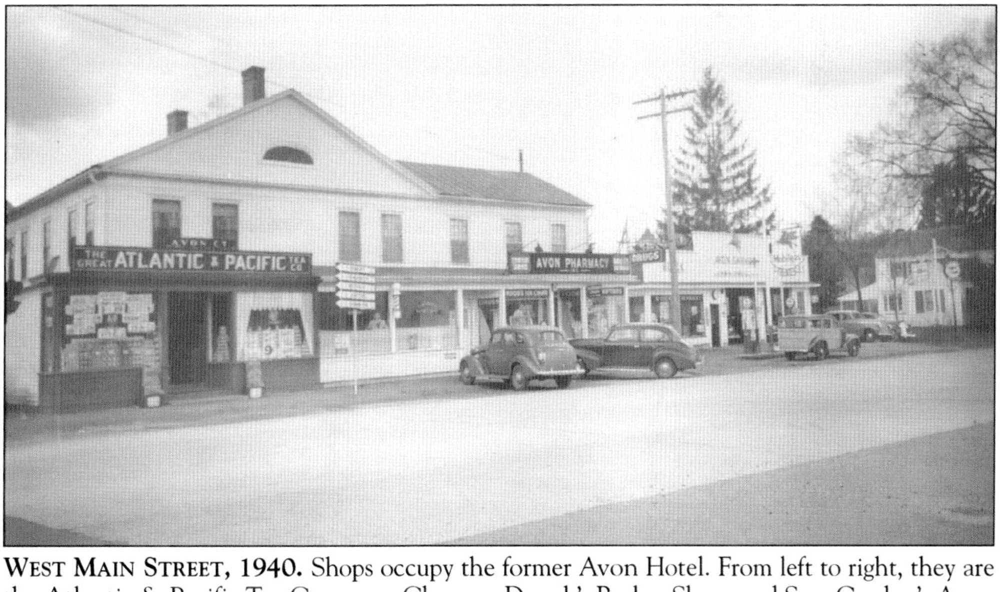

WEST MAIN STREET, 1940. Shops occupy the former Avon Hotel. From left to right, they are the Atlantic & Pacific Tea Company, Clarence Drezek's Barber Shop, and Sam Gordon's Avon Pharmacy. Parked at O'Neil's Mobil Garage is Ostrom and Alice Enders's Ford station wagon. At the far right is the Avon Congregational Church parsonage. (Anthony O'Neill Collection.)

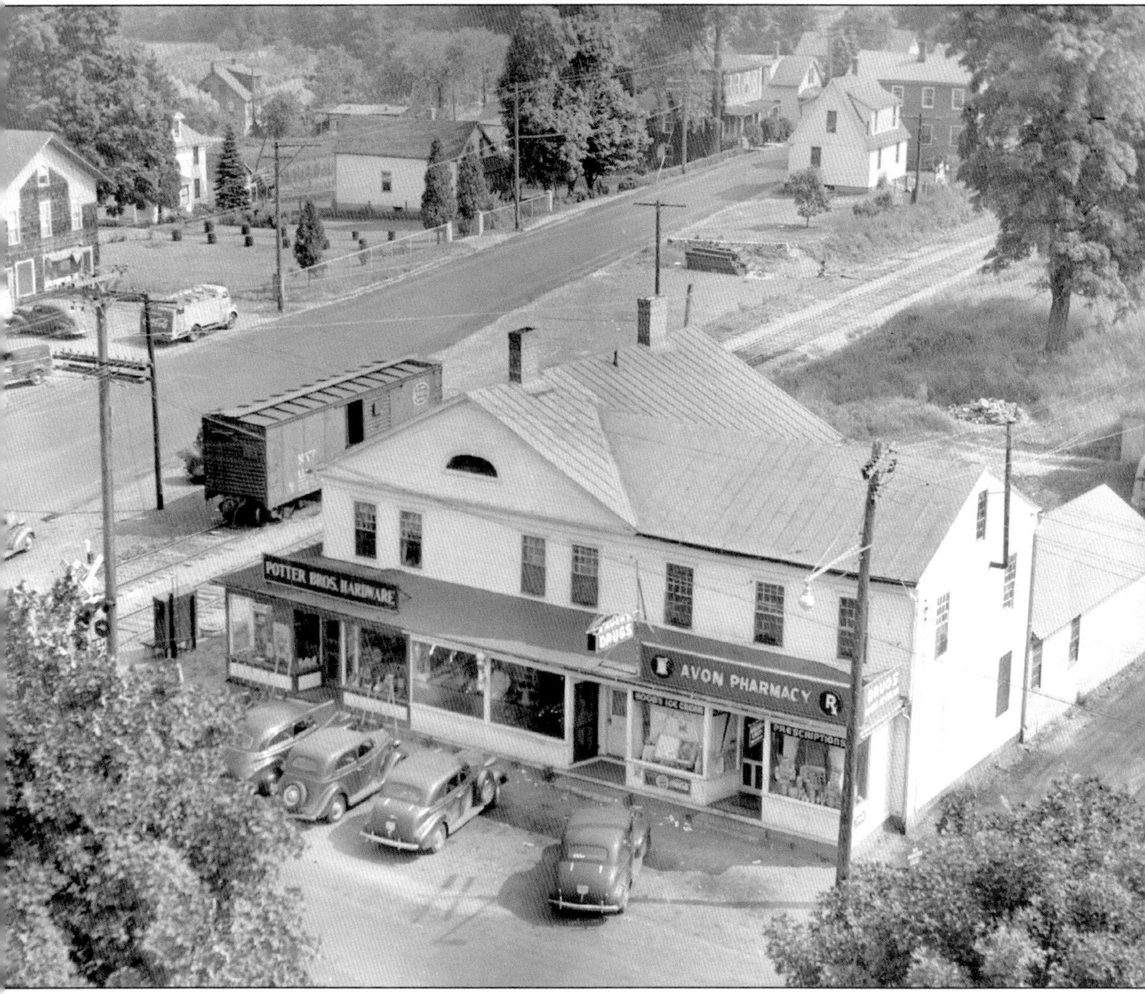

West Main Street, May 1946. Potter & Brothers Hardware moved into the former Atlantic & Pacific Tea Company in November 1945. Operated by World War II veteran Jack Potter, it was Avon's first exclusively hardware and paint store. This photograph was taken shortly before the fire that destroyed the building. The *Farmington Valley Herald* reported that when the O'Neill block caught fire, "Avon's new Volunteer Fire Department won its first major engagement . . . by saving the entire center of Avon from sure destruction." (Anthony O'Neill Collection.)

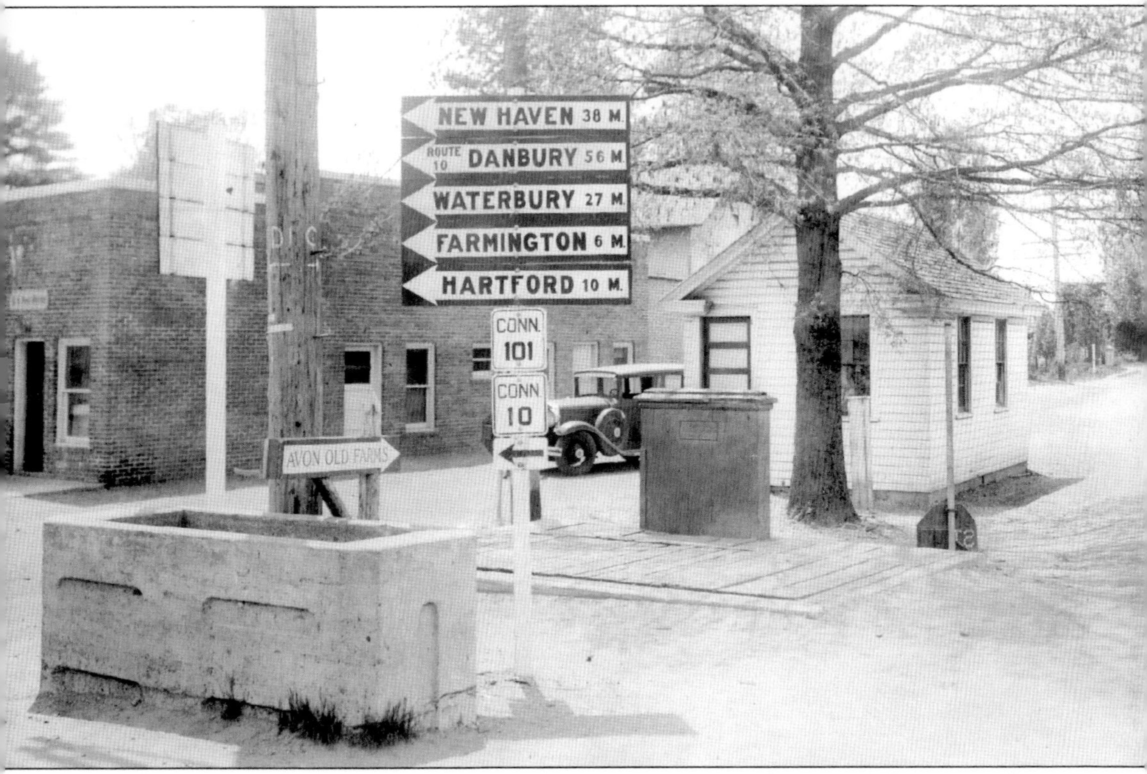

AVON CENTER, 1935. Republican Willis Chidsey (1868–1957) erected the post office (center) after his appointment as postmaster in 1922. Chidsey and assistant Lavinia Hadsell (1883–1968) took turns working in the 11-by-17-foot room. After Democrat Franklin Roosevelt was elected president, George "Ted" Manion succeeded Chidsey in 1934 and moved the post office to the brick building (left). The photograph shows truck scales, a watering trough for horses and cows, and the Constitution Oak tree grown with seed from Hartford's famous oak. (Avon Collection.)

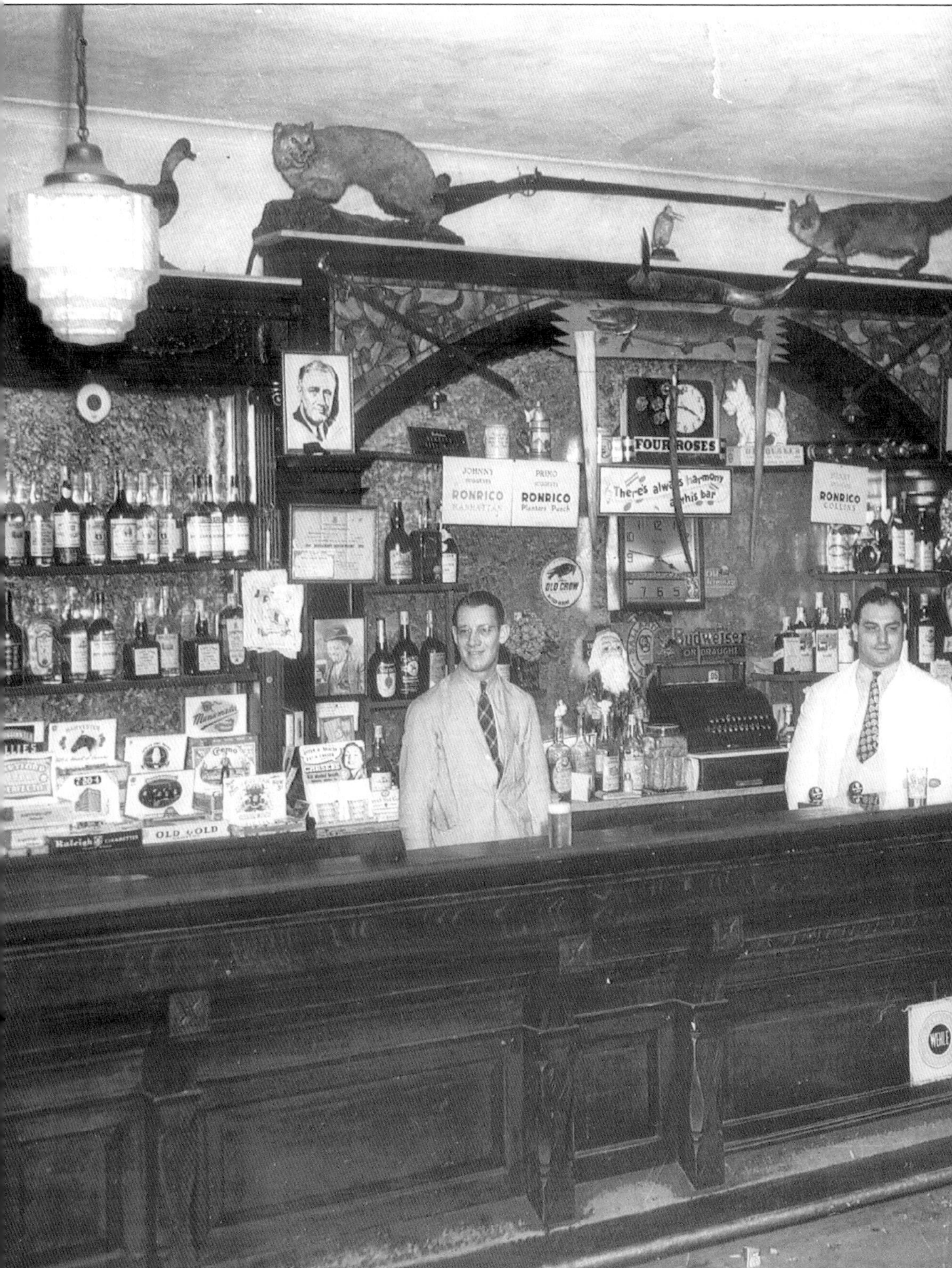
FOUR ROSES
RONRICO
MANHATTAN
RONRICO
Planters Punch
There's always harmony at this bar
RONRICO
COLLINS
OLD CROW
Budweiser
ON DRAUGHT
OLD GOLD
Raleigh
WEHLE

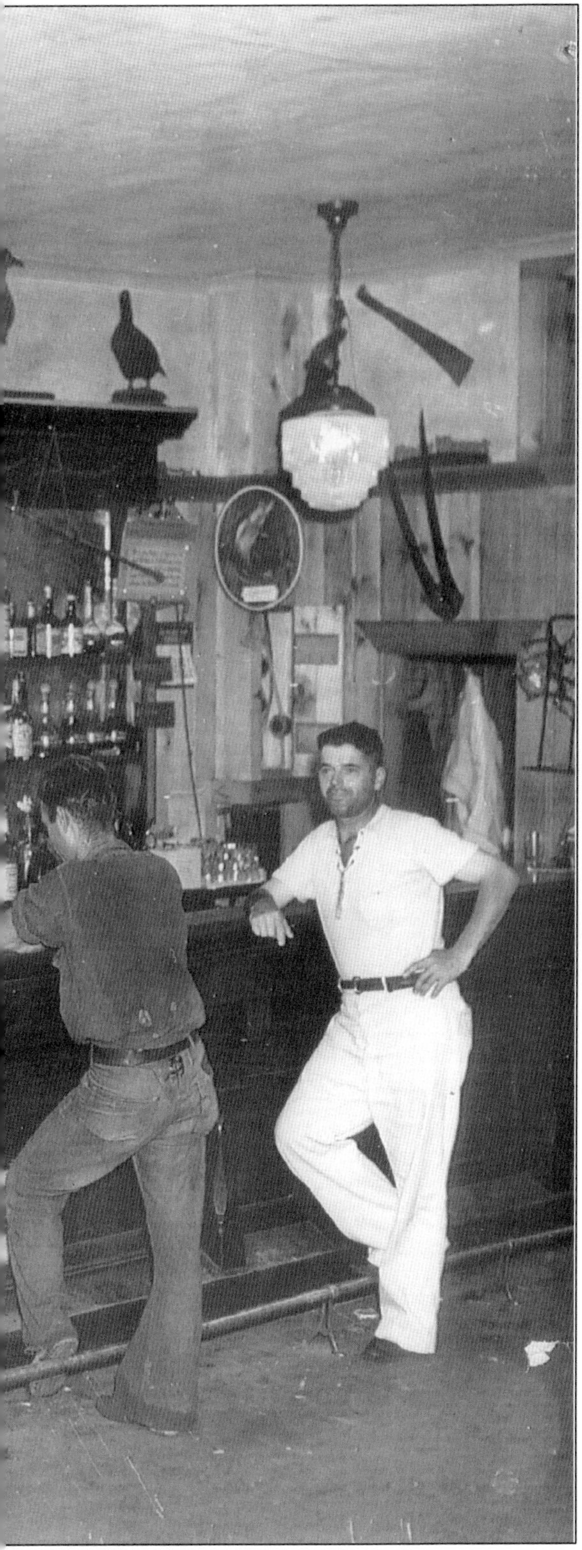

THE OLD TOWN TAVERN, 1930S. The tavern was located in the commercial block east of Old Farms Road. Behind the bar, at the right, is owner Primo Viti. Co-owner Henry Kopp is not pictured. A photograph of Pres. Franklin Roosevelt hangs on the wall. Wildlife includes a fox, a bobcat, ducks, and a fish. The shelves are fully stocked with liquor and cigars. This building replaced the Canal Warehouse, which burned on March 5, 1932. (Avon Collection, courtesy of Carl Candels.)

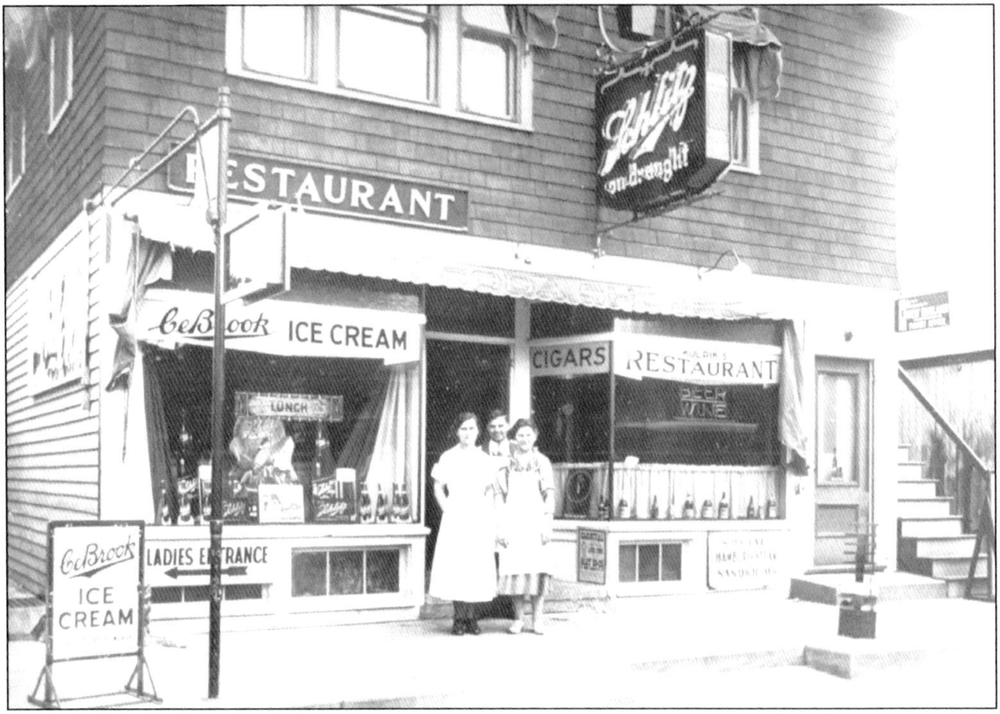

KULPIK'S RESTAURANT AND BAR, 10 EAST MAIN STREET. The exterior view was taken c. 1932 and shows, from left to right, Margaret Kulpik, Adam Piacik, and Edith Adam. Not pictured is owner Tony Kulpik. The ladies' entrance allowed women to enter the restaurant without going into the bar, which opened in 1933. The building later became Flo's Inn. The interior view was taken c. 1940 by Marvin Deming. (Avon Collection.)

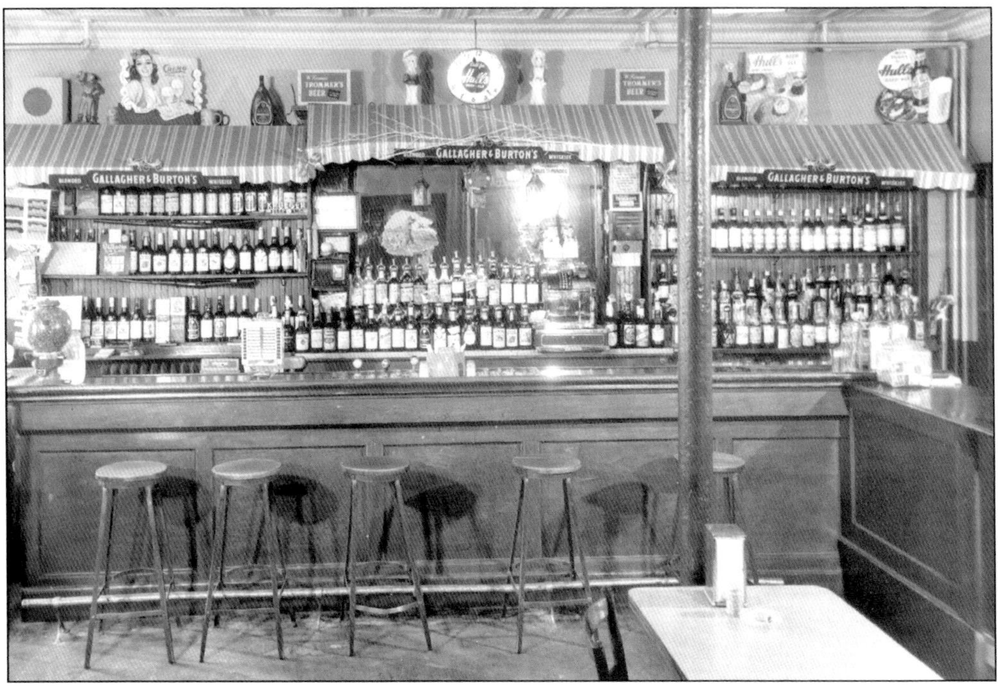

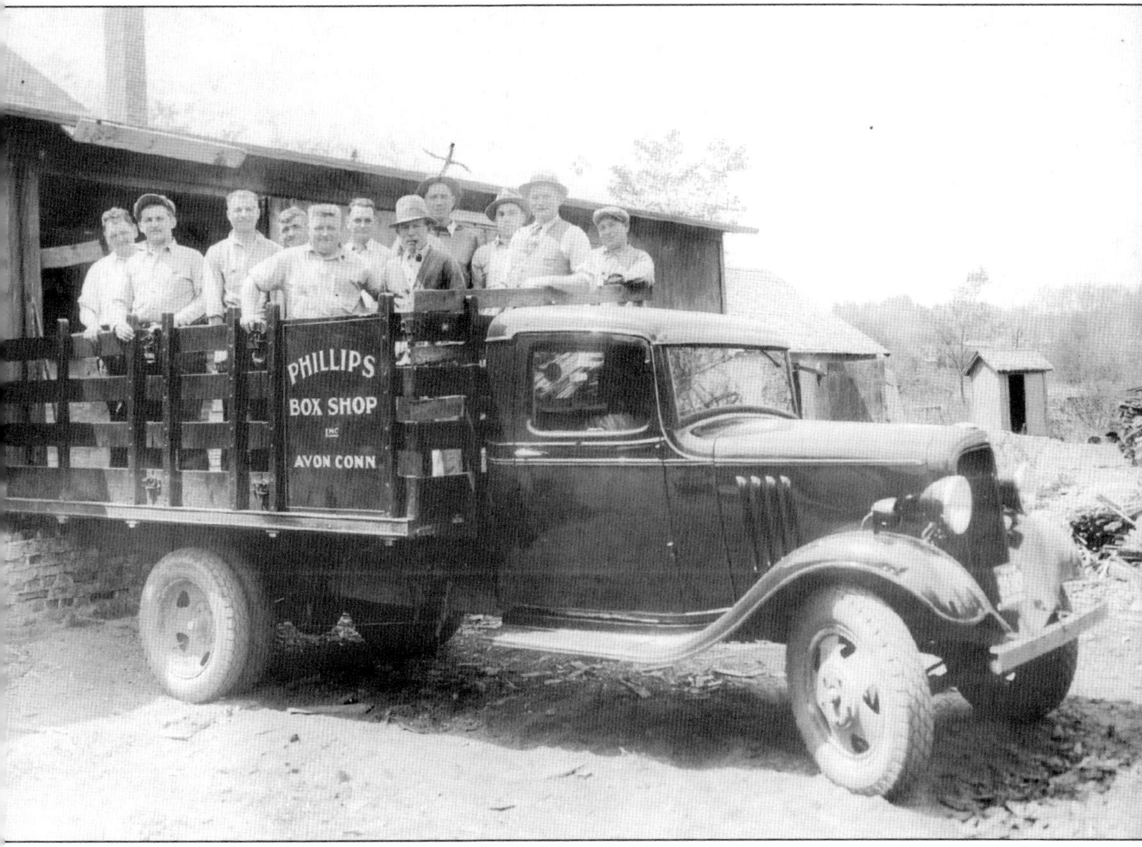

PHILLIPS BOX SHOP, C. 1940. These men made wooden boxes with dovetail corners. Also known as Harry's, the shop was located on the west side of Simsbury Road, opposite Towpath School. Pictured in the 1935 Chevrolet are, from left to right, John Anderson, John Swider, Dindo Salvadori, unidentified, Joe Tanganell, Ken Anderson, Fifo, Harry Wilcox, Austin R. Hunter, Frank A. Phillips, and Paul Marchelli. (Avon Collection.)

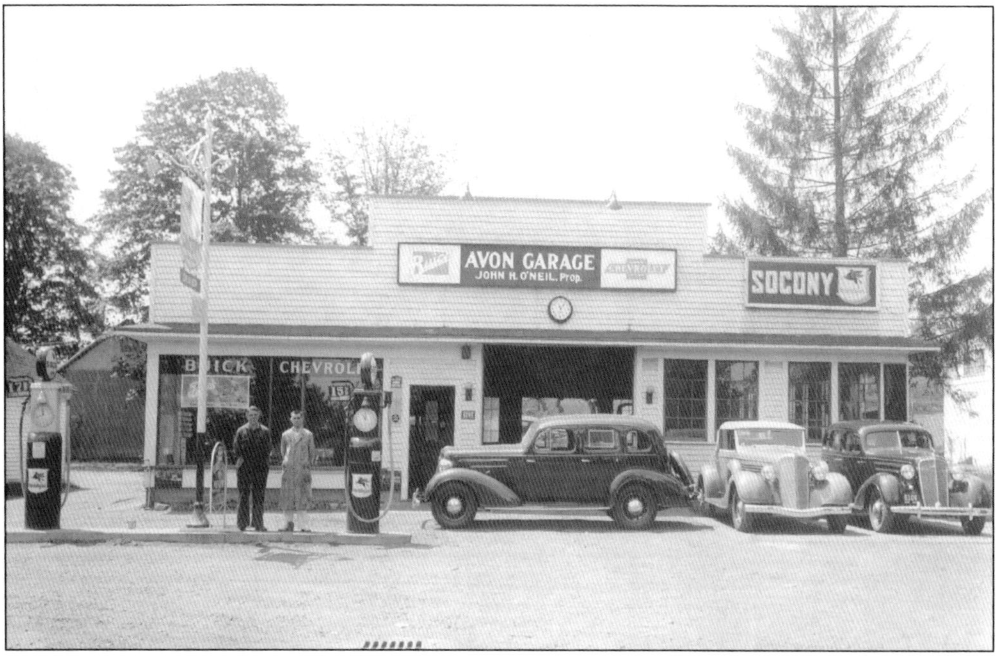

AVON GARAGE, 5 WEST MAIN STREET, 1935. Pictured at John H. O'Neill's garage and Buick and Chevrolet dealership are, from left to right, Charlie Hunter of Avon and Bob Lamb of Simsbury. West Main Street at this time was two lanes wide. (Anthony O'Neill Collection.)

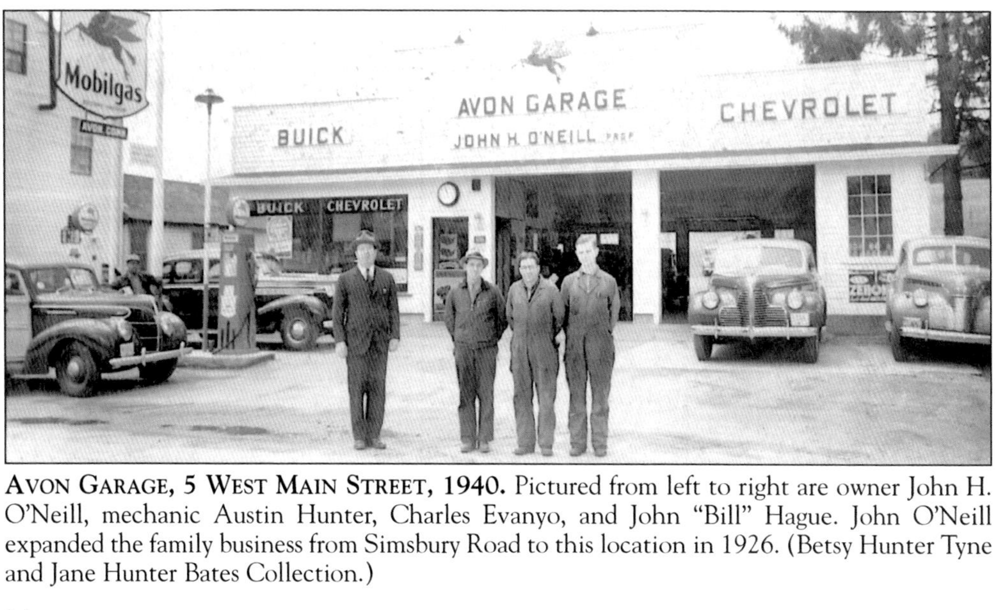

AVON GARAGE, 5 WEST MAIN STREET, 1940. Pictured from left to right are owner John H. O'Neill, mechanic Austin Hunter, Charles Evanyo, and John "Bill" Hague. John O'Neill expanded the family business from Simsbury Road to this location in 1926. (Betsy Hunter Tyne and Jane Hunter Bates Collection.)

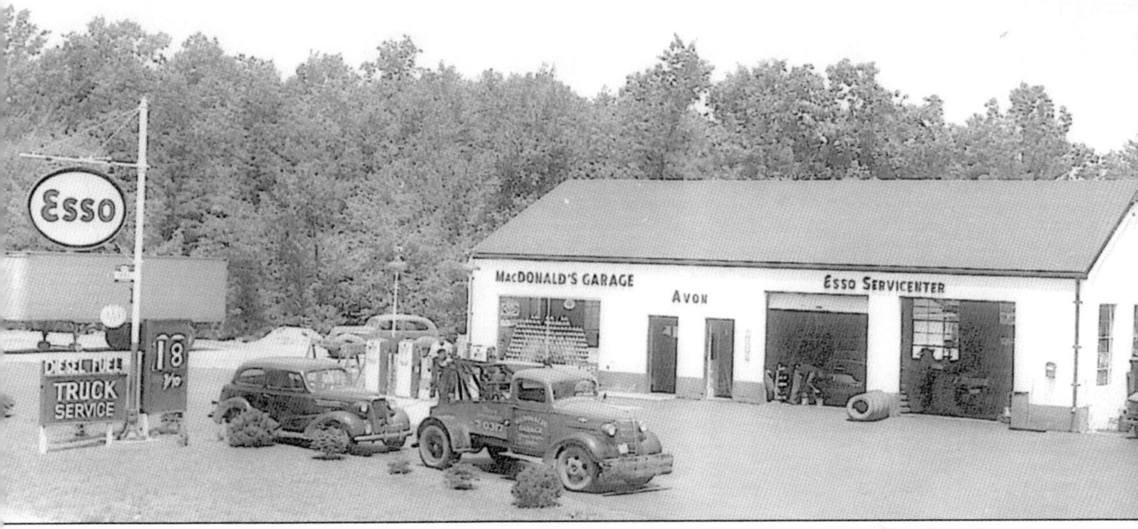

MacDonald's Esso Garage, 75 East Main Street, 1949. This photograph was taken the year the garage opened, when gas sold for 18.9¢ a gallon. (Thomas E. MacDonald Collection.)

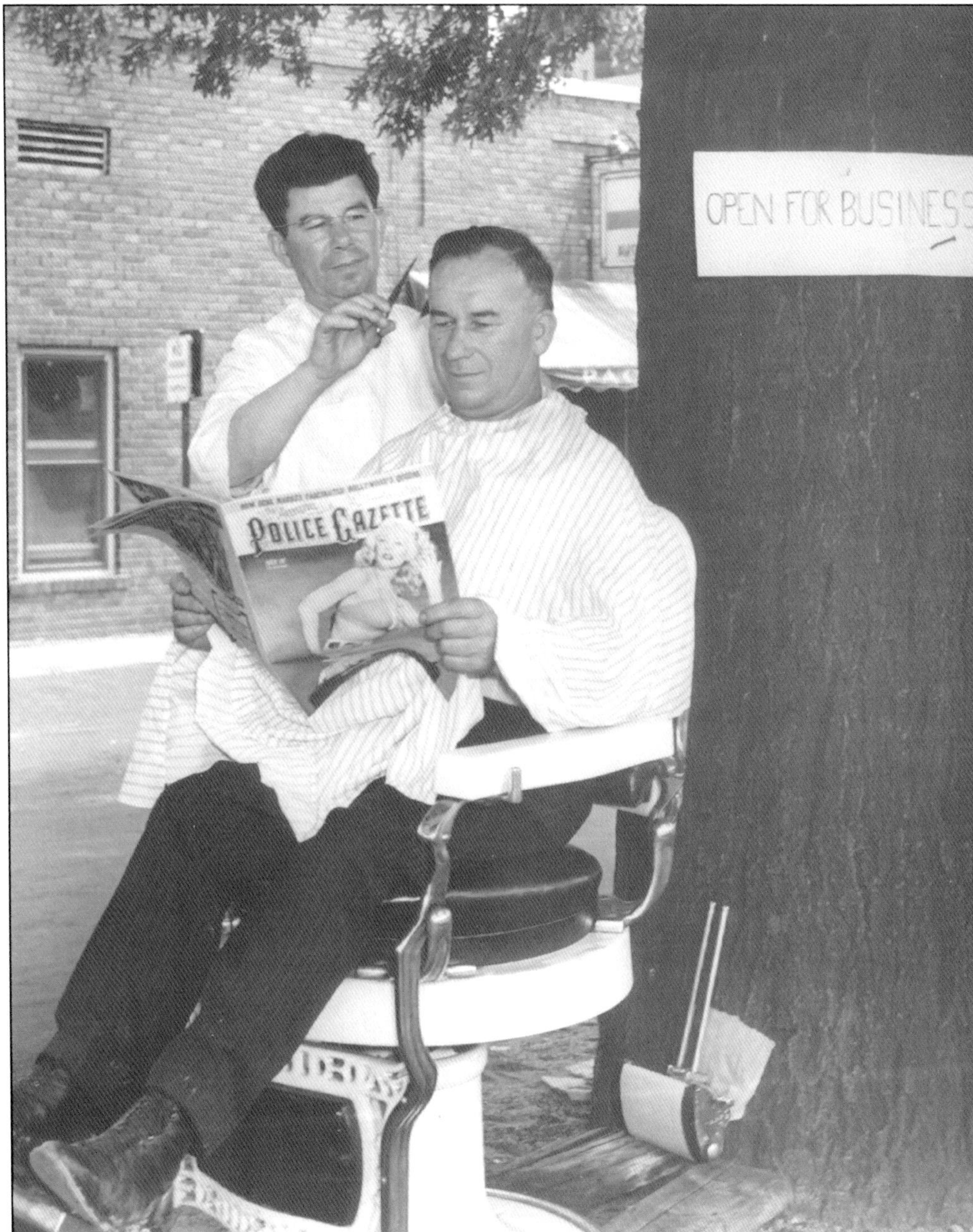

A HAIRCUT, 1946. After the O'Neil block burned on June 26, 1946, barber Clarence Drezek removed his chair to set up shop in his home across the street at 20 Old Farms Road. En route, he gives Fire Chief Peter Bonesio a haircut. (Dwight Douglas photograph, Avon Collection.)

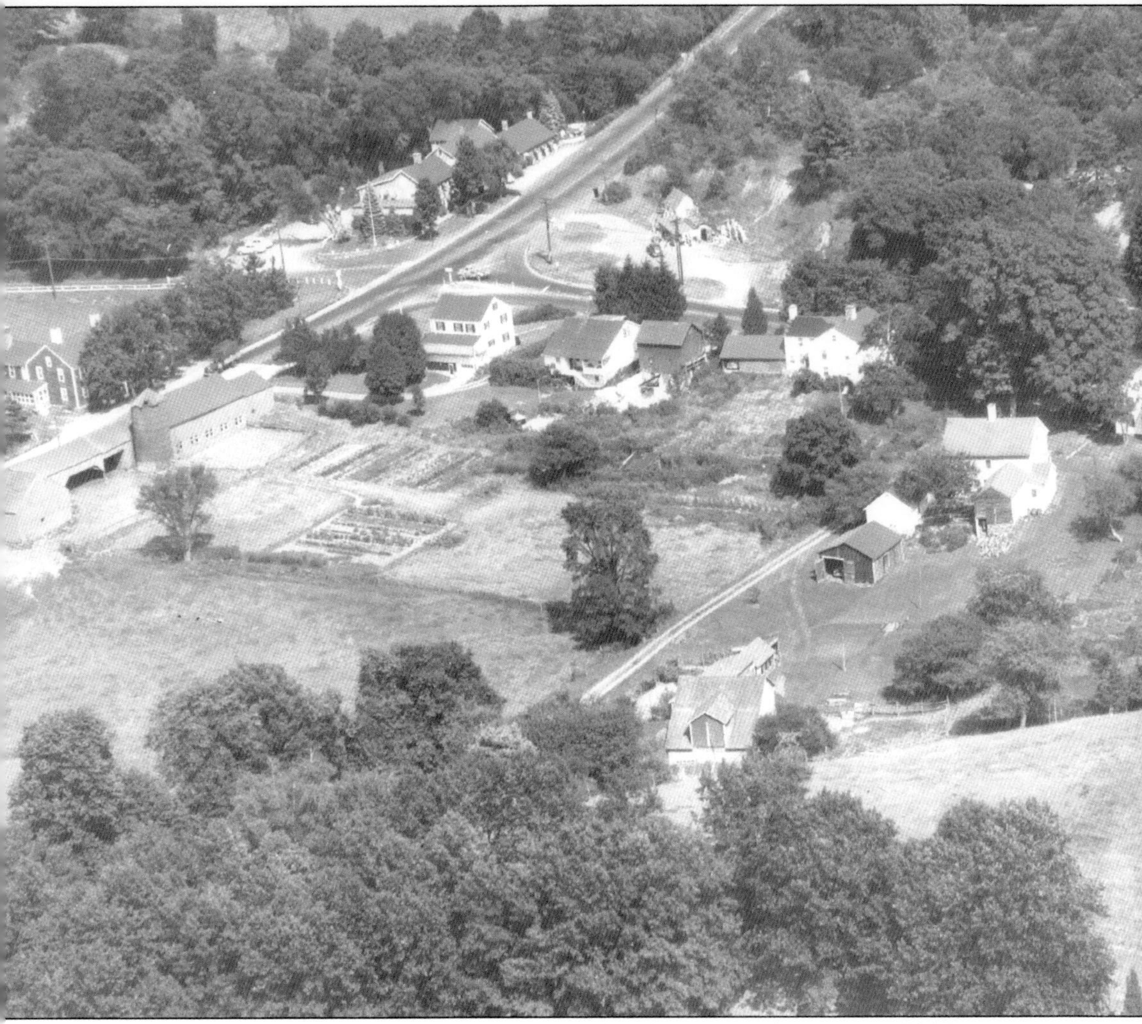

NOD CORNERS, 1949. This view of Waterville Road and Route 44 shows Avon Old Farms Inn at the top left. Across Route 44 is Sam Baba's fruit stand, now the location of the Avon Old Farms Hotel, owned by the Brighenti family. West of Waterville Road are the Togni House, Jack and Charlotte Brighenti's house, and Brighenti's Avon Plumbing. At the far left is a Wood Ford Farm employee house, and across Route 44 are Wood Ford Farm barns and employee gardens. (Avon Collection.)

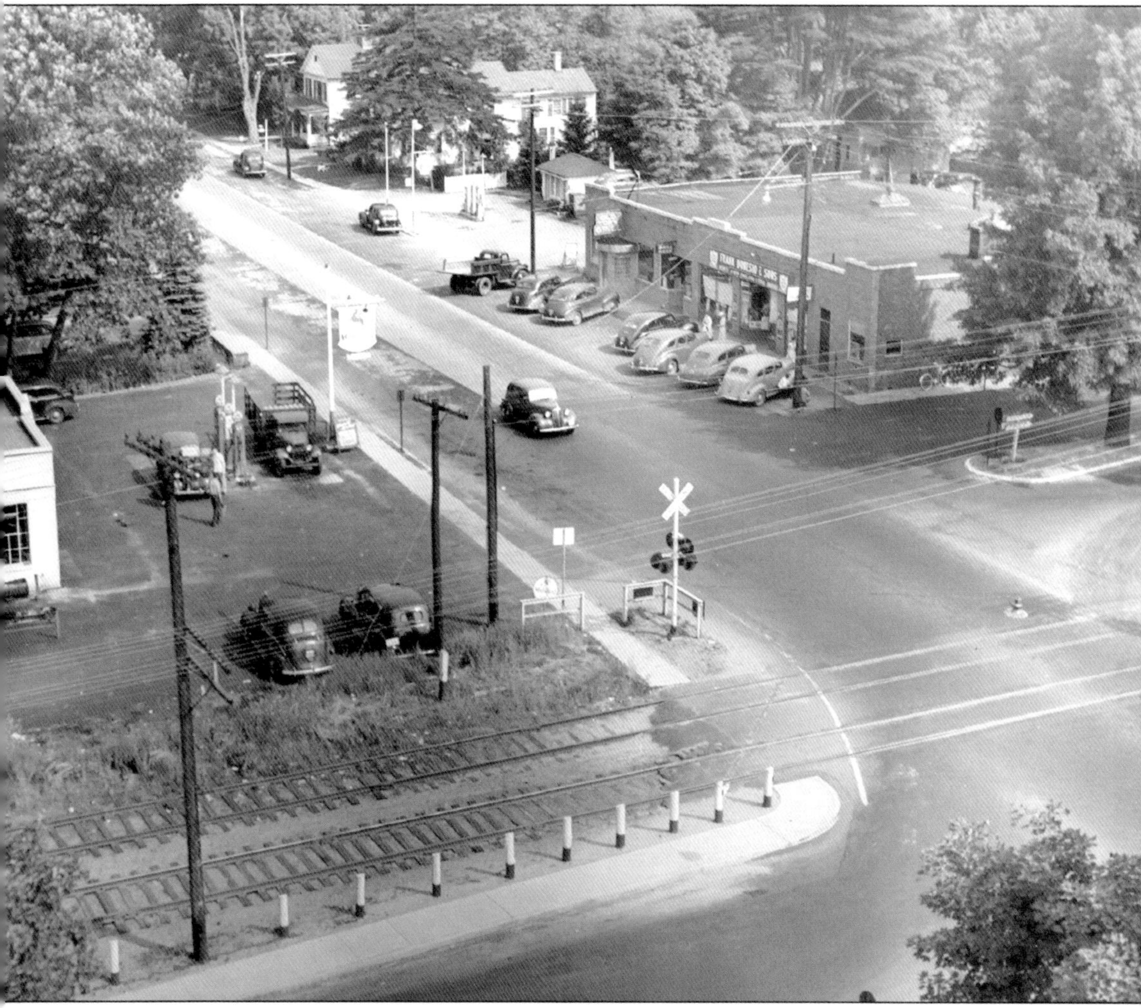

AVON CENTER, 1946. Taken from the Avon Congregational Church steeple, this view looks onto East Main Street. At the left is Rene Ruez's Mobil Station. Across the street is Lucien's Shell Station (small white building), the Old Town Grill, and Frank Bonesio & Sons, Avon's largest grocery store. (Marvin Deming photograph, Anthony O'Neill Collection.)

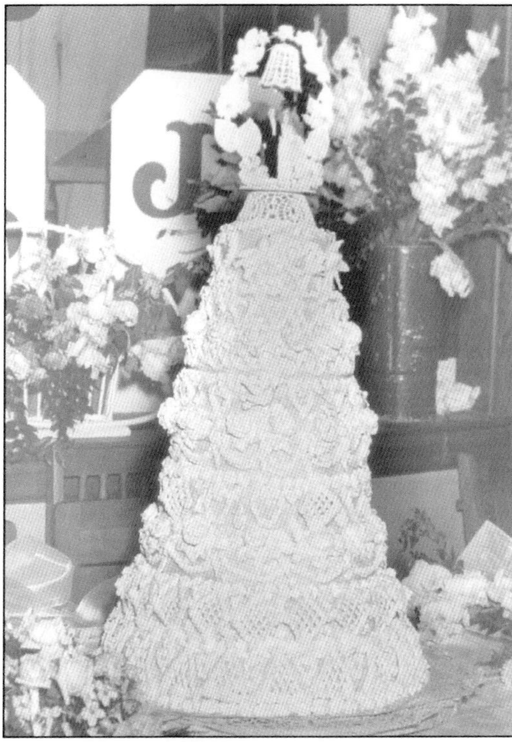

A WEDDING CAKE BY ANTHONY CANDELS, DECEMBER 25, 1948. Anthony and Martha Candels came from Germany to Hartford in 1927. Four years later, Candels became Avon Old Farms School's chief steward and chef. He made and gave this cake to Lorraine and Eddie Drezek for their wedding reception. During the Great Depression, he brought baked treats and unused sports equipment from the school to children in his Climax Road neighborhood. (Norman Taillon photograph, Carl Candels Collection.)

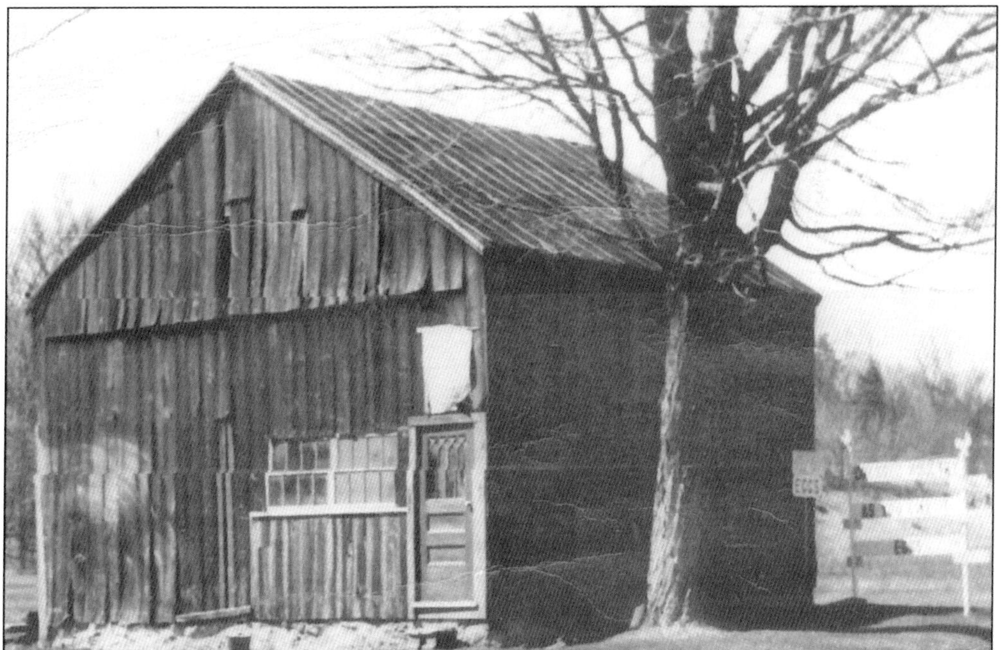

STAIANO POULTRY MARKET, WEST AVON ROAD, C. 1945. Built in 1766, this barn was originally used as a powder magazine for storing ammunition. The poultry market was owned by Charles and Roma Carmine. The sign reads, "Dressed Poultry, As you like it, Eggs." (Robert J. Campbell Collection.)

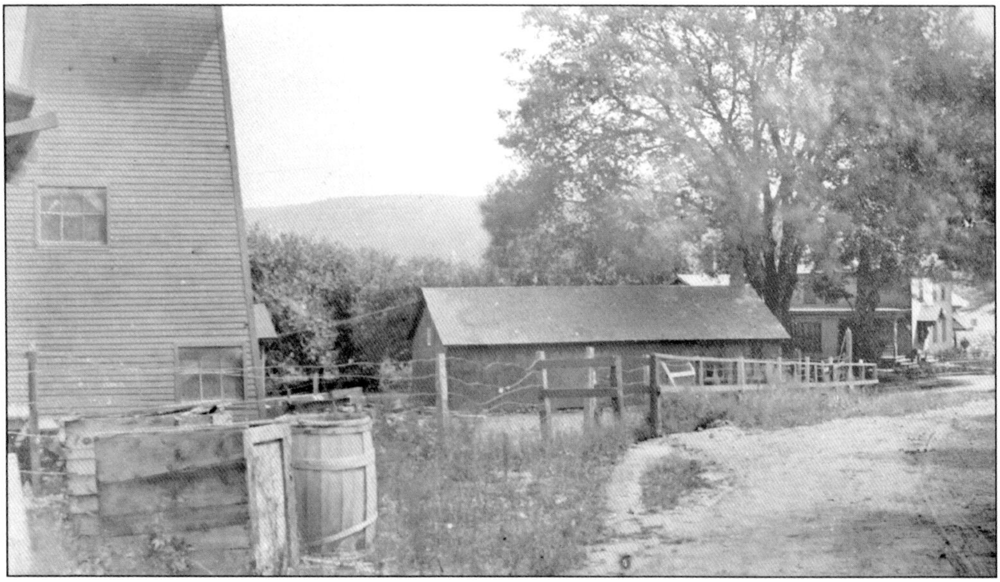

THE CLIMAX FUSE COMPANY, 1889. Romeo Andrews & Sons Company began fuse manufacturing in 1852 and continued until a fatal explosion in 1873. Albert Andrews and John Andrews brought the business back, incorporating the Climax Fuse Company in 1884. The Ensign-Bickford Company of Simsbury, which also made fuses, acquired a one-half interest in the company in 1892, replacing the wooden buildings with safer stone buildings. Climax Fuse merged with Ensign-Bickford in 1907. (Avon Collection.)

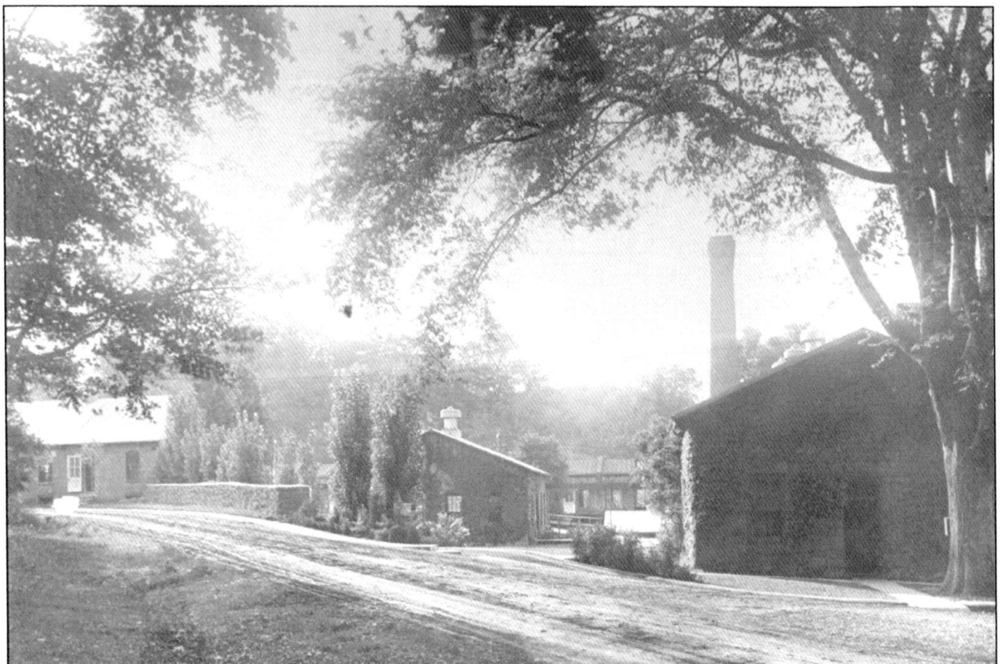

THE ENSIGN-BICKFORD COMPANY (FORMERLY CLIMAX FUSE). This undated photograph shows buildings used today by the Town of Avon. In the center is the town clerk and probate office; on the right is the town manager's office. (Avon Collection.)

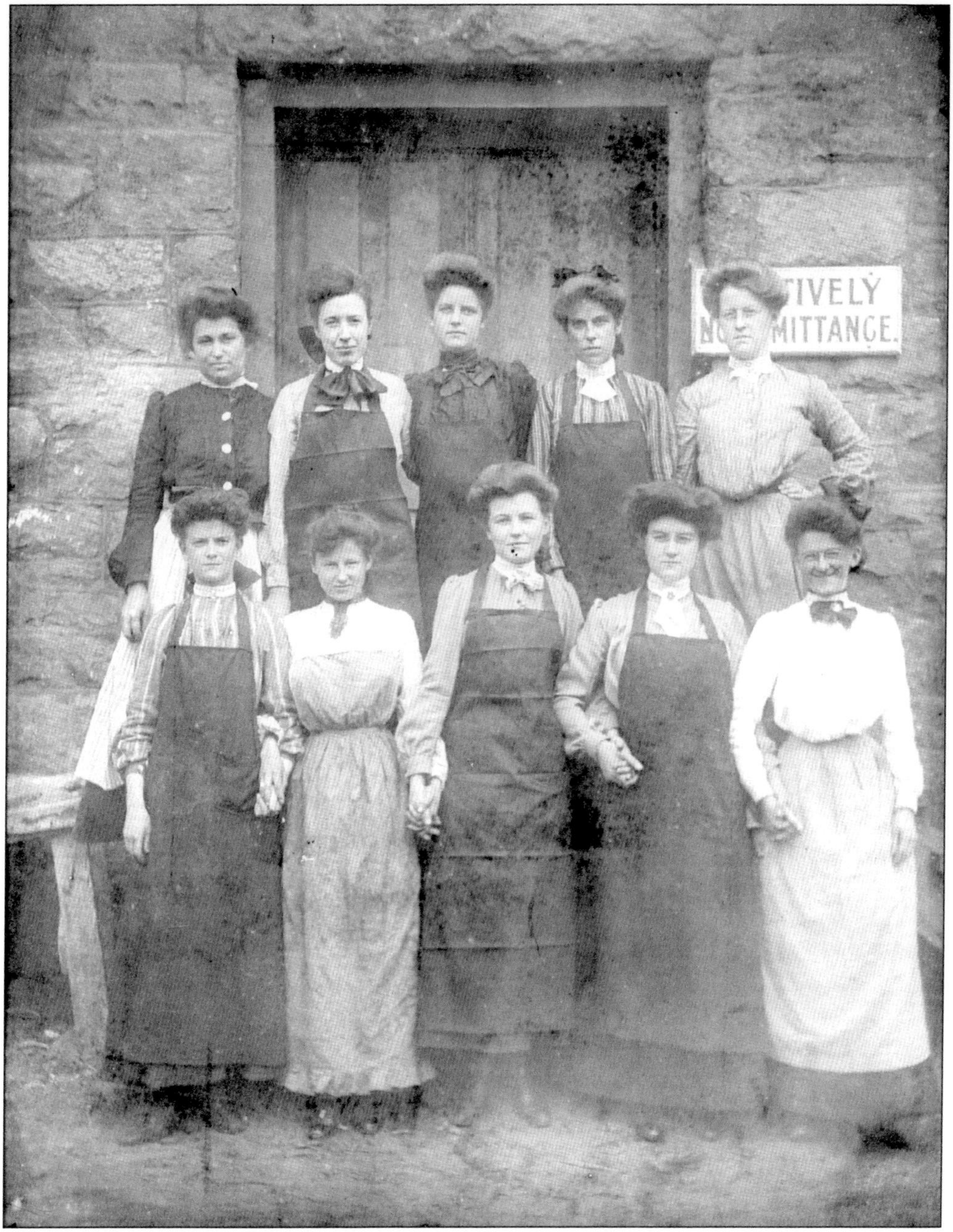

The Climax Fuse Company, c. 1905. Immigrants from Hungary, Poland, Russia, and other countries arrived in Avon *c.* 1903 to work at the fuse company. According to Frank Hadsell, company superintendent, they were "green as grass." Pictured third from the left in the front row is Nellie Collins; in the second row, second from the left, is Mary O'Neil. The sign reads, "Positively No Admittance." Hadsell wrote that "there was considerable competition in the fuse business from concerns in Denver and California and it was thought in 1892 that the western concerns were endeavoring to spy out the secrets of our process of manufacture, and we had orders from Mr. Ensign not to permit anyone not an employee to enter the shop unless written permission was given from Simsbury and presented to me." (Anthony O'Neill Collection.)

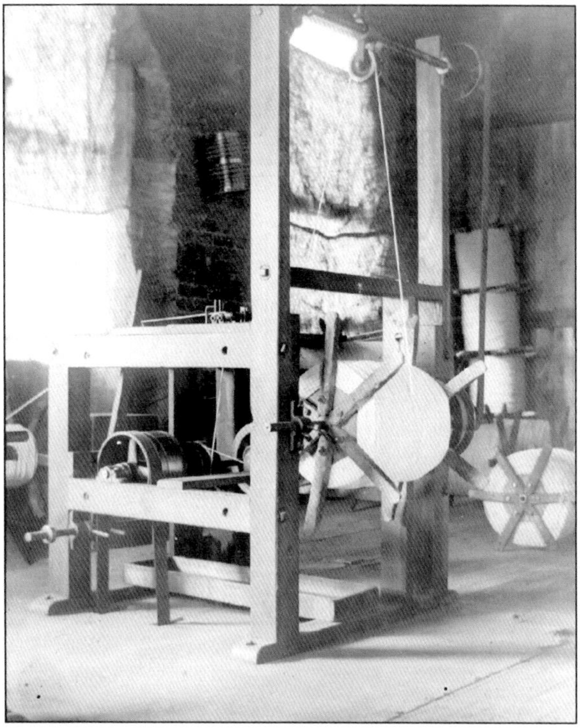

INSIDE THE CLIMAX FUSE COMPANY. This photograph shows a typical workroom at the Climax Fuse Company at the time of the 1905 fire. Note the rolls of fuse and flimsy window coverings. (Avon Collection.)

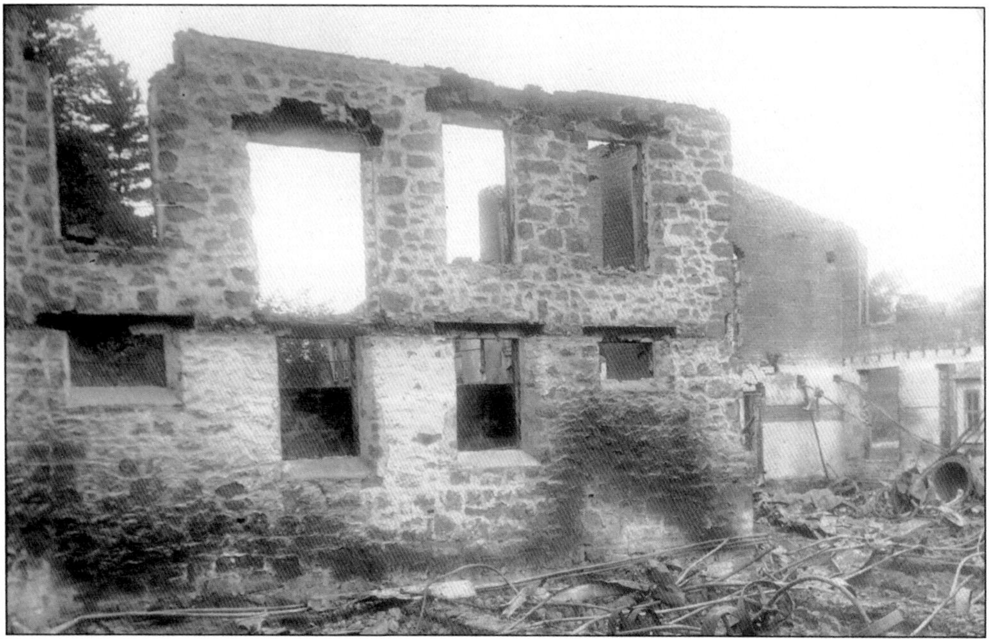

THE CLIMAX FUSE COMPANY FIRE, SEPTEMBER 15, 1905. Frank Hadsell, company superintendent, wrote that "the thing dreaded by me for so long happened." With the oil-soaked floor, powder dust and yarn for taping machines and fuse inspections, "at once the room was ablaze all over." Seven men and eight women died. Although the fuse-making rooms were not involved in the fire, only one Avon fuse maker returned to work. The Ensign-Bickford Company in Simsbury sent replacement workers, and business resumed by January 1906. (Avon Collection.)

Two

FAMILIES, FRIENDS, AND CHARACTERS

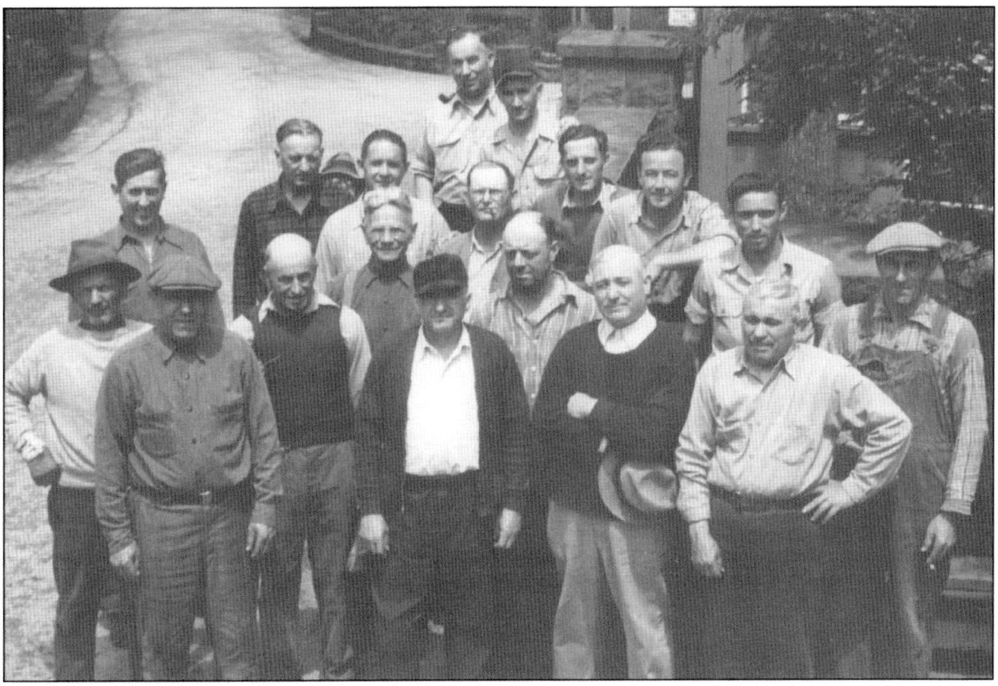

ENSIGN-BICKFORD COMPANY EMPLOYEES, EARLY 1940S. Pictured from left to right are the following: (first row) John Desimoni, Fedele Baraglia, Silvio Viti, and Leo Tarca; (second row) Peter Brunoli, Sebastian Masini, Felix DelBon, Pat Brighenti, and Bill Mommertz; (third row) John Kulikowski Jr., John Kulikowski Sr., Harold Guidetti, and Ted Ksiazek; (fourth row) Harold Miller, Buster Brown, and Pay Vedovelli; (fifth row) Tom Crowley (barely visible), Peter Bonesio (with pipe), and Dennis Bogino. (Anthony O'Neill Collection.)

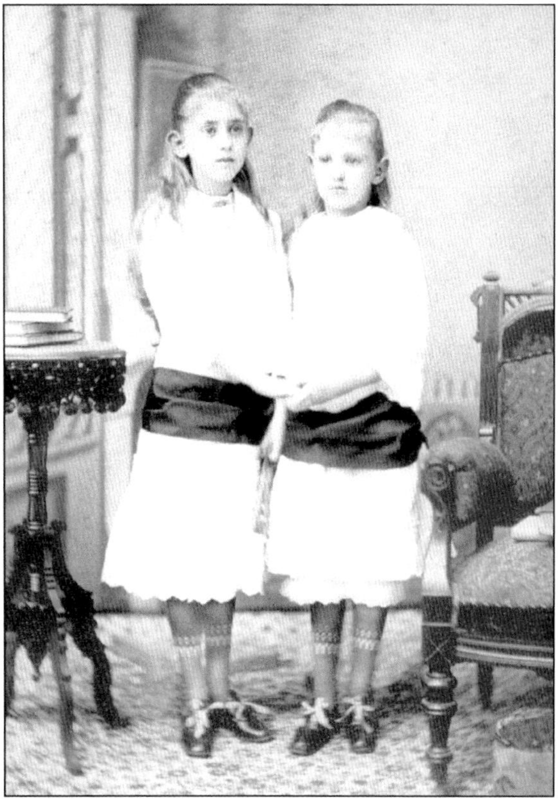

THE BISHOP SISTERS, C. 1883. Pictured, from left to right, are Sarah Roxanna and May Belle Bishop. Both girls attended Miss Porter's School in Farmington and never married. May studied in Paris and became an artist. (Cider Brook Miller & Bishop Families' Collection.)

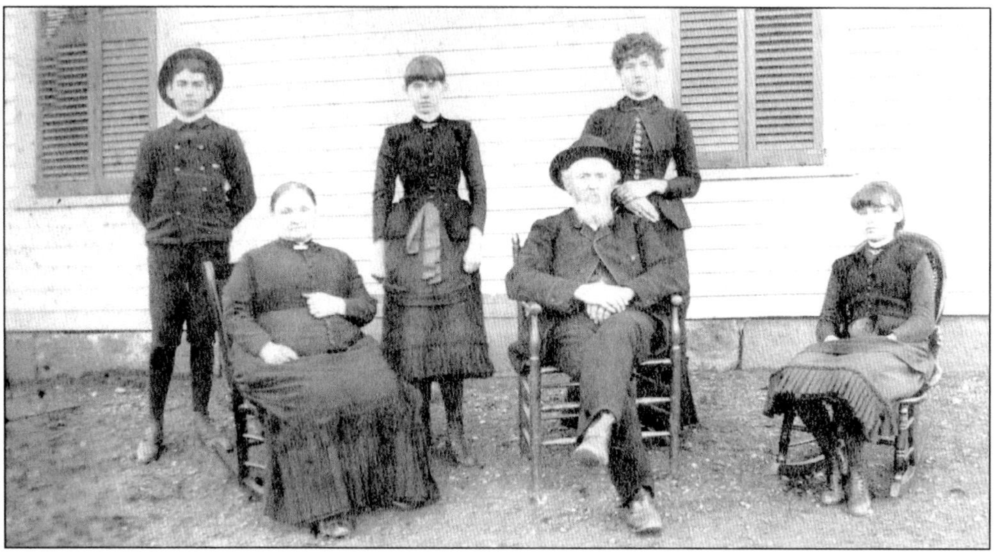

THE BISHOP FAMILY, BEFORE 1886. Pictured from left to right at 7 Bishop Lane are Truman Bishop Miller (1863–1931), Jane Bishop (1833–1912), Sarah Roxanna Bishop (1872–1962), Fitch L. Bishop (1829–1900), May Belle Bishop (1874–1953), and Ellen Bishop (1865–1950). Ellen Bishop later married Truman Miller. Fitch Bishop owned over 300 acres and was a partner in F. Ripley and Company, tobacco dealers. From 1799 to 1842, the Bishop family operated the town library out of this house. (Cider Brook Miller & Bishop Families' Collection.)

MARY ROSE ST. CLAIR, HIGH SCHOOL GRADUATION, 1902. Mary Rose St. Clair (1885–1957), was raised in Avon, the granddaughter of Nicholas and Margaret White. She taught school in New Milford, retiring to the White farm to care for her aunt Elizabeth White (1854–1955), who had raised her after her mother, Margaret White St. Clair (1849–85), had died in childbirth. (Florence Lacy Cellini Collection.)

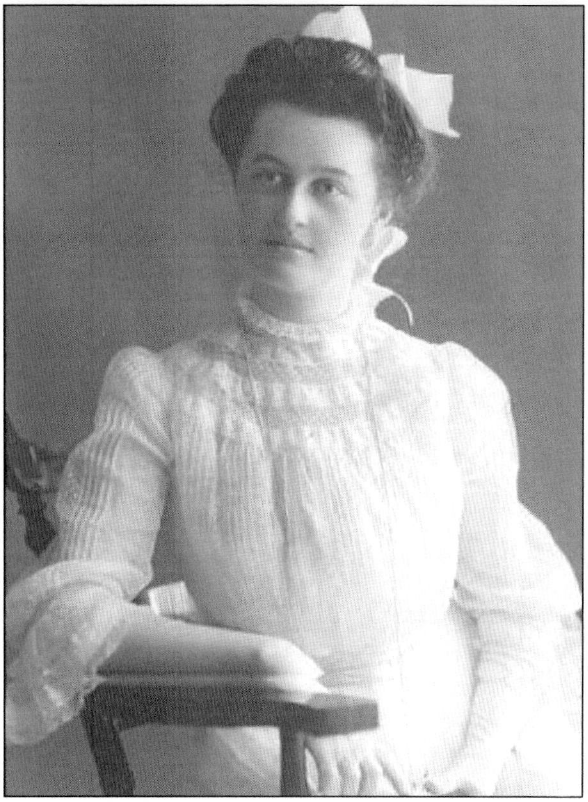

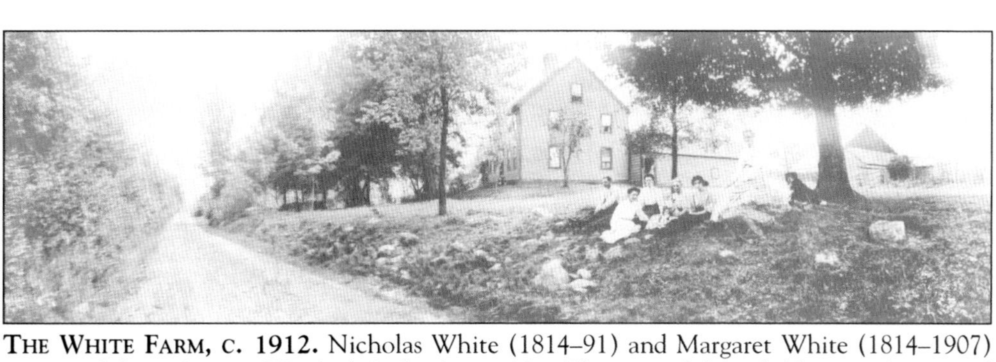

THE WHITE FARM, C. 1912. Nicholas White (1814–91) and Margaret White (1814–1907) emigrated from County Wexford, Ireland, in 1854. They raised five children in Avon, and daughter Elizabeth White inherited the farm. This postcard shows the farm at Huckleberry Hill and Edwards Roads. Pictured from left to right are farmhand Otto Schinkel, Mary Lacy, Mary Rose St. Clair, Elizabeth White, and two unidentified persons. The house was demolished in the 1950s. (Florence Lacy Cellini Collection.)

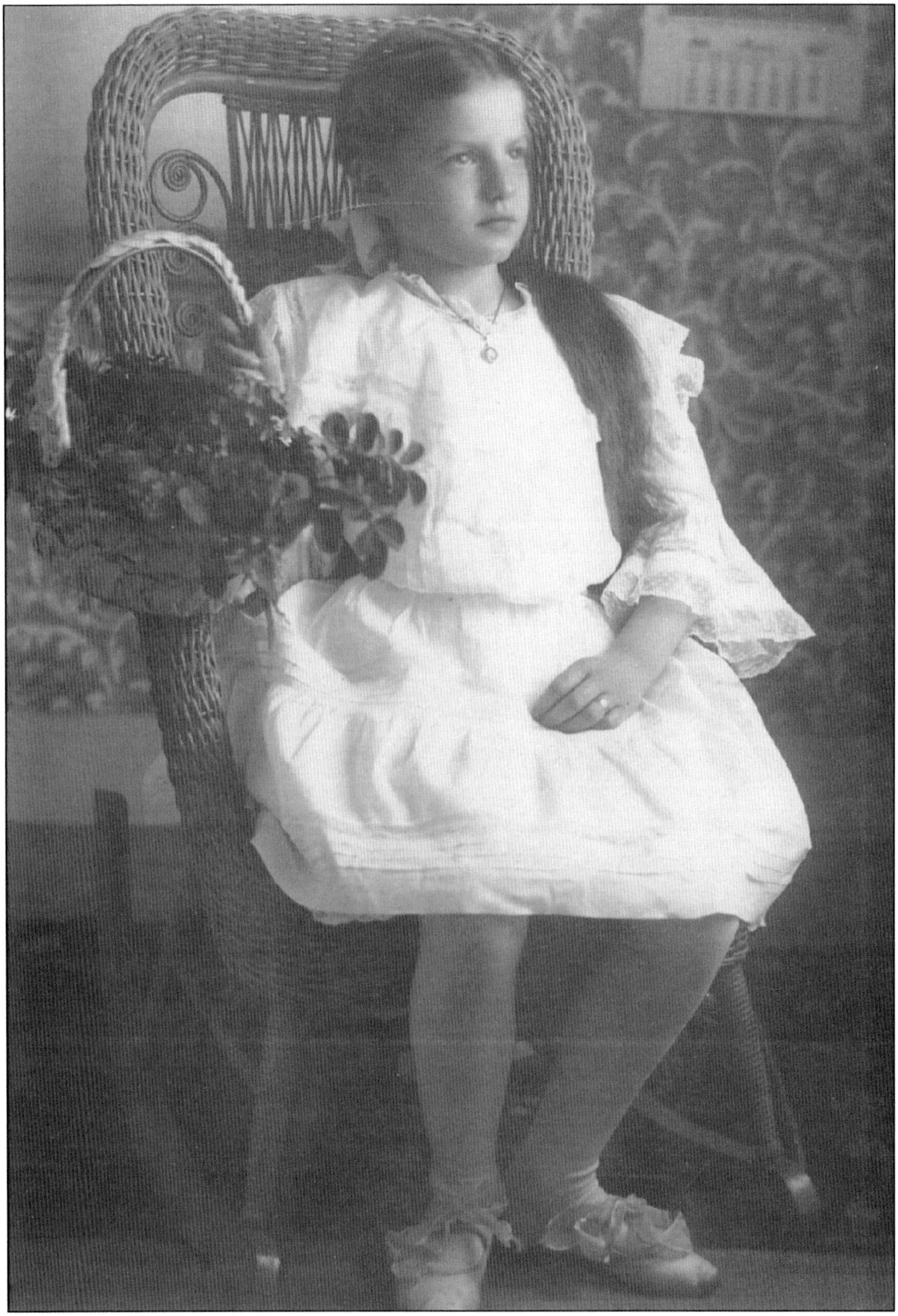

A Flower Girl, 1904. Anna Schell, flower girl at the Chidsey wedding, poses with her necklace and ring, her long hair tied in a ribbon and fancy bows on her delicate shoes. (Collection of Anthony O'Neill.)

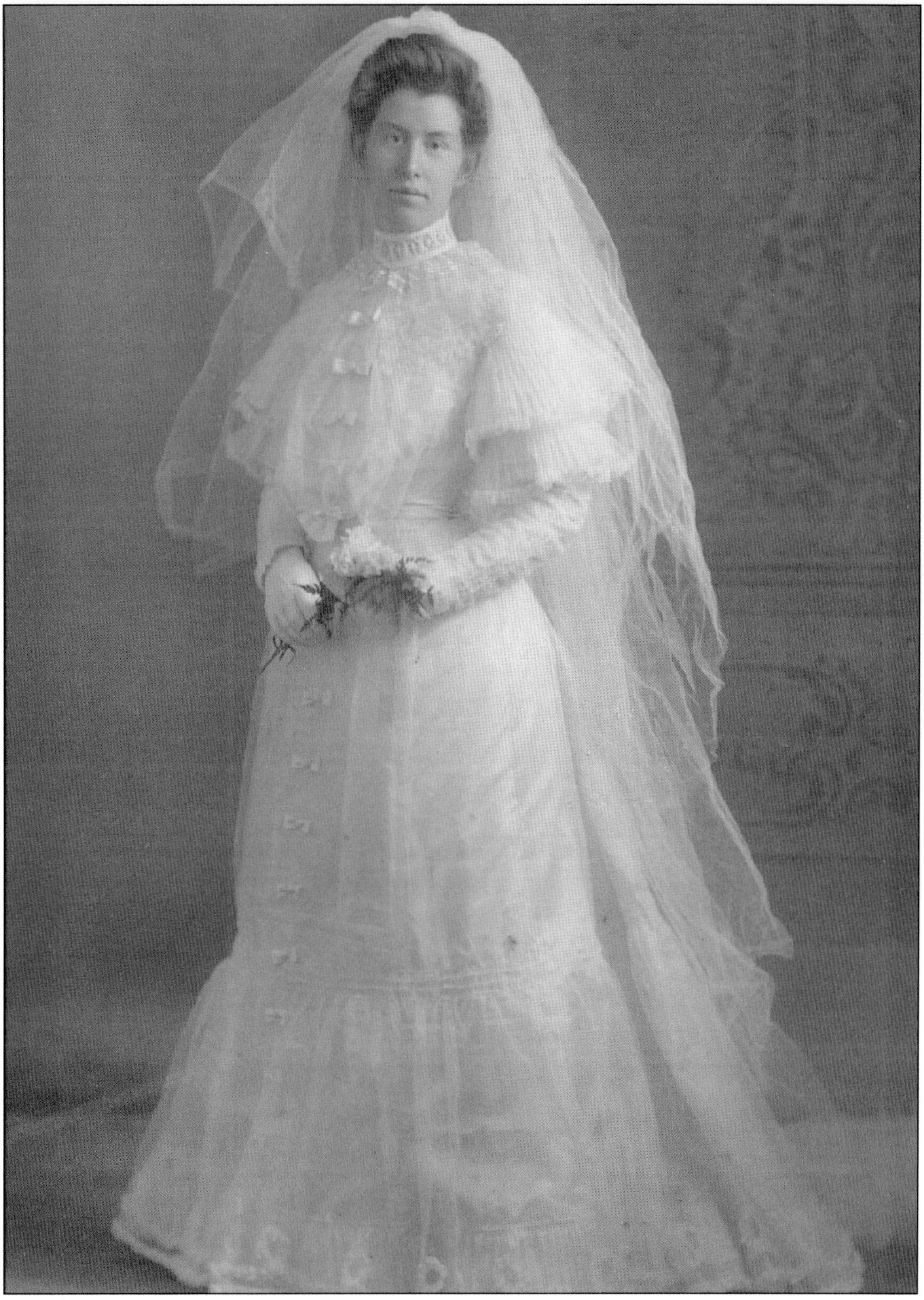

THE CHIDSEY WEDDING, 1904. Luella Sarah Fish Chidsey (1884–1978) married Louis A. Chidsey (1881–1945) on October 19, 1904, one of nine couples married in Avon that year. Luella had joined the Avon Congregational Church in 1902, and the wedding was presumably held there. The Chidseys lived and farmed in West Avon. (F.M. Johnson photograph, Anthony O'Neill Collection.)

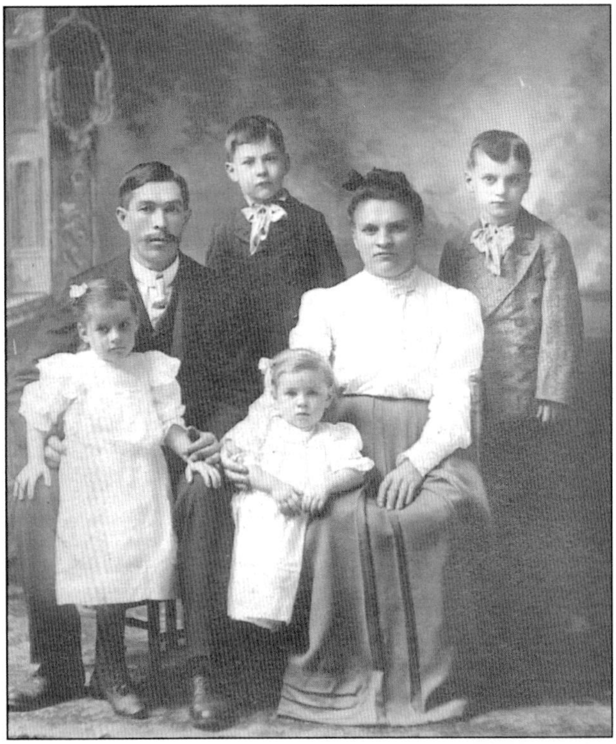

THE BEKALIK FAMILY, C. 1910. Pictured from left to right are the following: (front row) Anna Bekalik, Mary? Bekalik, and Victoria Kubik Bekalik; (back row) Joseph Bekalik, George Kubik, and Frank Kubik. Victoria Kubik emigrated from Vysne Ruzbachy, Slovakia, was widowed, and ran a boardinghouse on New Road. Her second husband, Joseph Bekalik, who also emigrated from Slovakia, was a boarder there and made plows at the Collins Company. They later owned Verveil Farm. (Doris Kubik Zumbroski Collection.)

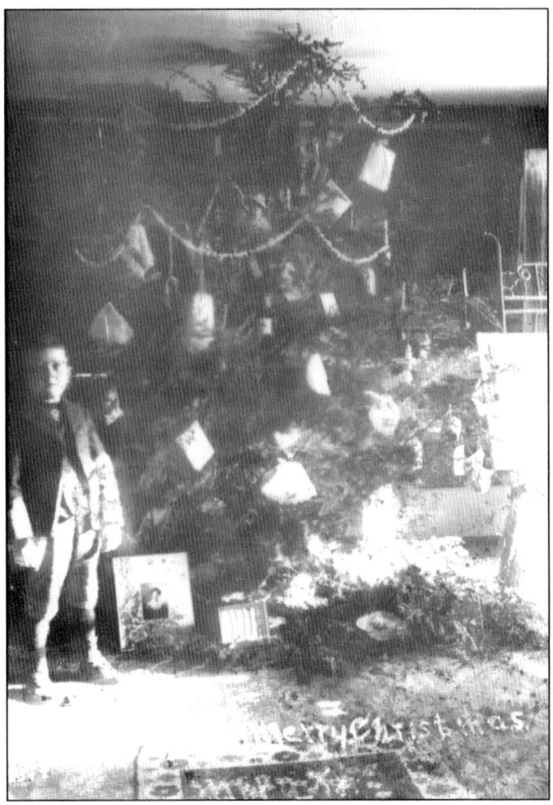

"ARNOLD'S TREE, DEC. 27, 1900." Arnold Miller stands by a Christmas tree. A framed woman's portrait stands at his feet. Decorations include garlands, a large doll, and candles. Written out on the glass plate negative is "Merry Christmas." The plate, damaged over time, is a rare view of a child's Christmas in Avon. (Clinton Hadsell photograph, Avon Collection, courtesy of Seth Stewart.)

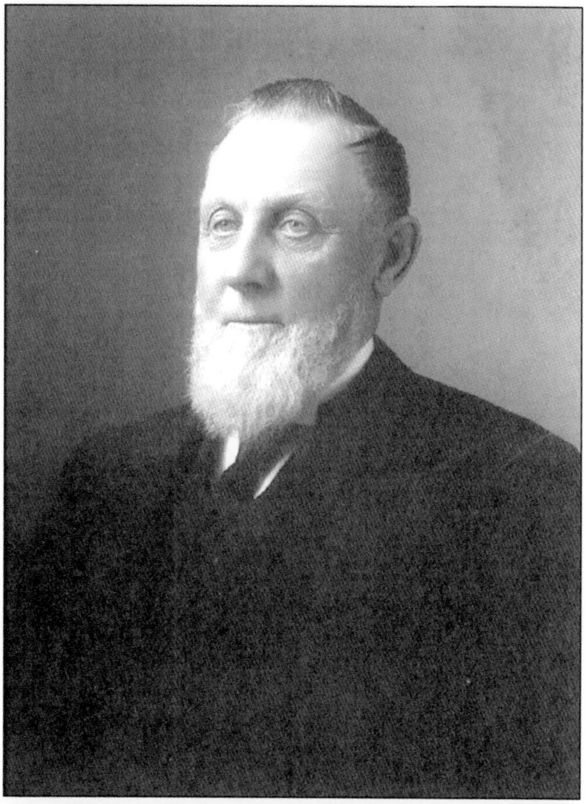

CHARLES MILLER, EARLY 1900S. Charles Miller (1840–1922) built the house at 290 Waterville Road near his birthplace. His wife was Francis Bishop Miller (1841–1903). A dairy farmer, Miller worked property on both sides of the road with his brother, Emory Miller, who lived at 331 Waterville Road. (Peg Curtin Collection.)

"VIN, FLORENCE NORTH, AND BESS. JULY 1912." Pictured from left to right are Lavinia Miller Hadsell, Florence North, and Lavinia's sister Bess Miller (1886–1970). Lavinia Miller married photographer Clinton Hadsell in 1902 and was Avon's librarian from 1913 to 1947. Florence North attended seminary in New Jersey, and Bess Miller worked as a telephone operator in Farmington. (Clinton Hadsell photograph, Avon Collection, courtesy of Doris Miller.)

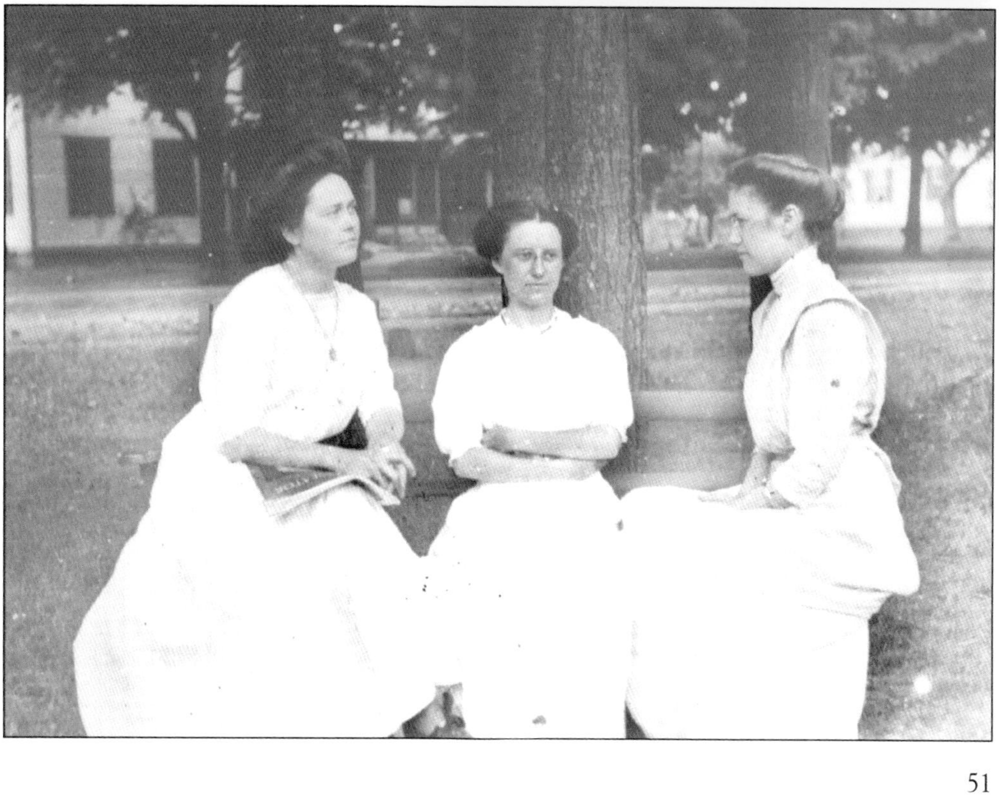

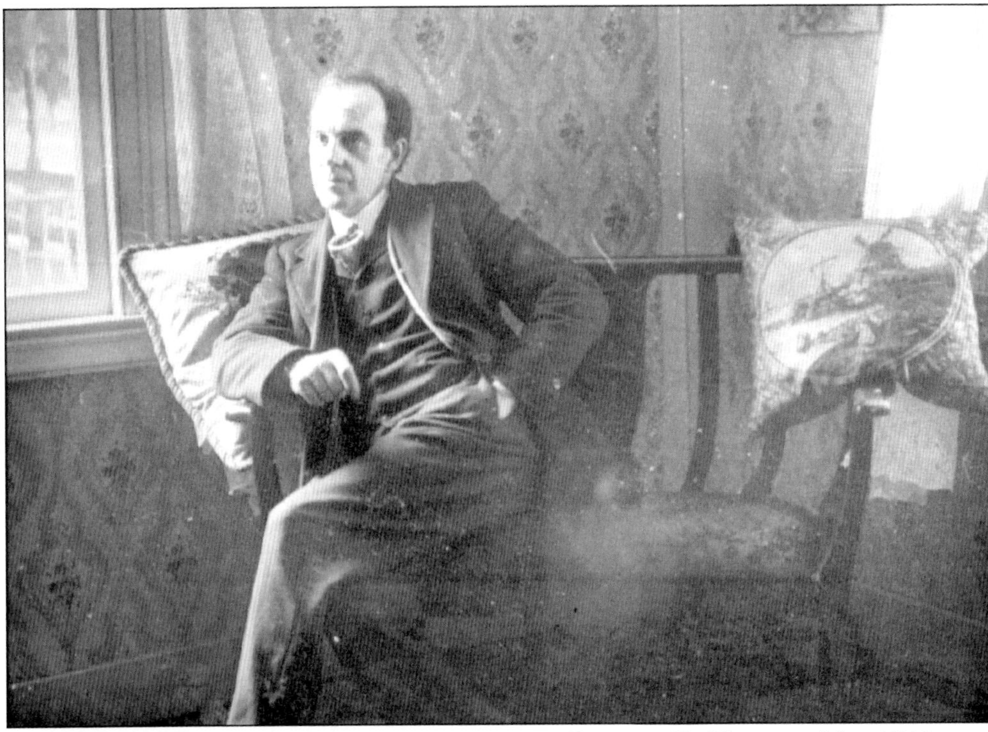

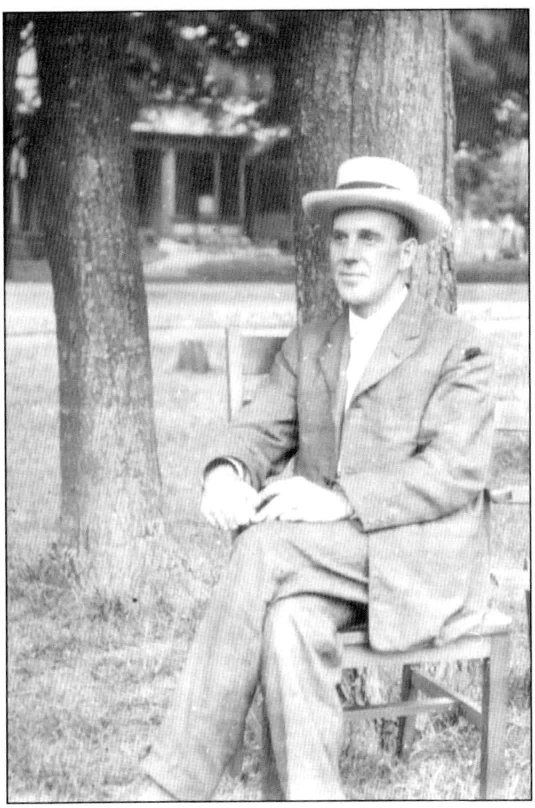

CLINTON B. HADSELL, MAY 1912. Clinton and his brother Frank Hadsell (1858–1949) created detailed records of Avon's past. Frank worked at the fuse company, ran Avon's telegraph, and was probate clerk. From his variety store, he sold postcards, groceries, books, fireworks, and many other items. His journals about Avon begin in 1845 and cover almost a century. Describing Avon in 1870, he wrote later that "little by little, the picturesque aspect of Avon Village [was] being destroyed." (Clinton Hadsell photograph, Avon Collection, courtesy of Doris Miller.)

CLINTON B. HADSELL, JULY 1912. More than 250 glass plate negatives of Avon by Clinton Hadsell (1872–1947), most of them dating from 1899 to 1918, are in the Avon Collection. Hadsell worked for the fuse company as foreman and inspector. His brother, Frank Hadsell, wrote in 1903 that Clinton Hadsell "had an instinctive flair for system and regularity and kept his wild bunch of coilers in that place attending to their work." (Avon Collection, courtesy of Doris Miller.)

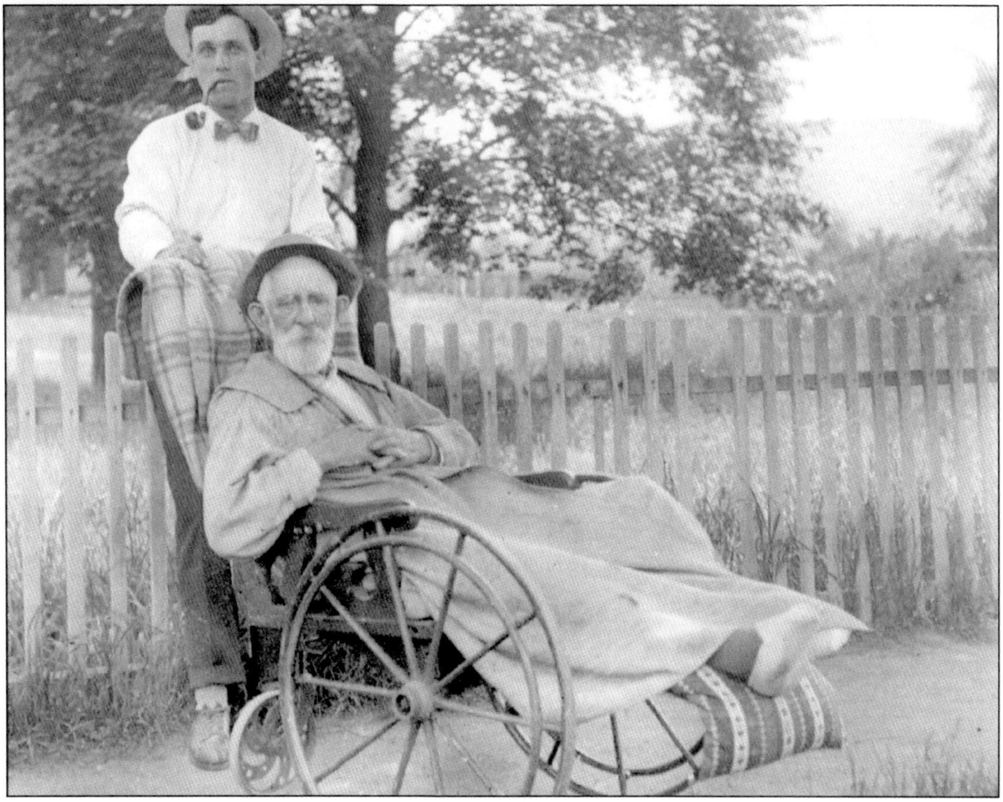

"FREDERICK RIPLEY IN A PUSHCART, MAY 27, 1912." Frederick Ripley operated Francis Woodford's hotel from 1844 to 1847. He later owned F. Ripley & Company, which sorted and packed tobacco in the Canal Warehouse, and was founding director of the Avon Water Company. When he died, Frank Hadsell wrote that Ripley "was a very honest man and a good neighbor." (Clinton Hadsell photograph, Avon Collection, courtesy of Doris Miller.)

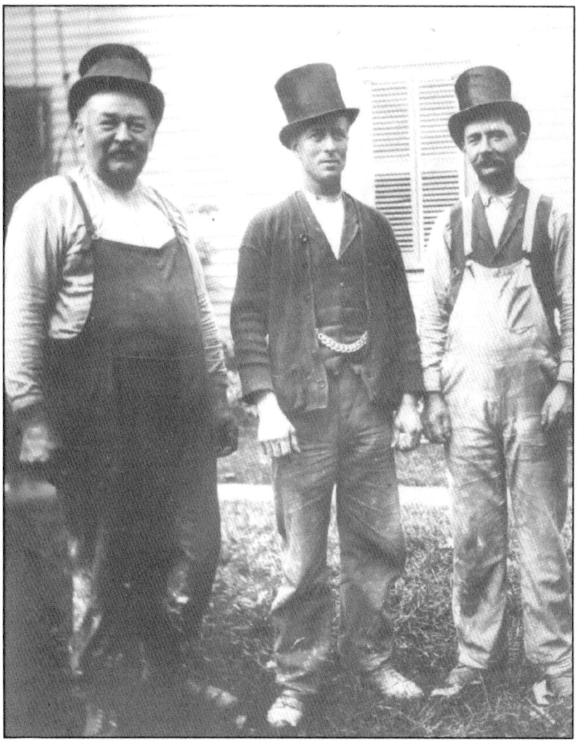

CHIMNEY WORK, C. 1906. This postcard shows, from left to right, Watson Hodge, Gux Arlander, and Laurence Scheidel. (Avon Congregational Church Collection.)

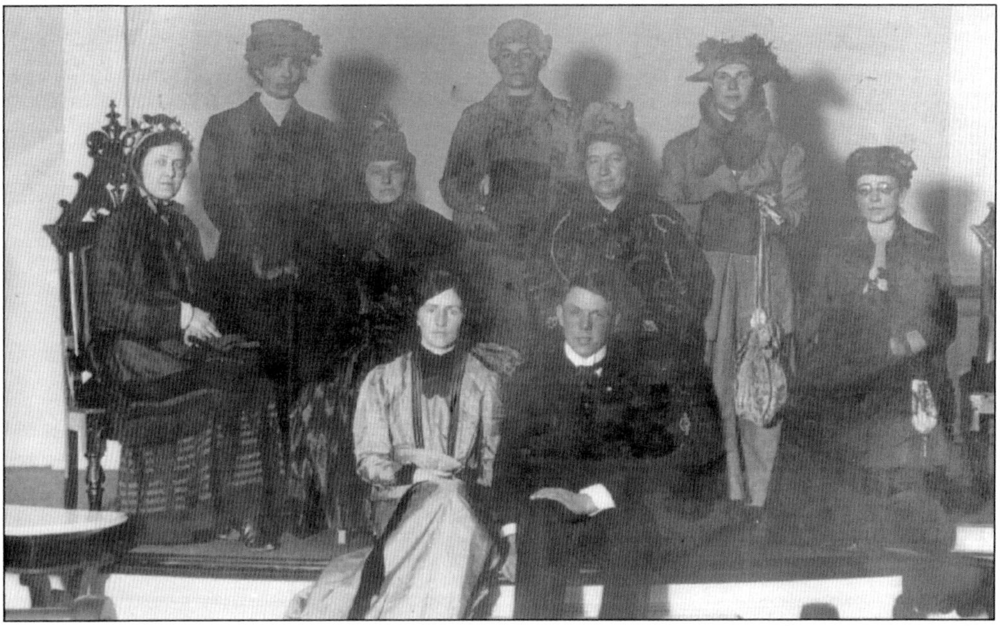

THE AVON CONGREGATIONAL CHURCH, MAY 16, 1929. Pastor Cecil Pearson took this photograph of "the Old Peabody Pew" cast sitting near the altar. Pictured from left to right are the following: (front row) Freda Woodford and Charlie Hunter; (middle row) Mrs. Frank Holloway, Mrs. Clarence Sisson, Mrs. Lucien North, and Mrs. Walter Hunter; (back row) Mrs. Archie Saxby, Mrs. Sam Goodwin, and Mrs. Sherman Eddy. (Rev. Cecil Peterson photograph, Avon Congregational Church Collection.)

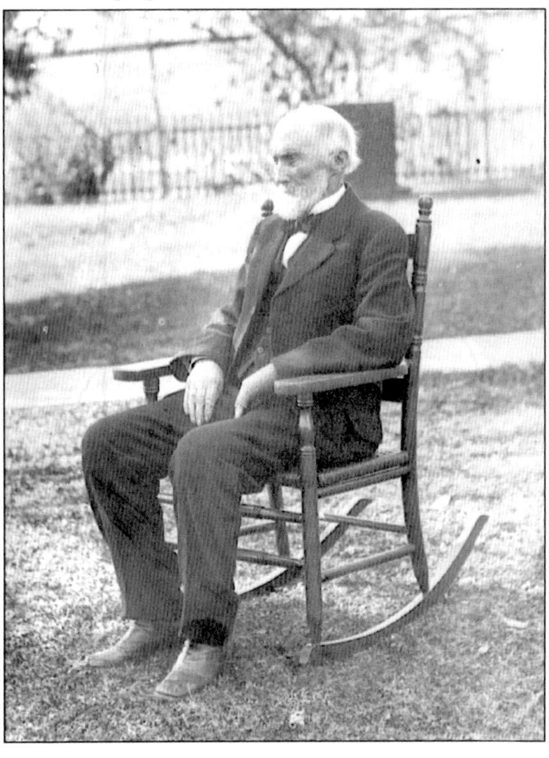

CHESTER RANDOLF WOODFORD, 1914. Chester Woodford (1814–1921) is shown on his 100th birthday in his rocking chair, a gift from his family. In 1838, lawyer Abraham Lincoln defended Woodford when he was accused of illegally selling clocks in Illinois. Woodford purchased 100 acres on Nod Road for dairying in 1841, was the first Avon farmer to grow tobacco, and introduced shade-grown tobacco in 1905. His grandson C. Frederick Woodford, chairman of the state Board of Agriculture and state representative, continued the C.F. Woodford & Son Farm, one of Connecticut's oldest family farms. (Avon Congregational Church Collection.)

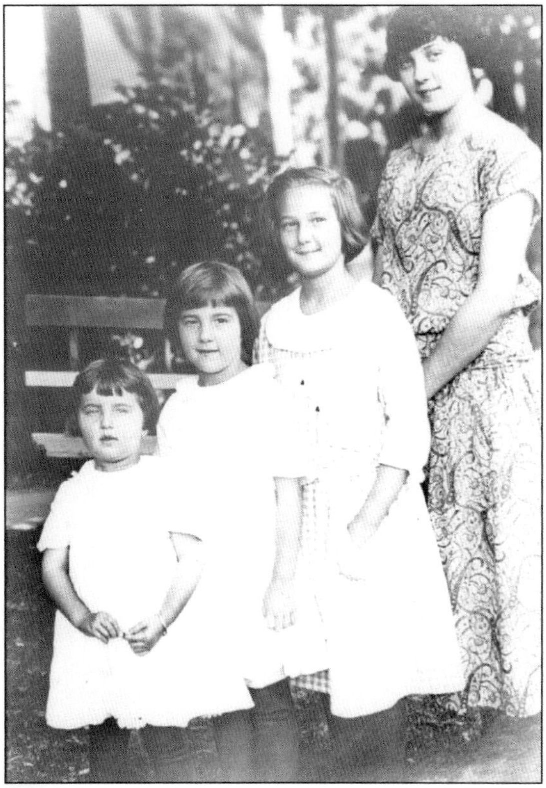

THE PLUDE SISTERS, C. 1923. Pictured at home at 89 Old Farms Road are, from left to right, Hazel, Carrie, Alice, and Gertie Plude. Their brothers were William, George, Ernie, and Howard Plude. Their mother, Martha Plude, emigrated from Germany in 1887, and their father, Eben Plude,worked at the Ensign-Bickford Company. (Barbara Plude Thomas Collection.)

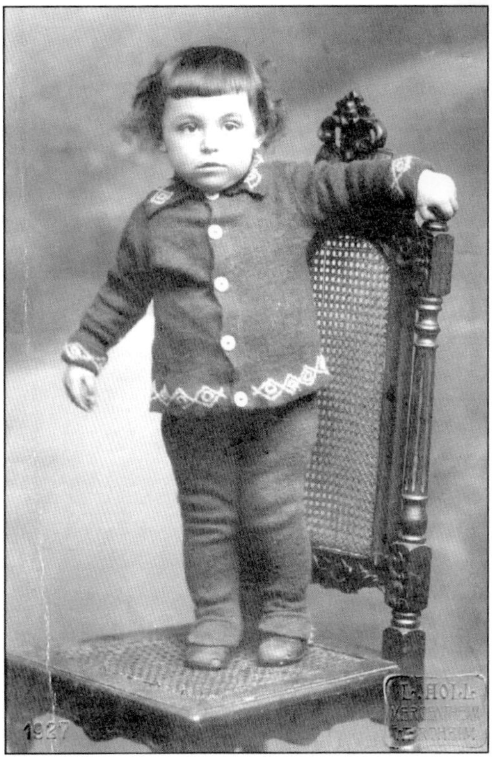

LOTHAR CANDELS, MARCH 13, 1927. Lothar Candels, the first full-time pediatrician in the Farmington Valley, opened his practice on Mountain View Avenue in 1957. Born in Germany in 1925, he came to Avon with his parents, Anthony and Martha Candels, in 1931. Dr. Candels graduated from Avon Old Farms School and New York Medical College. Named Avon Citizen of the Year in 1999, he retired in 2000 and was subsequently honored by the Prince Thomas of Savoy Society. (Carl Candels Collection.)

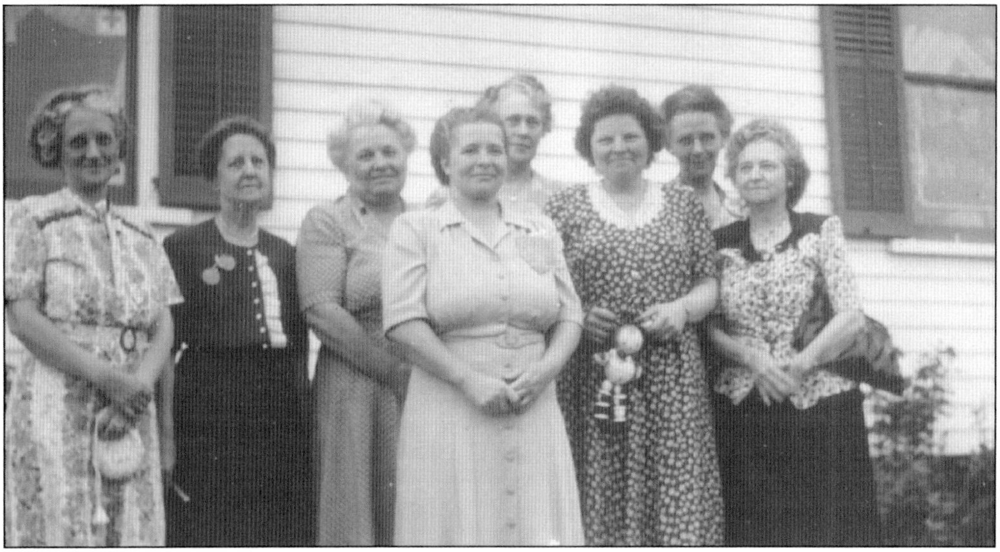

AVON FRIENDS, 1940S. Pictured from left to right are Grace Eddy, Lena Stowe LeGeyt, Nellie Read, Mildred Prowe, Lavinia Hadsell, Hazel Nelson Sisson, Maud Chandler, and Lulu Sisson. On display in the window is the Red Cross symbol. (Avon Collection.)

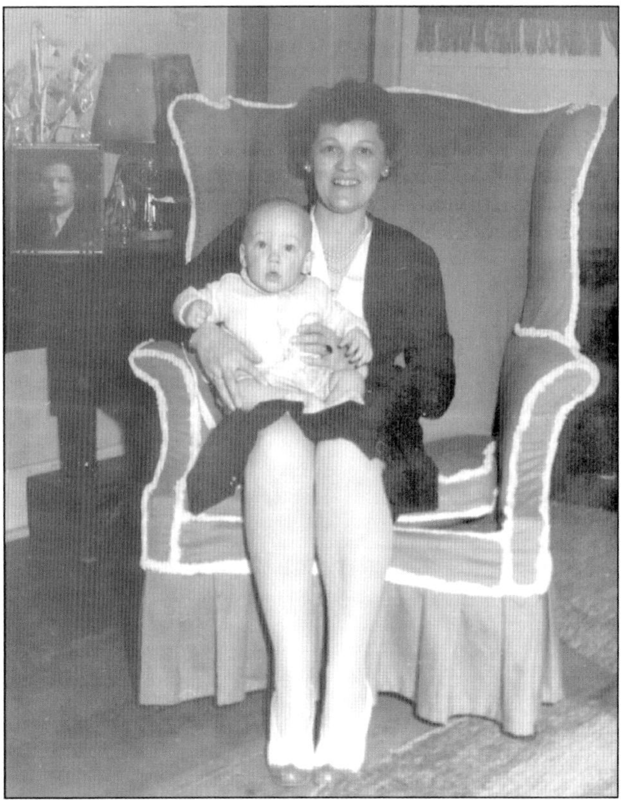

MITZIE JOYCE AND JIMMY, C. 1943. Mitzie's husband, John Joyce, was an accountant in Hartford and a stockholder of the Avon Water Company. The family lived at 37 West Main Street. (Avon Collection.)

Three

HOME SWEET HOME

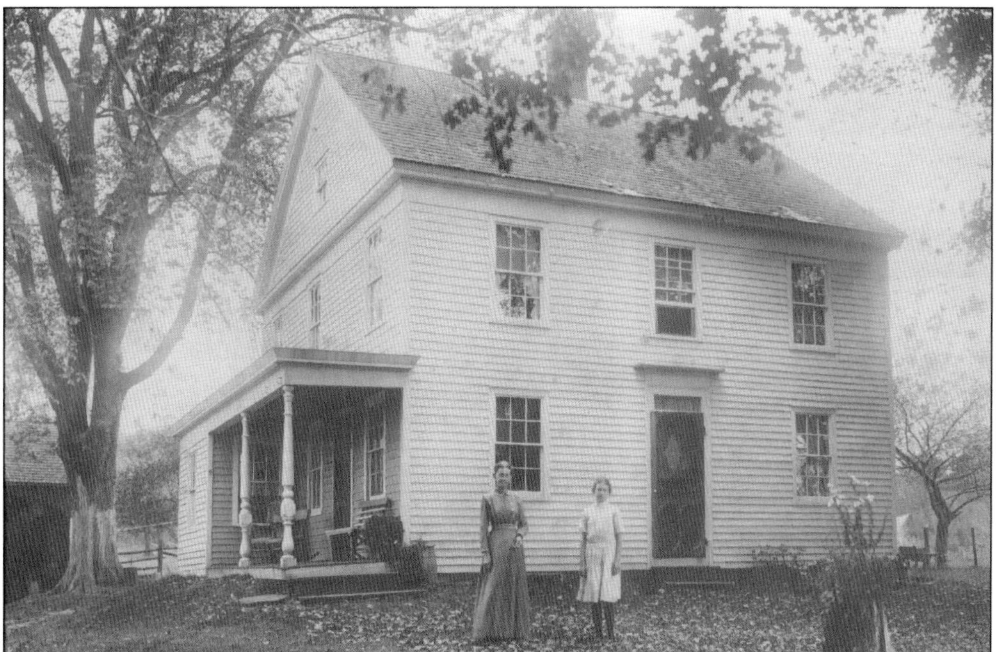

THE CHIDSEY HOUSE, C. 1915. Elizabeth Chidsey (1851–1933) stands with granddaughter Nellie Chidsey (1905–79) at 55 West Avon Road. Her husband, Edmund Chidsey (1852–1912), was a farmer, and her granddaughter was the fourth generation of the family to live in the house. Abraham Chidsey built the house *c.* 1790 and was keeper of the town poor. According to the 1910 census, Nellie Chidsey lived here with her mother, Luella Chidsey, and father, Louis Chidsey, a farmer and laborer. (Avon Collection.)

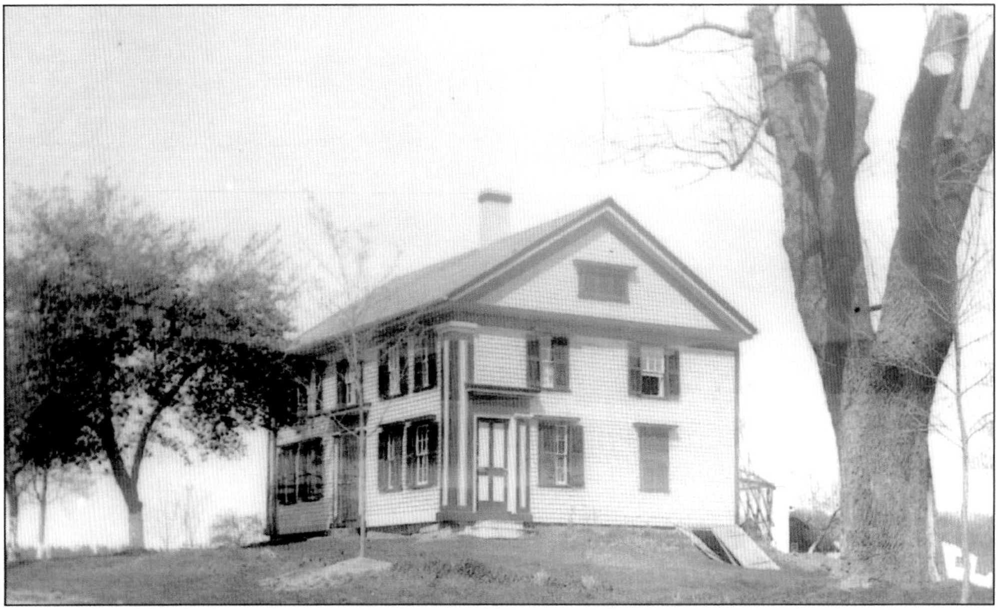

THE TILLOTSON FARM, C. 1906. This farm was established in 1776 by John Tillotson. It was later worked by son Elias Tillotson and grandsons Oliver, Shubael, and Romanta Tillotson, who farmed 380 acres and raised a herd of 140 sheep. Still standing at 164 Lovely Street, the house was built *c.* 1800 or earlier. (Avon Collection.)

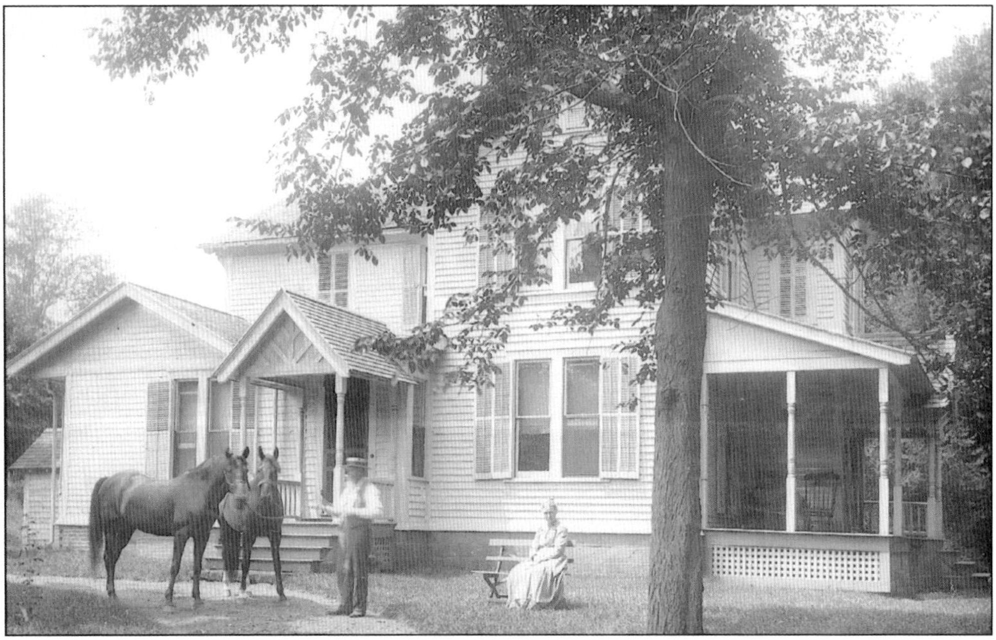

THE FRANKLIN AND LUCY ALFORD HOUSE, BEFORE 1908. This Victorian house still stands at 29 West Main Street. Franklin Alford (1840–1908) was wounded at Antietam during the Civil War. At the 16th Regiment's reunion in 1867, he wrote that those who attended "had a pleasant time but felt sad when we thought of the many brave comrades we had left buried in Southern soil." Discharged in 1863, he made bayonets for the army and began manufacturing fuses in Avon *c.* 1870. (Avon Collection.)

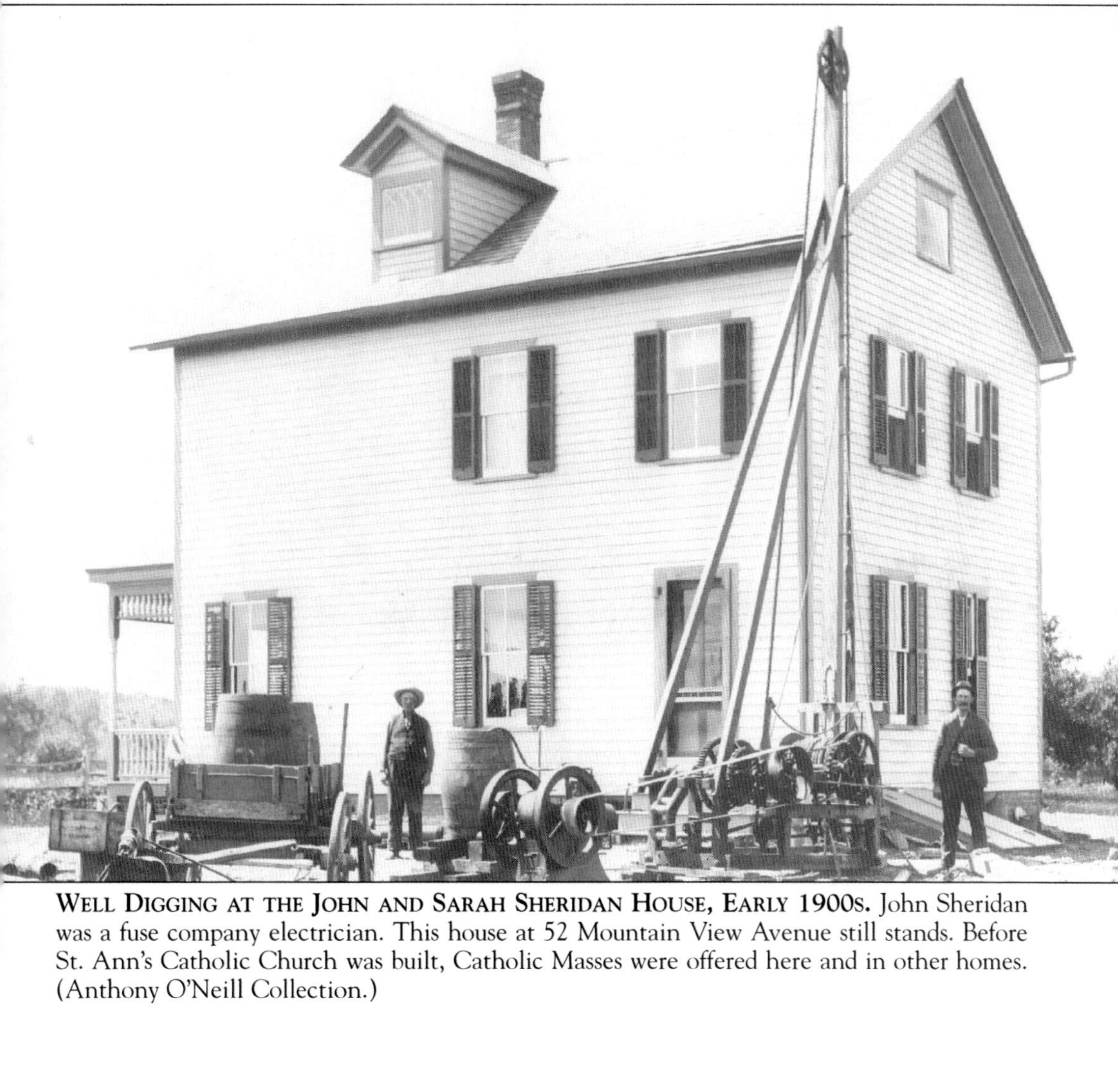

WELL DIGGING AT THE JOHN AND SARAH SHERIDAN HOUSE, EARLY 1900S. John Sheridan was a fuse company electrician. This house at 52 Mountain View Avenue still stands. Before St. Ann's Catholic Church was built, Catholic Masses were offered here and in other homes. (Anthony O'Neill Collection.)

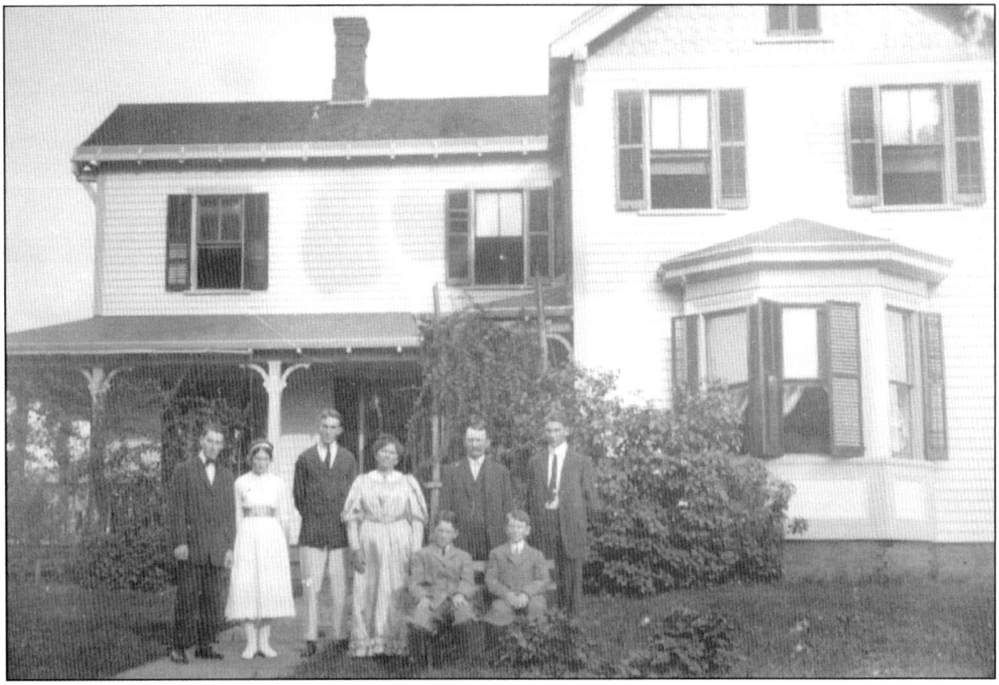

THE MANION FAMILY, JULY 1914. The house stands at 20 Mountain View Avenue. A few years after this photograph was taken, the Manion family donated property for the new St. Ann's Church. In 1910, the family included the following: William Manion, 42, a fuse company carpenter; Ellen Manion, his wife, 44; William, 15, a fuse company coiler; John, 14; Harold, 13; Dorothy, 10; George "Ted", 9; Raymond, 8; and a boarder. (Clinton Hadsell Photograph, printed in reverse. Avon Collection, courtesy of Doris Miller.)

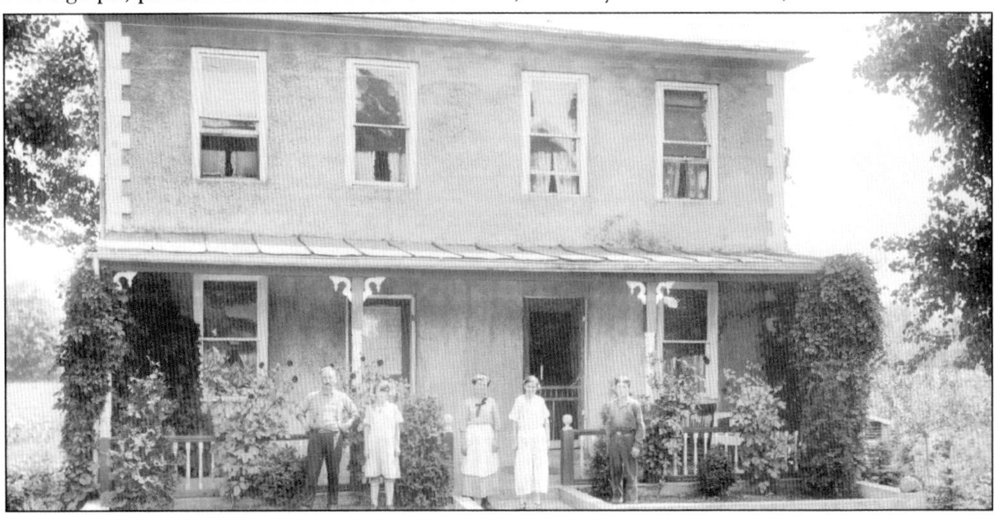

THE BONESIO FAMILY, C. 1918. Pictured is Joseph Bonesio with Alice, Rose, Theresa, and Louis Bonesio. Not pictured are sons Martin, Peter, and Frank Bonesio, the latter two serving in World War I. Joseph and Rose Bonesio emigrated from Italy in 1903. They ran a grocery store in their house and a tobacco farm on Old Farms Road. Peter Bonesio became Avon's fire marshall in 1941, setting up volunteer firefighting crews in different sections of town. His son Albert Bonesio became Avon's first fire chief in 1961. (Avon Collection.)

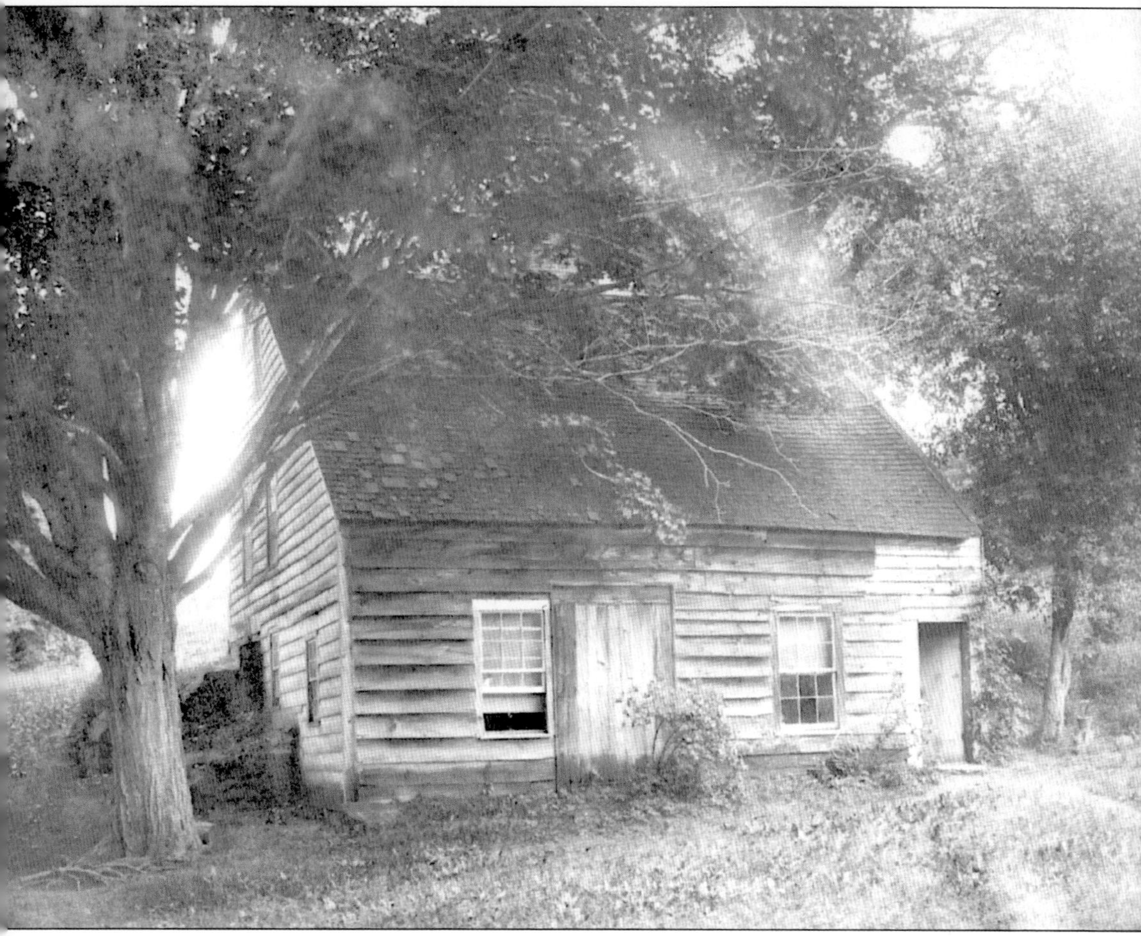

AN UNIDENTIFIED HOUSE. No longer standing, this house was in the Sleepy Hollow area of the Old Farms section. (Sunrise Farm Collection.)

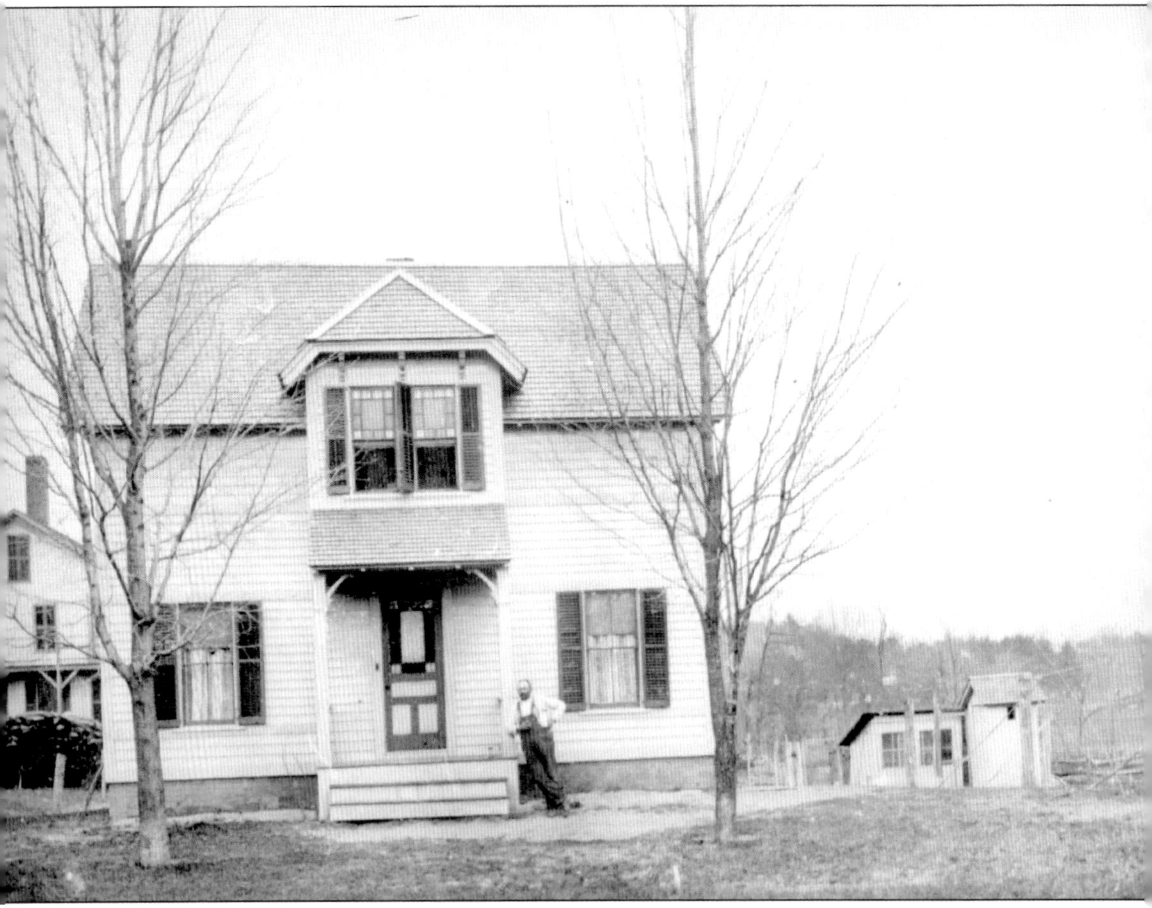

THE JOSEPH AND ELIZABETH SNYDER HOUSE, MAY, 1912. This photograph probably shows Joseph Snyder in front of his house. On the right is the outhouse. According to the 1910 census, the Snyder family had four children: Mary, 16, and Irene, 14, who worked as Ensign-Bickford fuse tapers; Joseph Jr., 12; and Gertrude, 11. The family had moved to New Jersey by 1917. (Clinton Hadsell photograph, Avon Collection, courtesy of Doris Miller.)

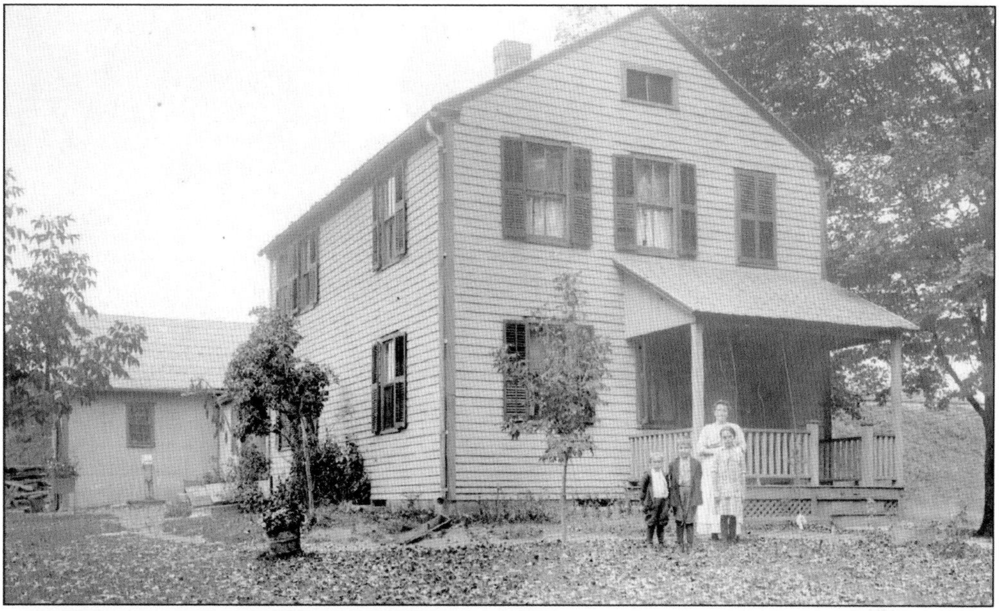

THE EBEN AND MARTHA PLUDE HOUSE, C. 1918. Located at 89 Old Farms Road and still standing, the house was owned by the Ensign-Bickford Company, which rented it to employees. Pictured from left to right are Ernie, Howard, and Gertrude Plude with their mother, Martha Plude. In back are railroad tracks leading north into Avon. (Barbara Plude Thomas Collection.)

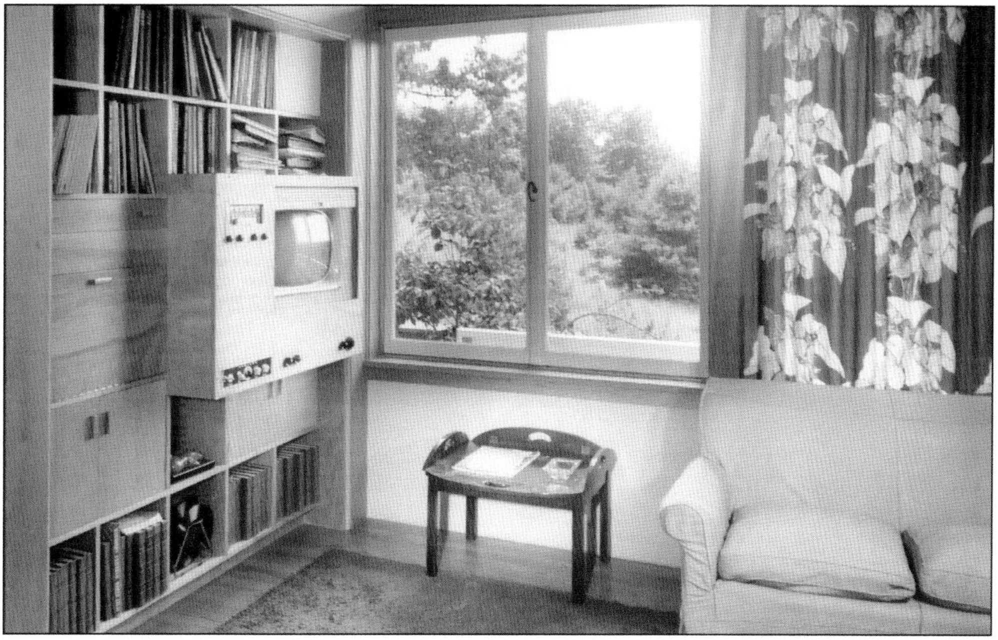

THE THOMAS AND ELINOR OAKES HOUSE, 1949. This home at 219 Cider Brook Road was built for a newly married Hartford insurance executive, Thomas Oakes, and his wife, Elinor Oakes, both veterans of World War II. Television had just been introduced to the public in 1946. The *Hartford Times* noted that "the postwar home building surge is opening new vistas for many . . . families . . . . The new homes represent the latest trends in contemporary design and construction." (Nora Howard Collection.)

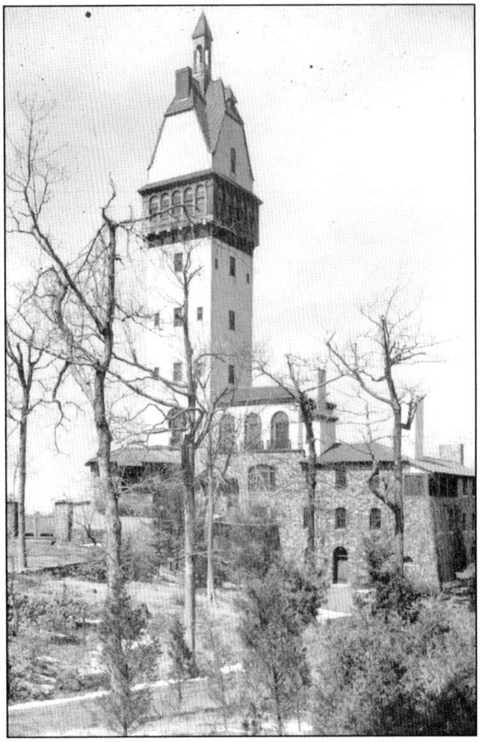

The Heublein Tower, c. 1914. Built in 1914 by Gilbert F. Heublein (1850–1937) and located just over the Avon line in Simsbury, this was the fifth tower atop Talcott Mountain since 1810. The Heubleins summered and entertained here from 1914 to 1937. The Hartford Times owned the tower from 1943 to 1966, the State of Connecticut opened it to the public in 1974, and it became a U.S. Department of the Interior Historic Place in 1983. (Friends of Heublein Tower Collection.)

General Eisenhower's Visit, 1950. Gen. Dwight David Eisenhower (on the left, smiling, with a circular design on his necktie) and Connecticut Gov. Chester Bowles attend a sheep barbecue at the Times Tower (Heublein Tower) in conjunction with the dedication of Bradley Field. While in town, Eisenhower was asked to run for the presidency of the United States. Leaving, he remarked to the Hartford Times publisher, "It's been a grand day." (Friends of Heublein Tower Collection.)

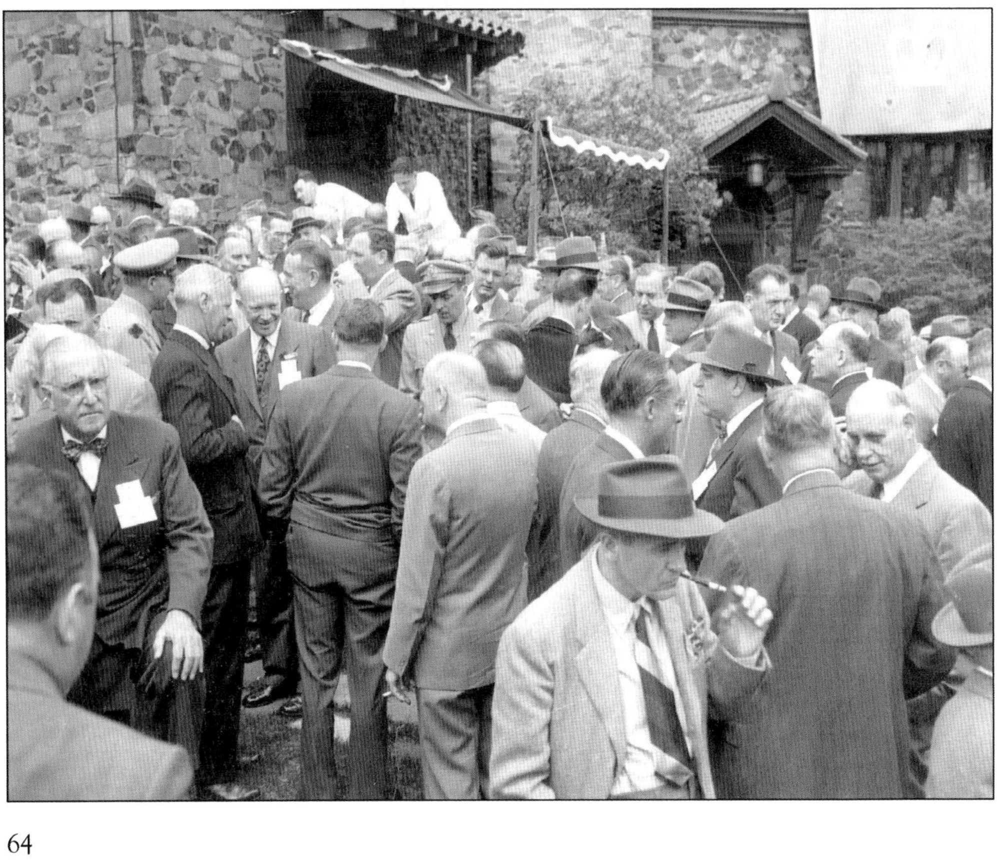

Four

SERVING TOWN AND COUNTRY

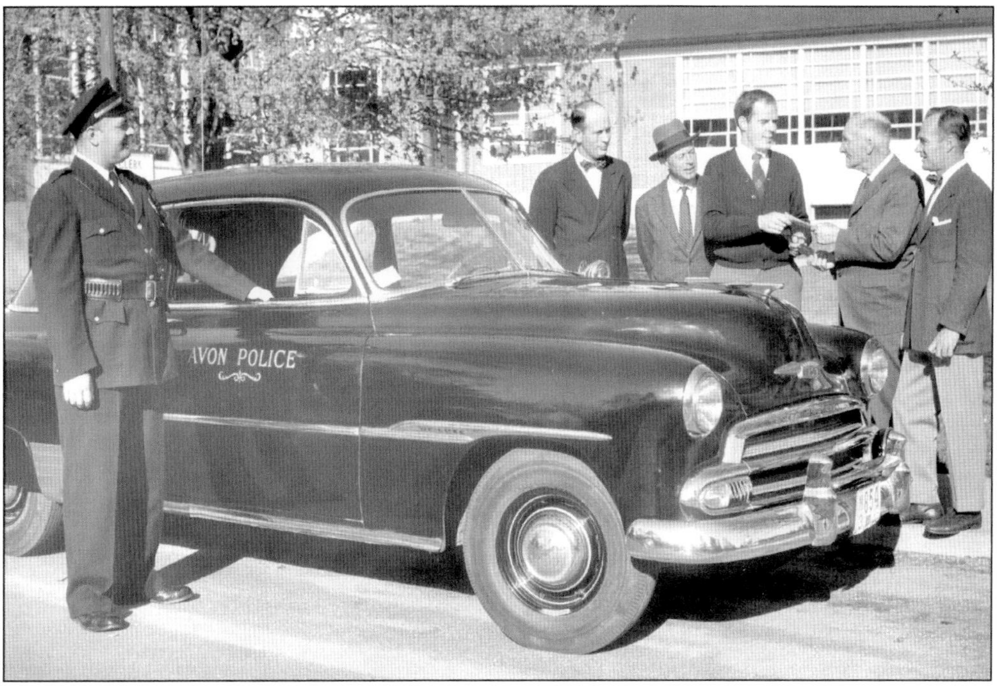

A NEW POLICE CRUISER. John H. O'Neill and his son John Anthony O'Neill gave Avon a new police car in 1952 or 1953. The O'Neills replaced this cruiser with a 1954 model "for a very nominal fee which was a great benefit to the town." Pictured from left to right are William Scott, police chief; Frank Holloway, police commissioner; Philip Hewes, selectman; John Anthony O'Neill; C. Fred Woodford, chair of the police commissioners; and an unidentified person. (Avon Police Department Collection.)

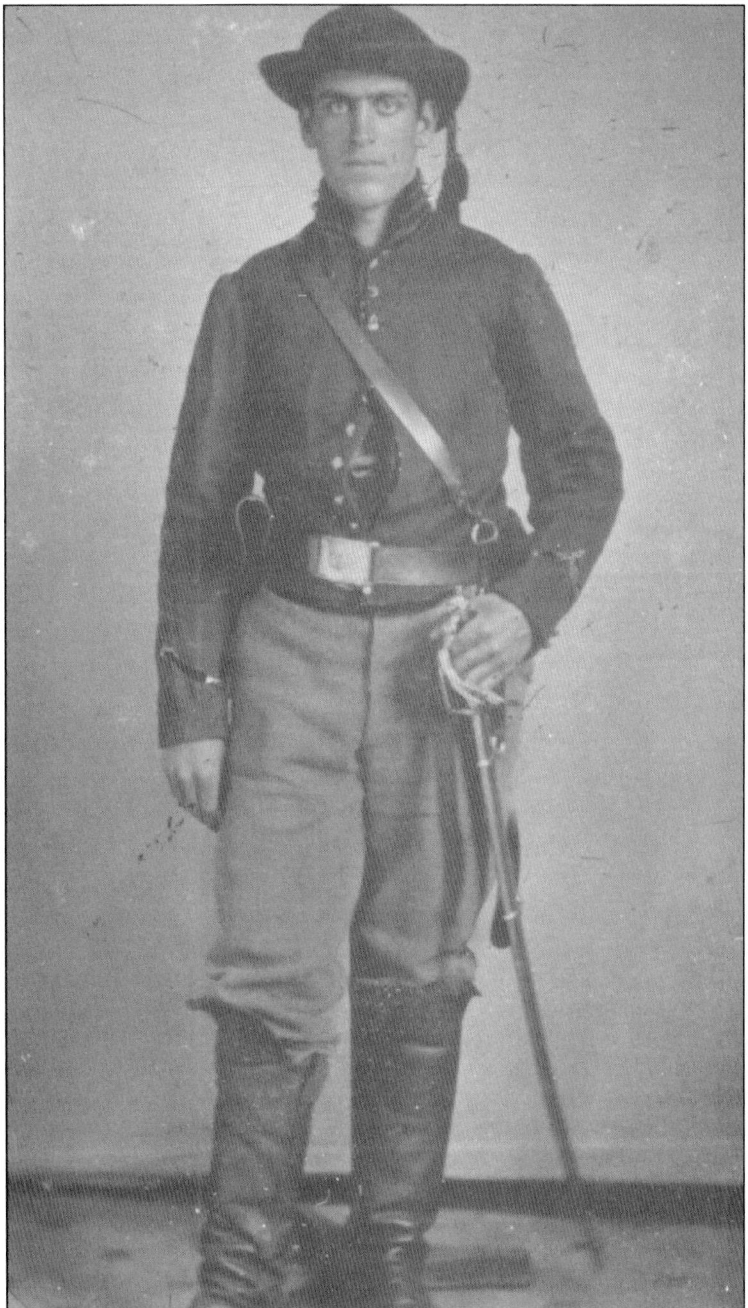

A Civil War Soldier, c. 1862. Robert Holmes (1841–1923), of East Granby, enlisted in 1862 in the 16th Connecticut Volunteers as a musician, fought at Antietem, was captured in 1864, and went to Andersonville Prison. Discharged on July 7, 1865, he never spoke of his war experiences. By the 1880s, Holmes was living in West Avon, where he operated a gristmill and sawmill. He served as a West Avon Congregational Church deacon and state legislator (1897–98). He lived with his daughter Alice Holmes at 621 West Avon Road after *c.* 1910. (Douglas Ross Collection.)

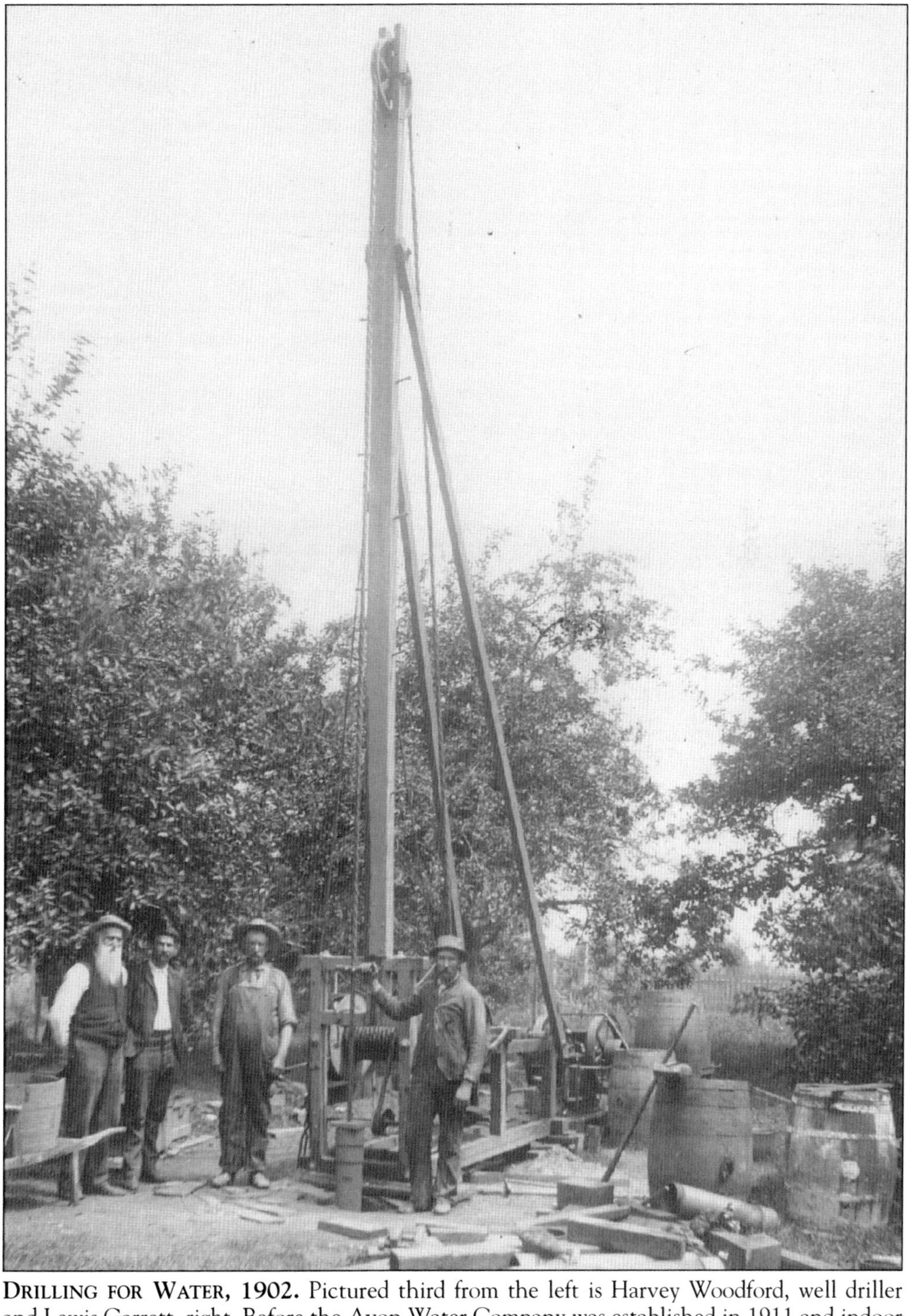

DRILLING FOR WATER, 1902. Pictured third from the left is Harvey Woodford, well driller and Lewis Garrett, right. Before the Avon Water Company was established in 1911 and indoor plumbing became available, residents had to use wells. Frank Hadsell opposed getting water piped into his home, not realizing, as he later wrote, "the wonderful convenience of running water at the sink." (Howes Brothers photograph, Anthony O'Neill Collection.)

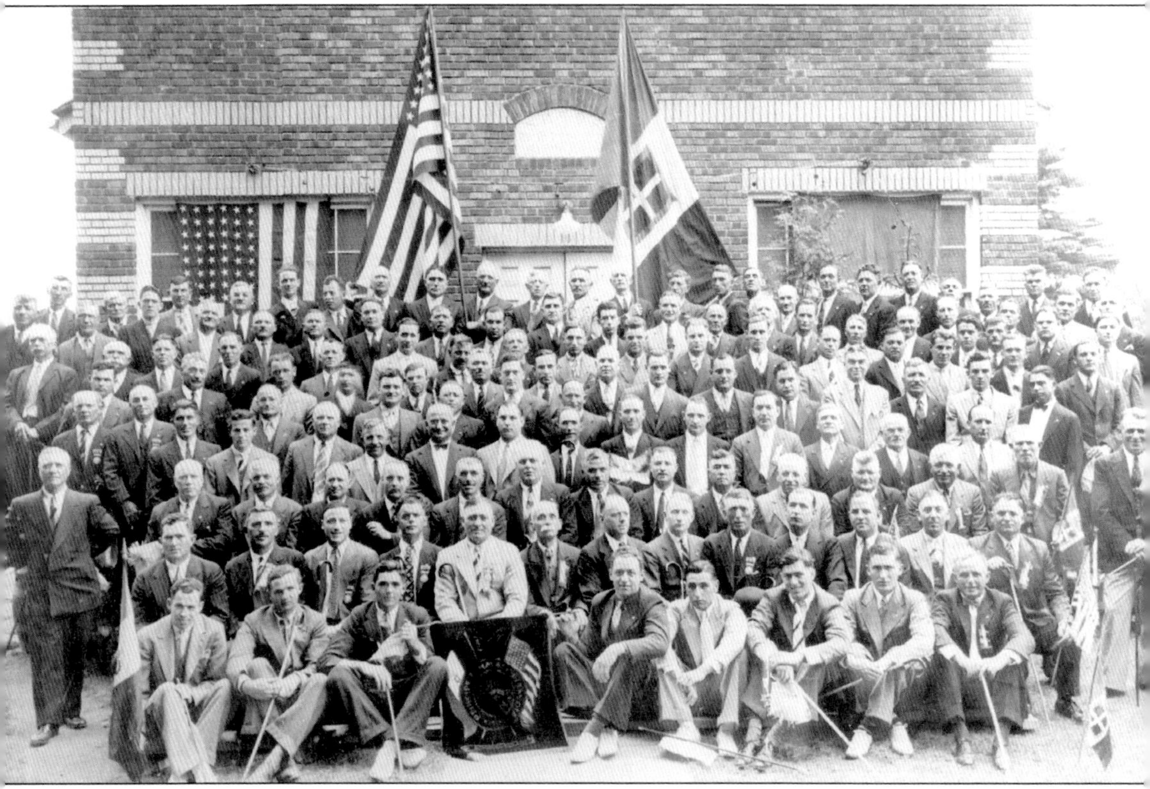

THE 20TH ANNIVERSARY OF THE PRINCE THOMAS OF SAVOY SOCIETY, 1937. This fraternal and civic society was formed in 1917 by the Italian community of Avon. The group met first in private homes until their meeting hall at 32 Old Farms Road was built in 1930. Donating to the building project were residents in Avon and surrounding towns and local leaders Arturo Fedrizzi and Silvio Viti. (Carl Candels Collection.)

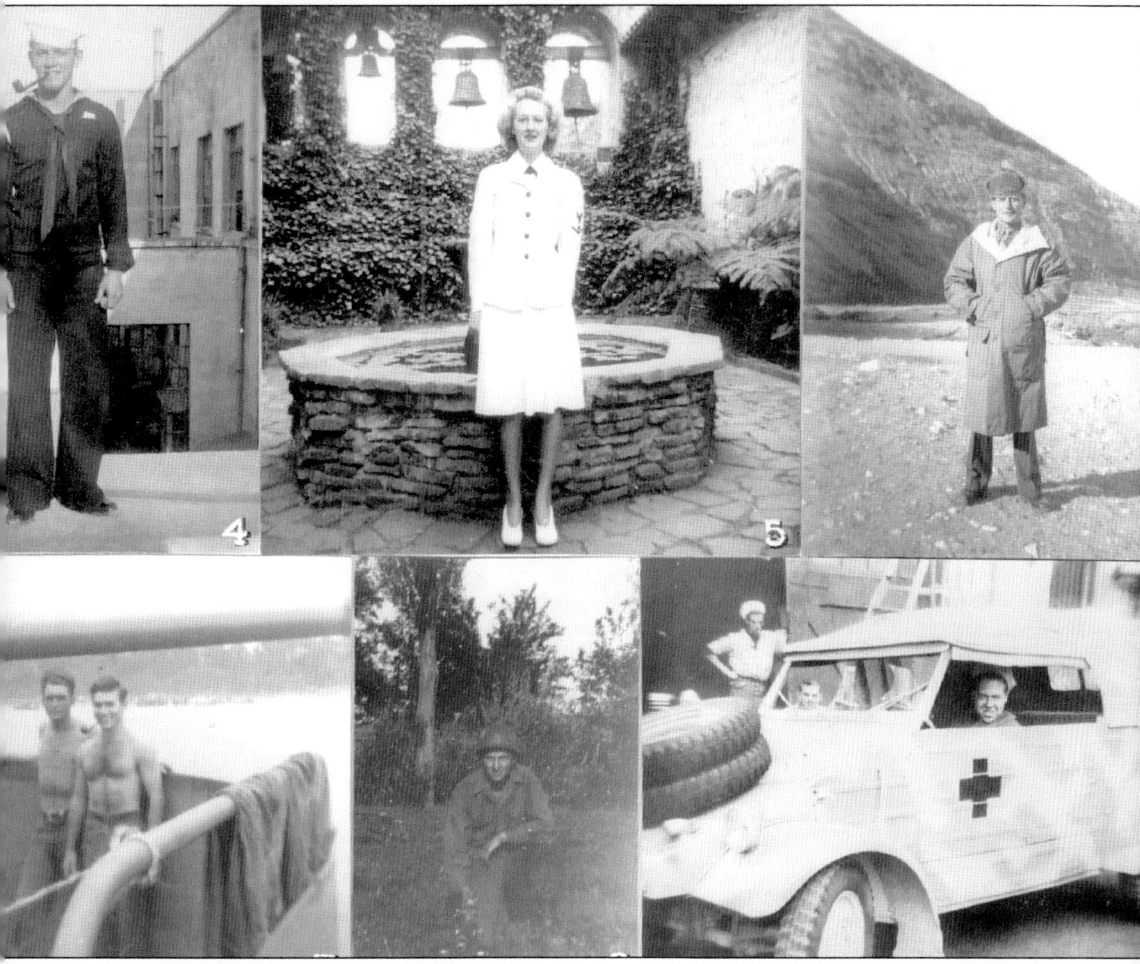

WORLD WAR II VETERANS. A total of 300 men and women from Avon are named on Avon's Veterans Memorial as serving between 1941 and 1946. Of that number, 13 lost their lives. The granite memorial on the Avon Town Green, dedicated to all who served after Avon's incorporation in 1830, carries the words "Avon Remembers" and "No Greater Gift." Pictured are, clockwise from top left, Victor Westerling in Italy, Dorothy Magnuson in California, Henry Goralski in Greenland, Russell Strunk in a German jeep in the United States, John Zanolli in Europe, and Gerald Steben (right) at Guadalcanal, 1944. These photographs appeared in the bimontly *Avon Newsletter*, issued by the Red Cross for "Avonites in the Services." (Avon Collection.)

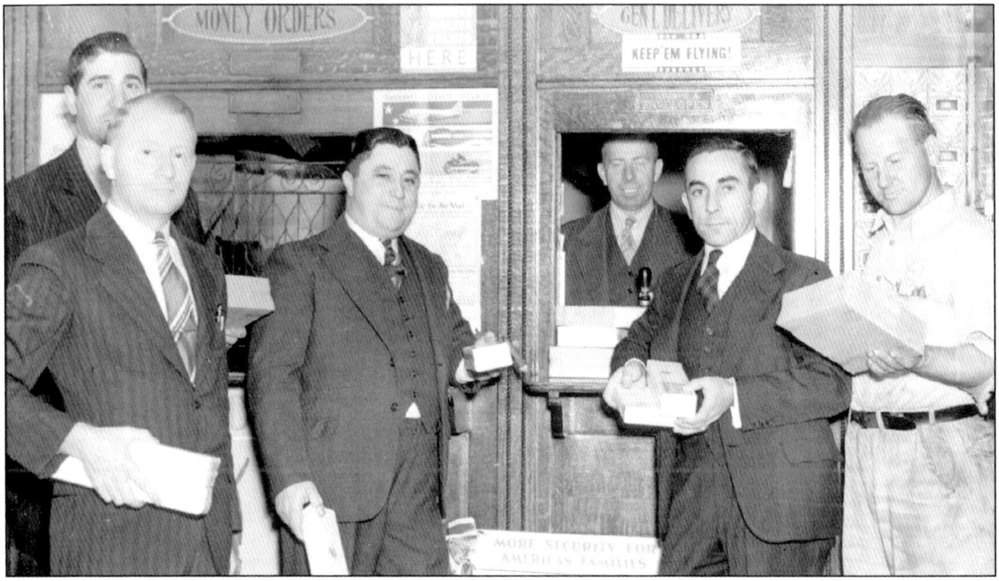

SENDING PACKAGES TO SERVICEMEN, 1943. Pictured in the post office, at 1 East Main Street, are members of the Red Men's Club, a fraternal group who hunted and fished together. Shown from left to right are Bill Gold; Ernest Tarca; Barto Roncaioli; Ted Manion, postmaster from 1934 to 1968; Dom Bogino; and Lucian Baranoski, fire chief. (Anthony O'Neill Collection.)

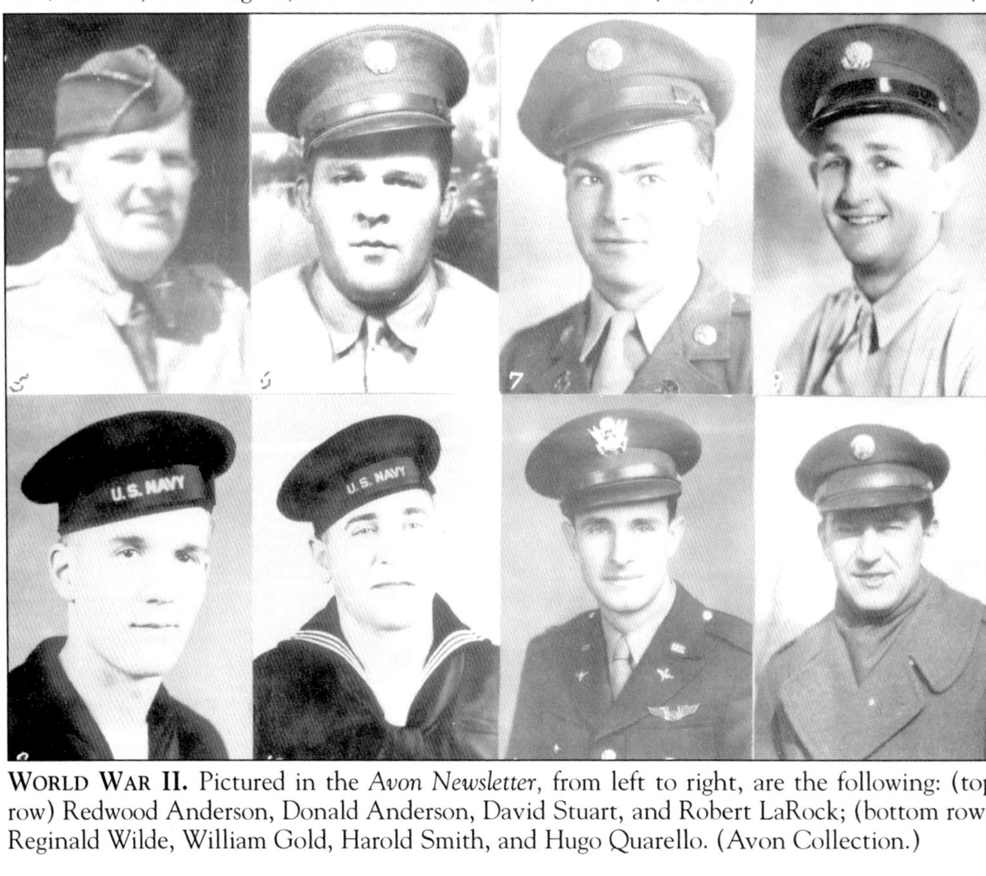

WORLD WAR II. Pictured in the *Avon Newsletter,* from left to right, are the following: (top row) Redwood Anderson, Donald Anderson, David Stuart, and Robert LaRock; (bottom row) Reginald Wilde, William Gold, Harold Smith, and Hugo Quarello. (Avon Collection.)

THE AVON HEALTH CENTER, C. 1945. Pictured are Gertrude Petersen (1901–91) and Nick Petersen (1891–1953). After selling their 200-acre Haynes Road dairy farm in 1941, and at the request of physicians, Gertrude Petersen and her children began caring for people in their home at 652 West Avon Road c. 1943. Selling the operation in 1955, it became the Avon Convalescent Home, the Farmington Valley's first (now the Avon Health Center). (Jeanette Petersen St. Peter Collection.)

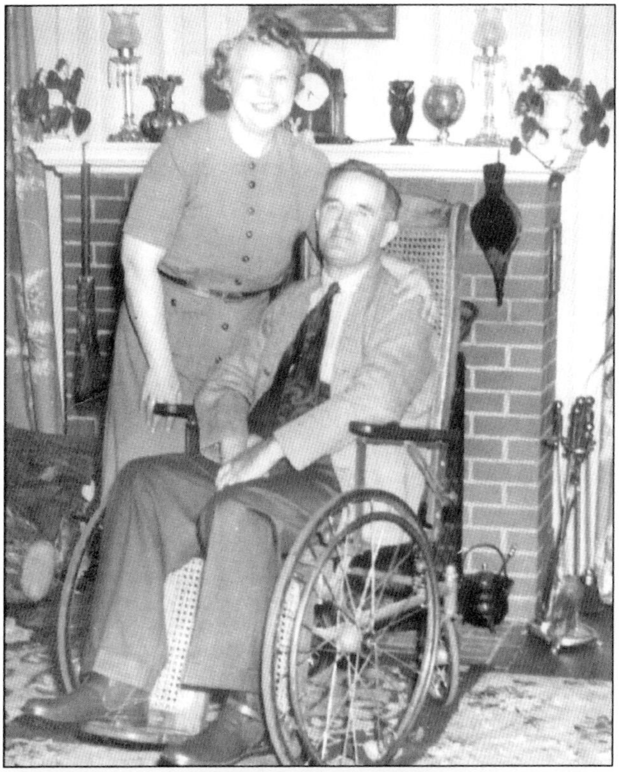

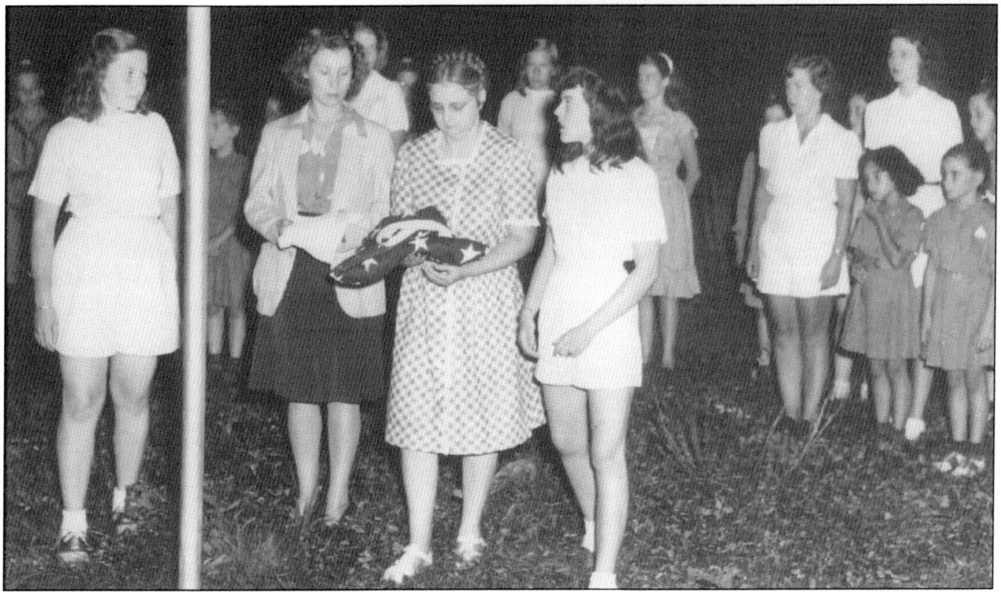

THE CAMP GERTRUDE BRYANT DEDICATION, AUGUST 26, 1947. Pfc. Gertrude Bryant (1917–44) served in the Women's Army Air Corps during World War II. Not wanting to share Camp Alsop for boys, Avon girls and Gertrude Bryant's mother, Mrs. J.A. Bryant, established a Girl Scout camp near the present high school. It operated until the 1960s. Pictured from left to right are Joanne Phillips, Dorothy St. Pierre, scout leader Dorothy Hunter, and Lois Heiman. (Sunrise Farm Collection.)

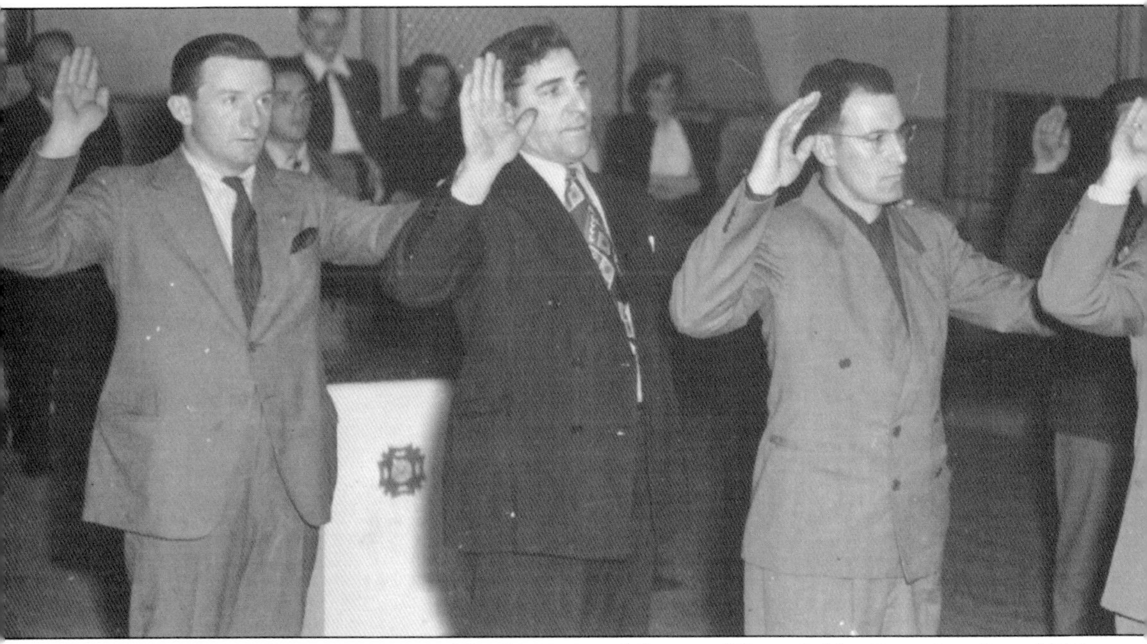

Swearing in Officers, 1949. The Veterans of Foreign Wars, Gildo Consolini Post 3272, was established in 1945 and met at the town hall. Its first commander was Arthur Neriani, and it served veterans from Simsbury, Unionville, Farmington, and Avon. The post was named in honor of World War II serviceman Gildo Consolini, Avon's first man to die in a foreign war.

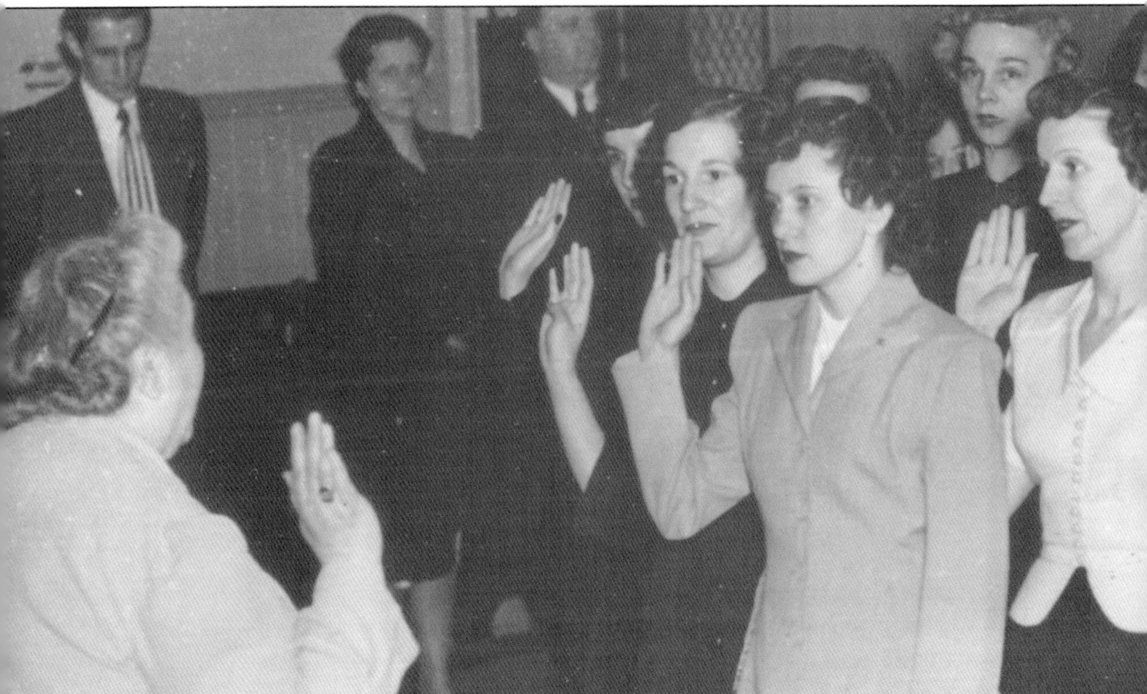

The VFW Auxiliary, 1949. Pictured in the front row are (facing forward) Dorothy Brunoli, Rose Gaioni Silver, unidentified, Margaret Gaioni Julian, and Edith Gold. To Dorothy Brunoli's

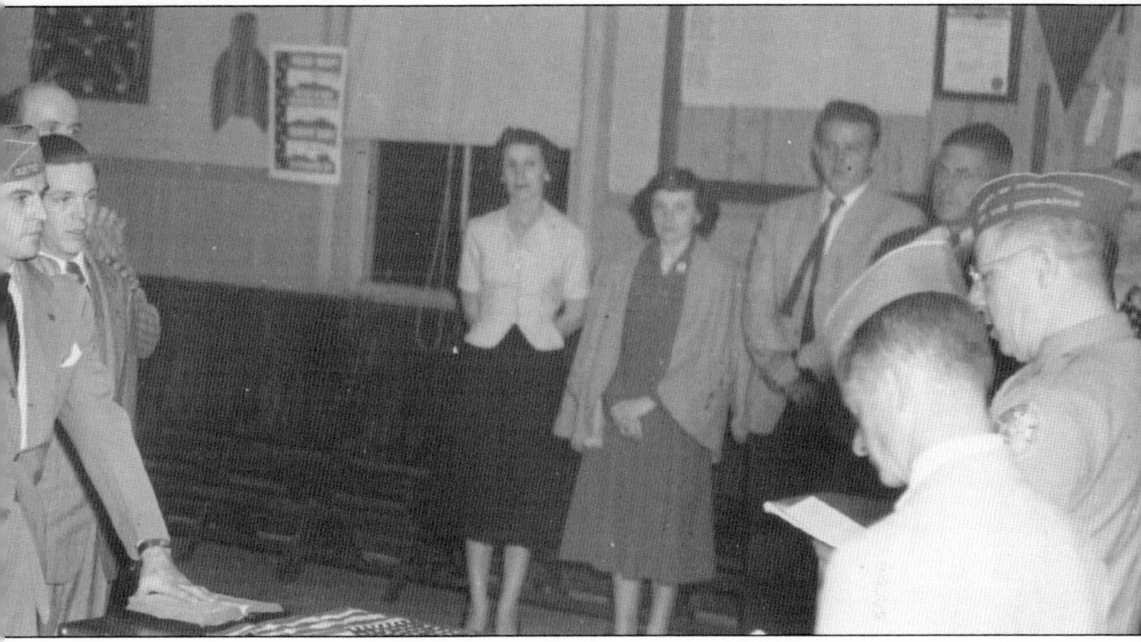

In this photograph, veterans—with their left hands on one another's shoulders—are sworn in as post members. Pictured from left to right are John Alsop; William Gold; Gino Consolini; John Gaioni, incoming VFW commander, with his hand on the Bible; and Abbot Rhodes, behind Gaioni.

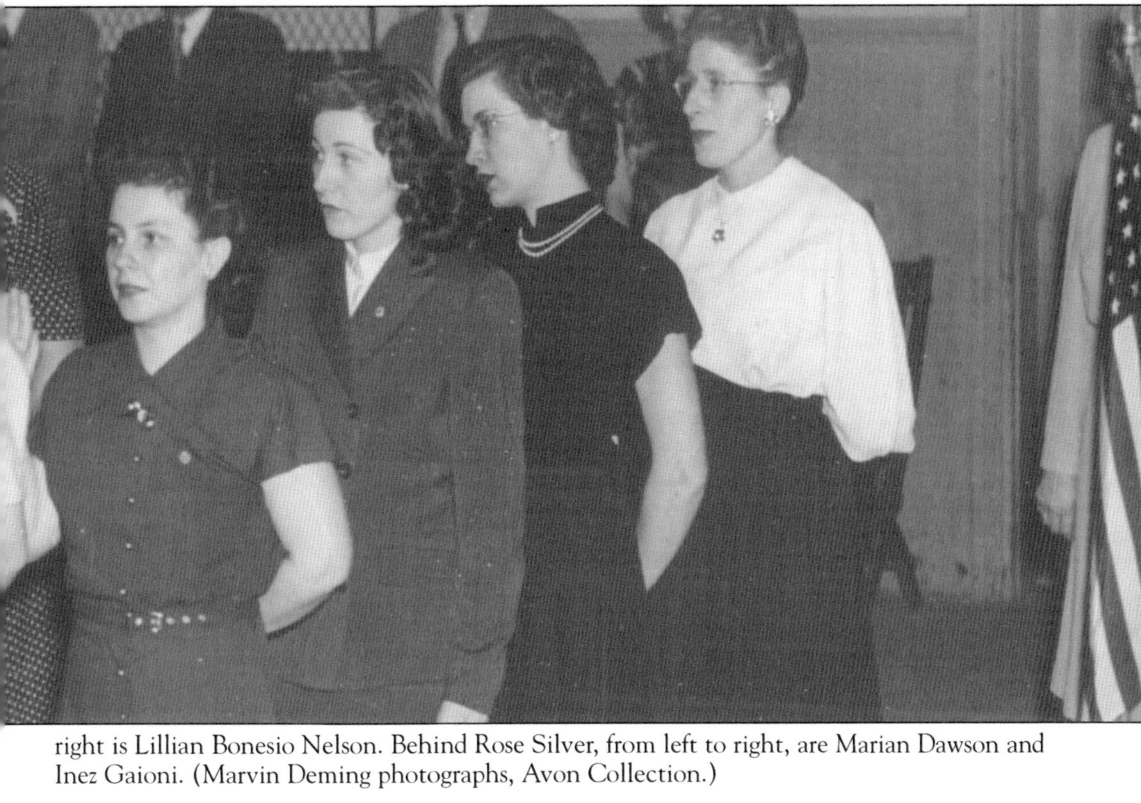

right is Lillian Bonesio Nelson. Behind Rose Silver, from left to right, are Marian Dawson and Inez Gaioni. (Marvin Deming photographs, Avon Collection.)

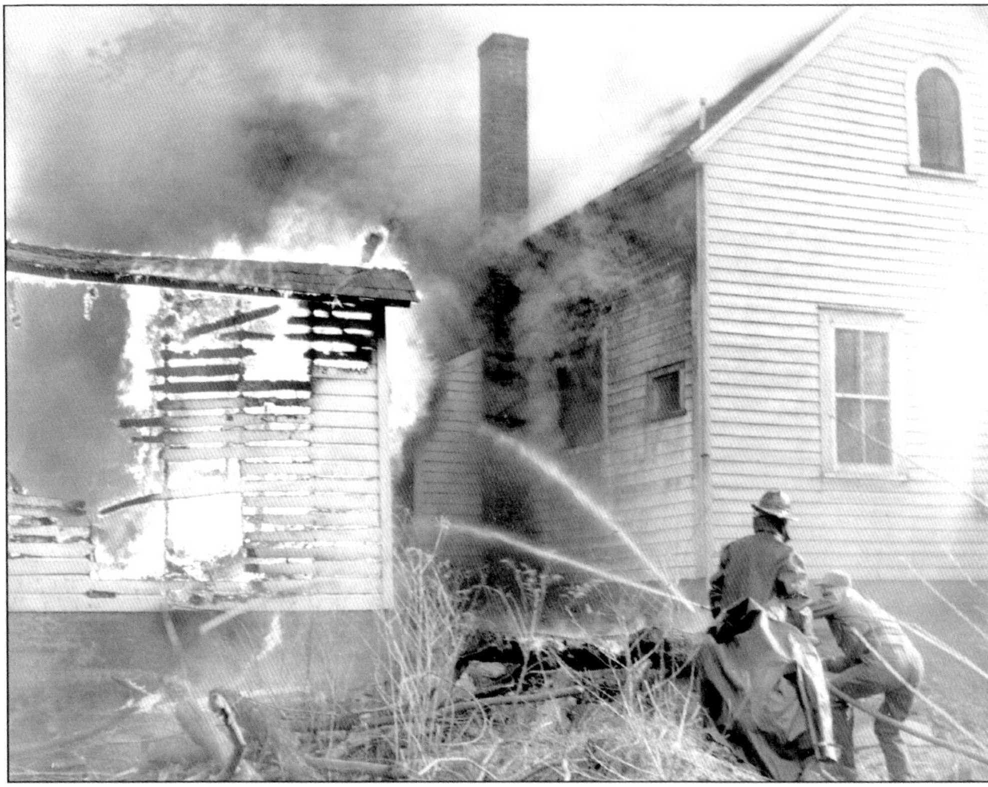

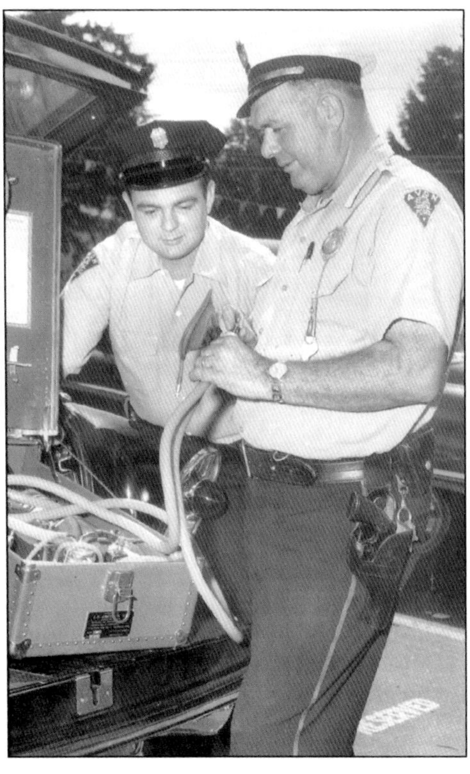

THE LUSK HOME, LOVELY STREET, C. 1950. Efforts to start a volunteer fire department began during World War II when Avon realized the possibility of enemy bombs falling on the town. The Avon Volunteer Fire Department was incorporated on August 5, 1943, one month after the town purchased its first fire engine. Today, the department has more than 120 active members and volunteers. (Marvin Deming photograph, Avon Collection.)

THE AVON POLICE DEPARTMENT, 1950S. Pictured inspecting a resuscitator are, from left to right, Malcolm Heath, Avon's second police chief (1958–61), and William Scott, Avon's first police chief (1953–58). Today, the police department has 31 regular officers. Under James A. Martino Jr., chief of police since 1983, the department became one of only 11 agencies in Connecticut to receive international accreditation by the Commission on Accreditation for Law Enforcement Agencies. (*Hartford Times* photograph, Avon Police Department Collection.)

Four

SCHOOL TIME
ASPIRATION AND PERSEVERANCE

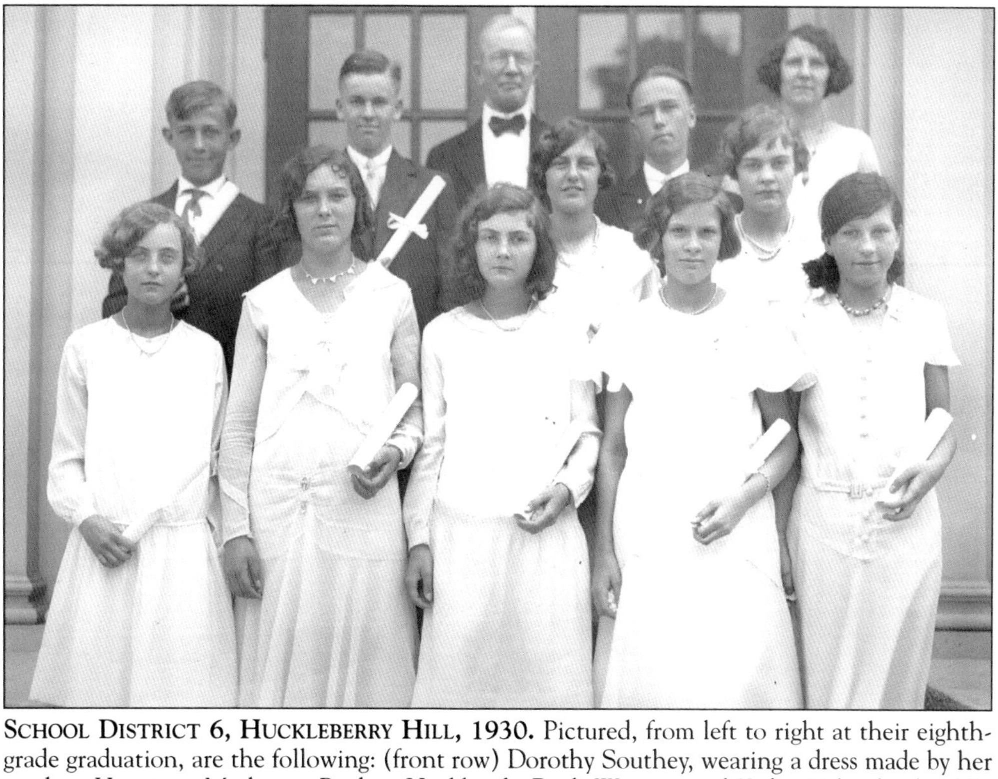

SCHOOL DISTRICT 6, HUCKLEBERRY HILL, 1930. Pictured, from left to right at their eighth-grade graduation, are the following: (front row) Dorothy Southey, wearing a dress made by her mother; Henrietta Maskaitis; Pauline Hackbarth; Ruth Wivagg; and Yadga Volovski; (middle row) Raymond Pomaski; Eino Pennala; Gertrude Demski; and Mary Grant; (back row) Fritz Lofgren, school board chairman; Otto Hanelius; and Adelaide Snow, teacher. (Dorothy Southey Dodge Collection.)

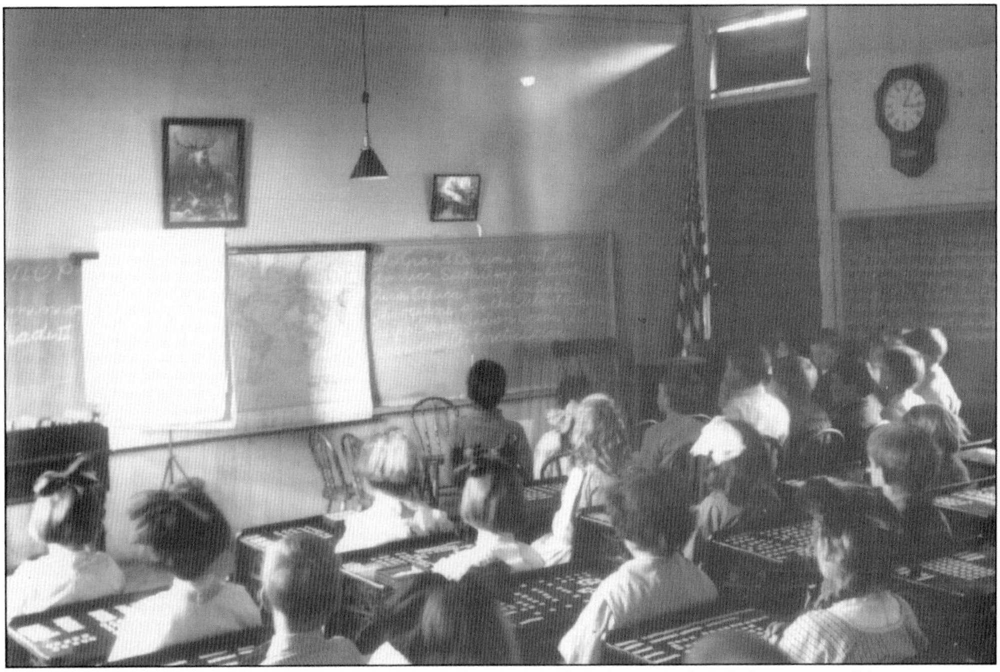

A Schoolhouse Interior, c. 1900. Students in this Avon school face a world map and a geography lesson on the blackboard. Also shown is the American flag and the teacher's desk. The shapes laid out carefully on each desk suggest an arithmetic lesson. (Kelley Lanahan Collection.)

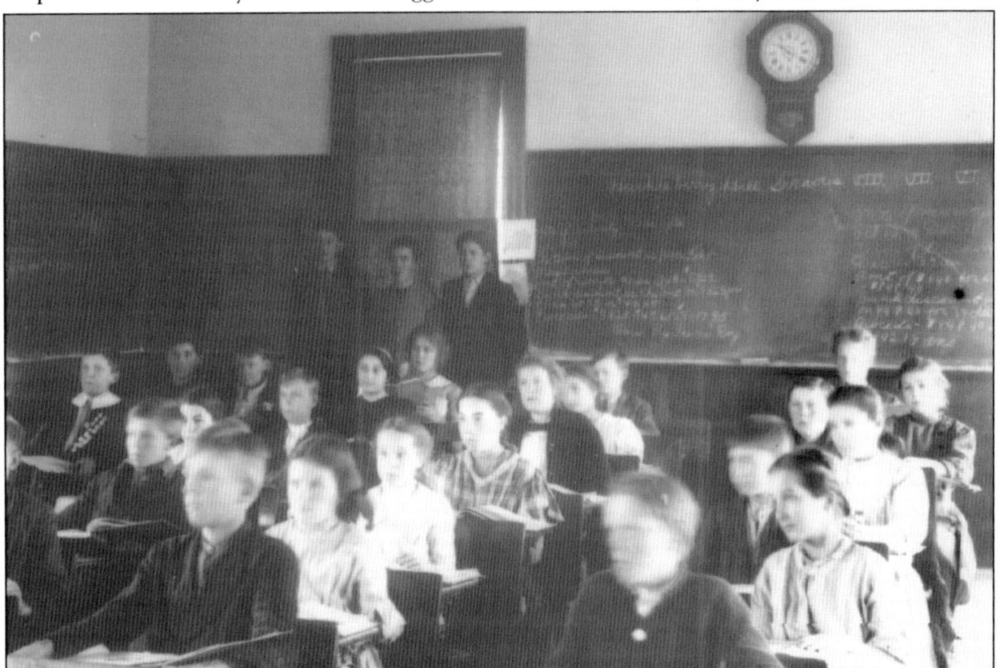

School District 6, Huckleberry Hill, c. 1900. Window shades cover the windows to lessen the glare from the photographer's light. Written on the board is "Grades VIII, VII, VI" and numerous math problems. (Kelley Lanahan Collection.)

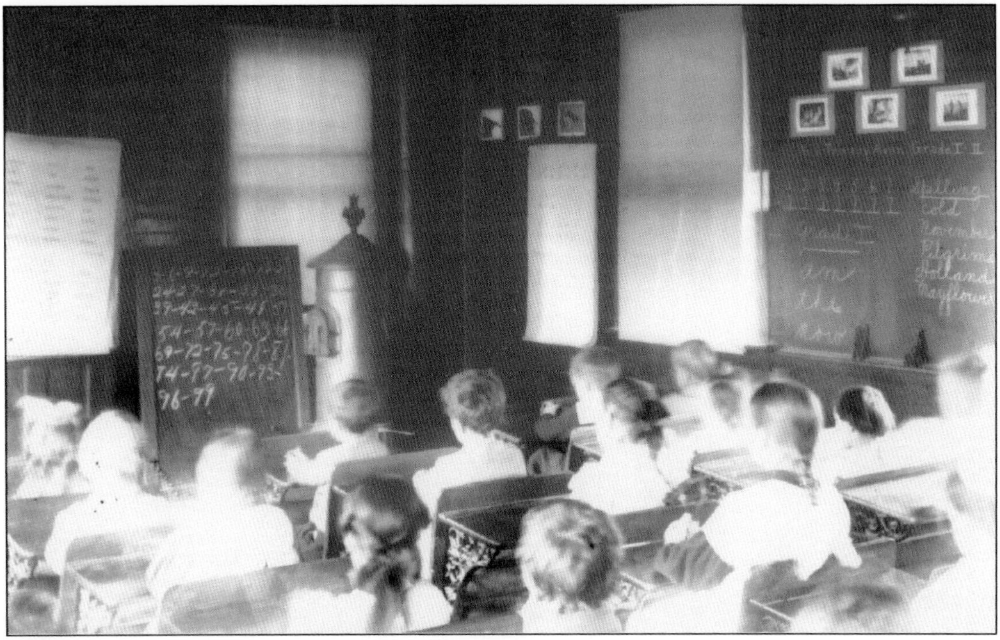

School District 6, Huckleberry Hill, c. 1900. A stove keeps the children warm on a cold autumn day. On the blackboard are lessons for grades one and two, including the spelling words *November*, *Pilgrims*, *Holland*, and *Mayflower*. (Kelley Lanahan Collection.)

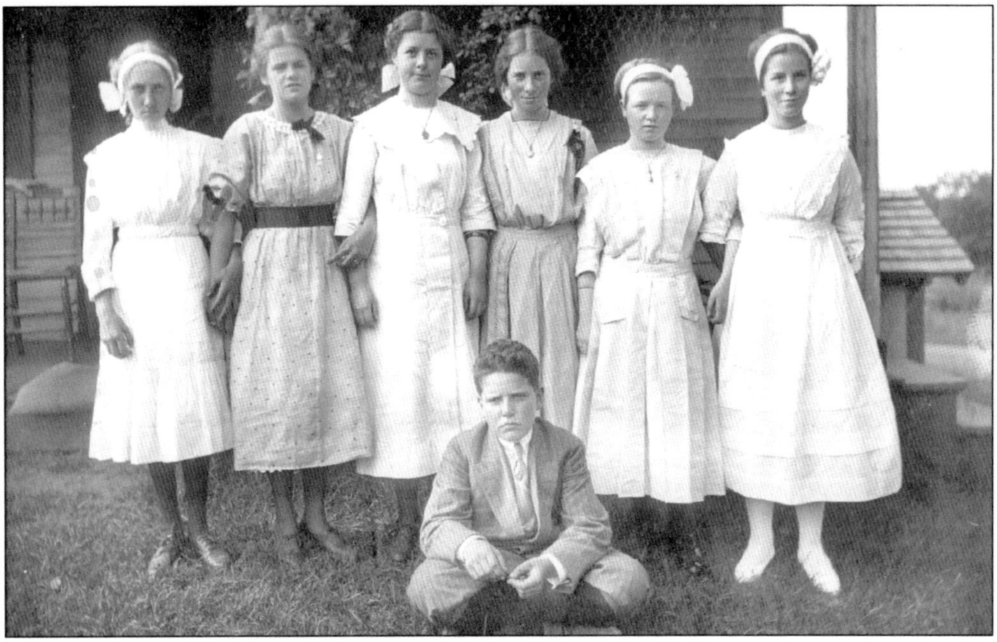

School District 5, Center School Graduation, 1912. The eighth-graders pictured from left to right are Mildred Williamson, Kathleen O'Neil, Dorothy Manion, Irene Collins, and Mildred Coles, with Edward Van Heusen. Kathleen O'Neil wrote the class song, which follows: "There's a pretty spot in Avon, which memory holdeth dear / It's a school-house on the hill-side, that we visit year by year / Many times we have been angry, many times we have been glad / But today we all are leaving, and our hearts are very sad." (Avon Collection.)

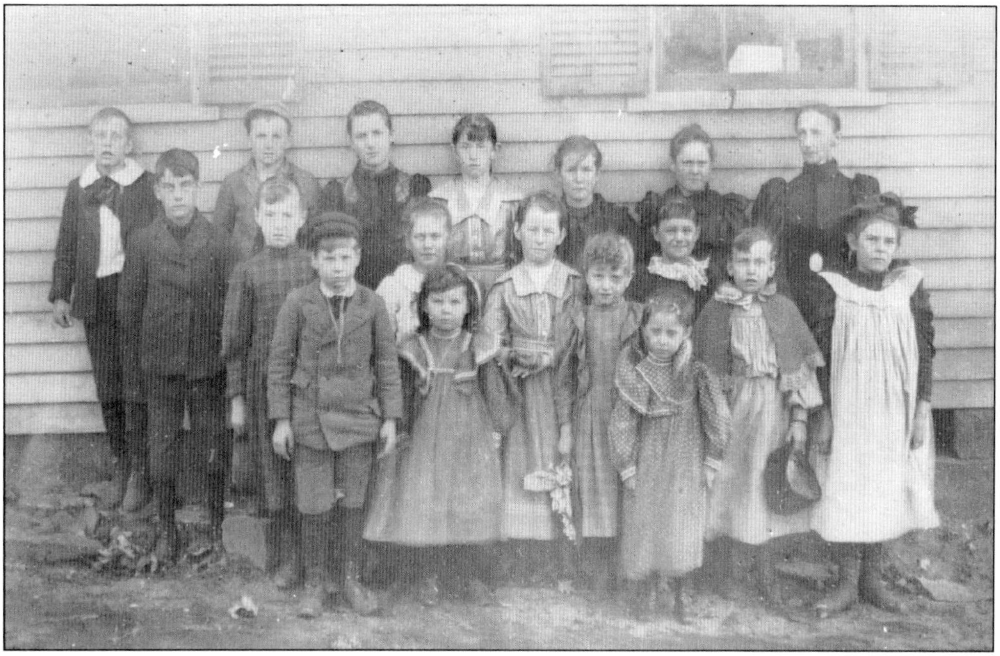

SCHOOL DISTRICT 3, NOD ROAD, C. 1900. Mary Woodford is shown with her students. The first Nod Road schoolhouse opened in 1767. In 1804, 58 children attended the school. A century later, 13 children attended. Located north of Hunters Run, the school closed in 1917 and the pupils transferred to School District 5. Nod Schoolhouse sold for $1,800 and became Wood Ford Farm manager Jesse Anderson's residence. (Avon Collection.)

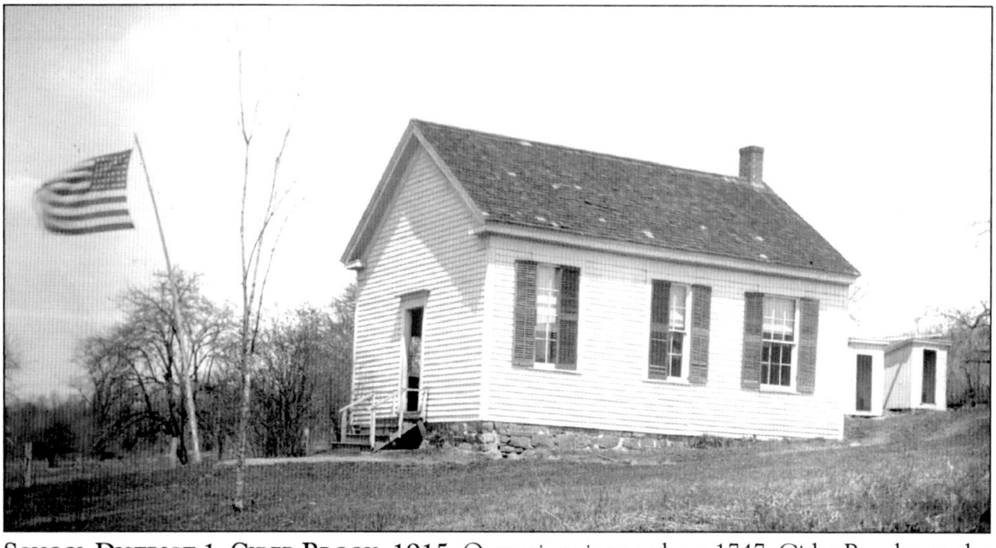

SCHOOL DISTRICT 1, CIDER BROOK, 1915. Operating since at least 1747, Cider Brook was the only school in the Northington Society of Farmington until 1767, when Nod School opened. In 1804, 41 children attended Cider Brook School. Located on the west side of Waterville Road, the building pictured was the third schoolhouse, built in 1871. It closed in 1918 with attendance at about ten students, reopened when parents objected, and closed permanently in 1920. (Lewis S. Mills photograph, Avon Collection.)

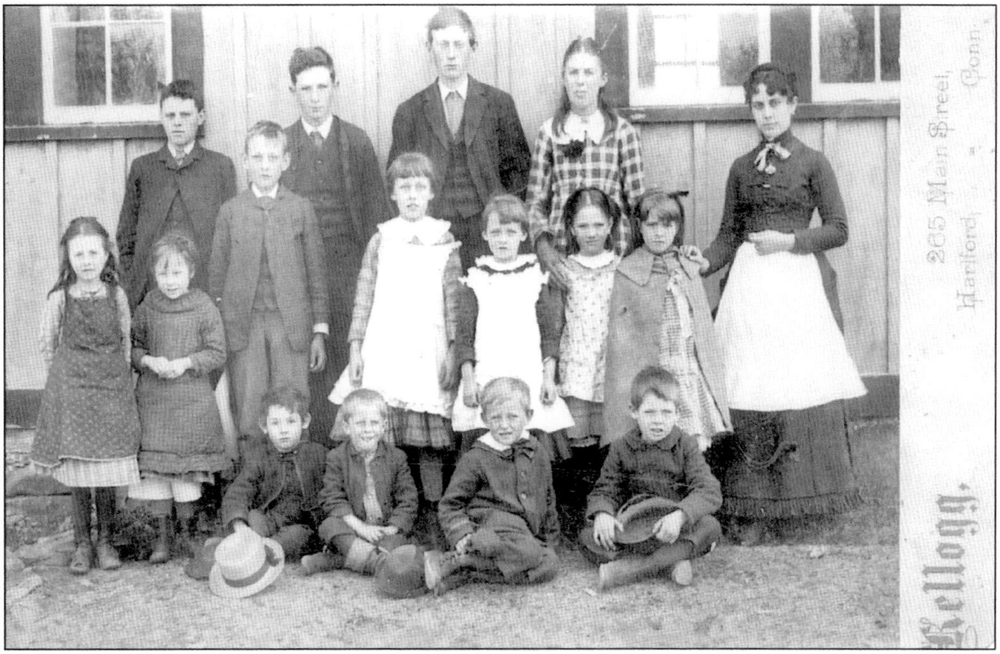

SCHOOL DISTRICT 7, PINE GROVE, C. 1885. This schoolhouse was built in 1865 for $1,538 and was renamed Pine Grove in 1927. Pictured, from left to right in the back row, are Winthrop Woodford, William Smith, Joseph Thompson, Lura Colvin, and the teacher. (Sunrise Farm Collection.)

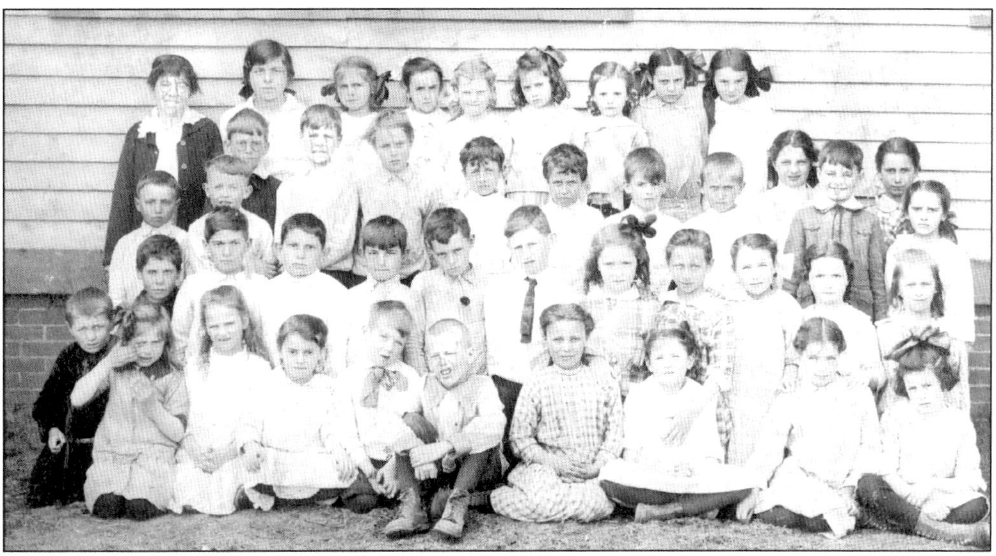

SCHOOL DISTRICT 5, AVON VILLAGE, 1917. Identified in this photograph are the following: (first row) Speranza Tarca, fourth from the right; (second row) Hazel Sisson and Rose Wollman, second and third from the right; (third row) Peter Bussolini and Ernest Bonadeo, seventh and eighth from the right; (fourth row) teacher Miss O'Neill and Lena Turchi, first and second from the left. When Nod School closed in 1917 and Cider Brook School closed in 1920, the pupils were relocated to Towpath School, also called the Avon Village School. (Marilyn Dumas Collection.)

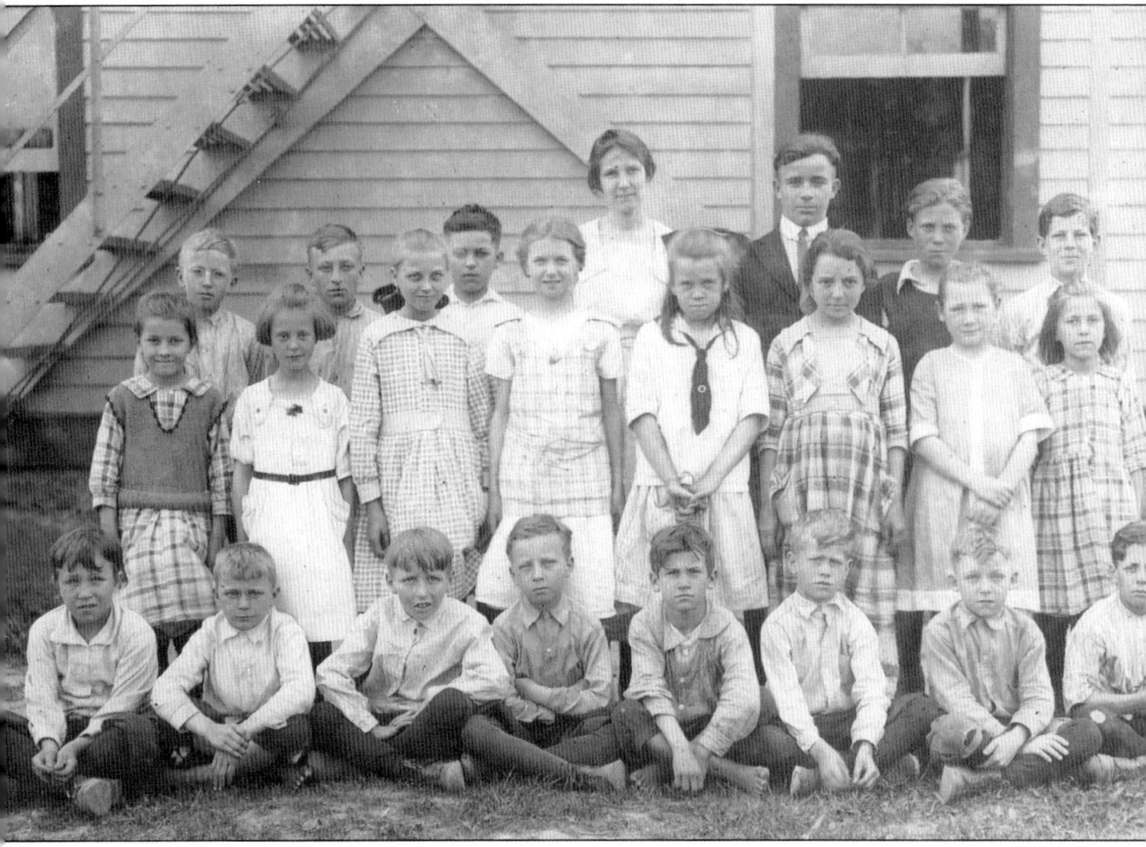

SCHOOL DISTRICT 6, HUCKLEBERRY HILL, JUNE 3, 1921. A class picture shows fire escape stairs and two shoeless boys, second and fifth from the left in the front row. Teacher Adelaide Snow stands at the rear. Identified in this picture are the following: (front row) Joseph Hanelius, left; (middle row) Hazel Fischer?, Agnes Fahr?, and Marion Nikstad, second, third, and fifth from the left. (Martha Fitzgerald Collection.)

THE HIGH SCHOOL BUS, 1939. Ninth-grader Martha Fitzgerald of Huckleberry Hill Road poses with one of Avon's first school buses. Driver Austin Hunter transported high school students to adjacent towns, as Avon did not have a high school until later, graduating its first completely Avon-educated class of 12th-graders in 1961. John O'Neill operated the buses and was commended by the State in 1933 for installing shatterproof glass and governors—devices to hold the vehicles' speed below 35 miles per hour. (Regina Pilitowski Collection.)

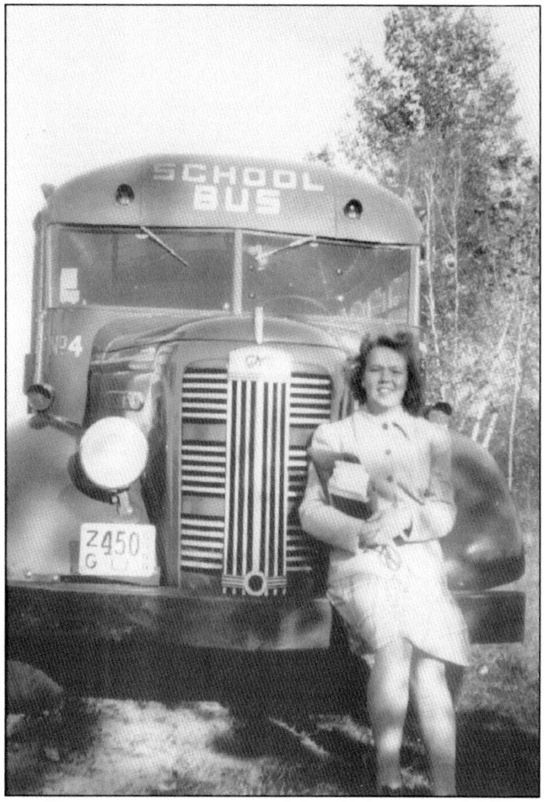

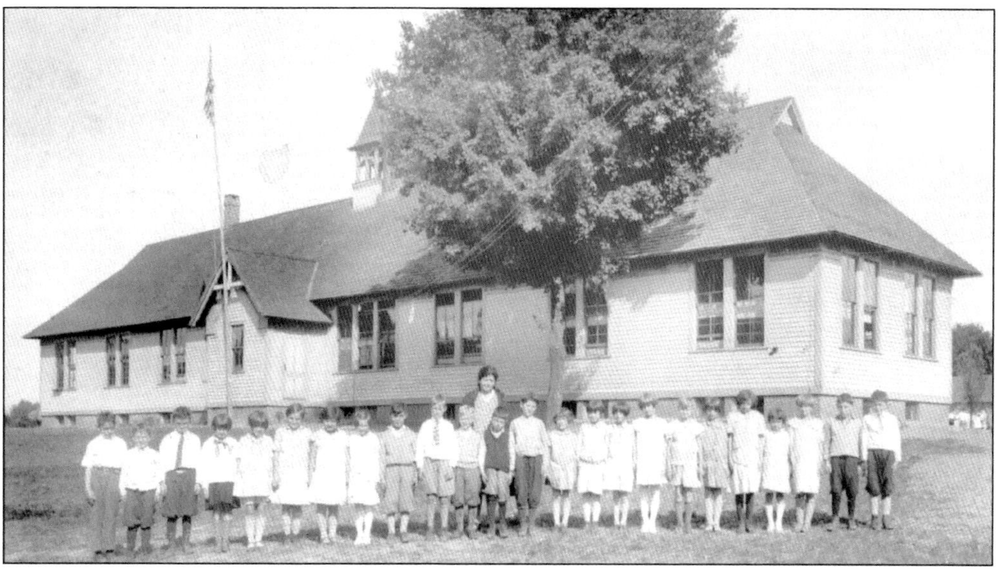

SCHOOL DISTRICT 5, TOWPATH (FORMERLY AVON VILLAGE SCHOOL), FIFTH GRADE, 1931. Located by the path on which mules had towed canal boats, Towpath School was built in 1879. Rooms were added in 1909, 1914, 1917, and 1923. To ease overcrowding, this building was replaced in 1949. (Doris Gaioni Collection.)

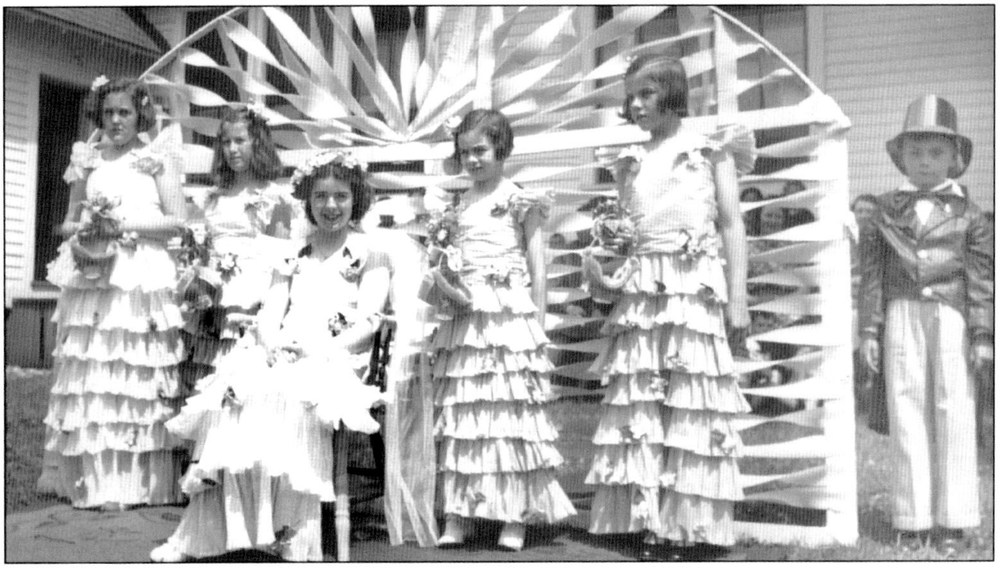

TOWPATH SCHOOL MAY DAY FESTIVAL, 1939. This was the first year that there was a crowning of a May queen. Pictured from left to right are Marjorie Case; Mary Hewes; Mary O'Neill, May queen; Patricia Smith; Virginia Peterson; and Carl Candels, crown bearer. (Carl Candels Collection.)

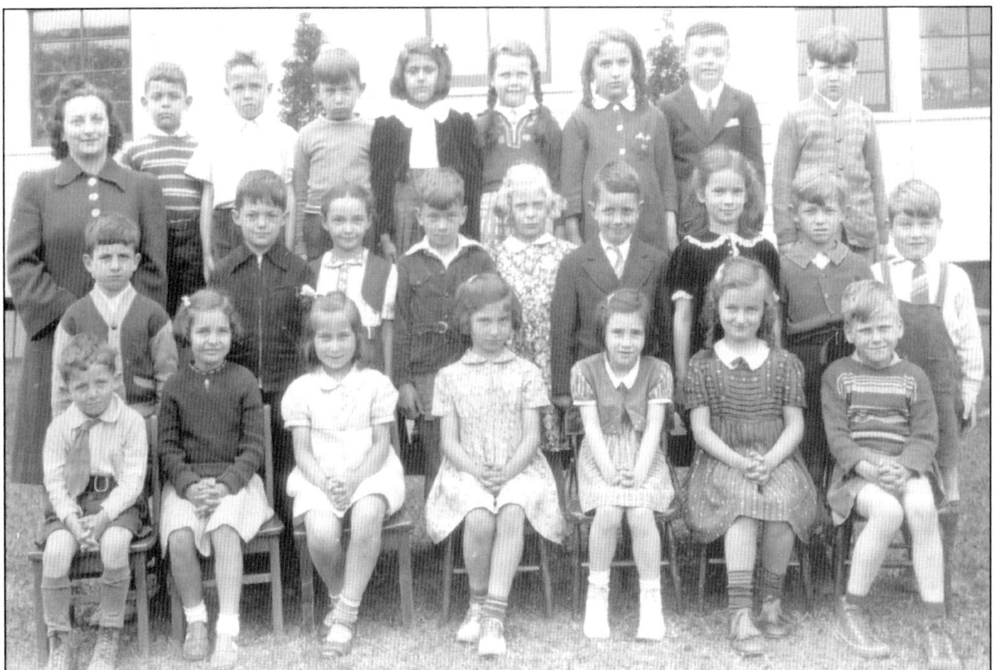

TOWPATH SCHOOL, FIRST GRADE, 1939–1940. Pictured from left to right are the following: (front row) Francis Lattizori, Betty Abbot, Priscilla Bolles, Helen Kowalski, Jacqueline Roncaioli, Laura Tarca, and Billy Cedar; (middle row) Benny Nascimbeni, Dennis Smith, Marie Plude, Ernie Plude, Lucy Panilaitis, Bruno DalBon, Dorothy Plude, Peter Sartori, and Paul Lignelli; (back row) teacher Ida Parrella, Charles Kopp, Paul Olsen, John Bolles, Janet Morelli, Edwina Jarvis, Dolores Rotondo, Carl Candels, and Robert Pilon. (Carl Candels Collection.)

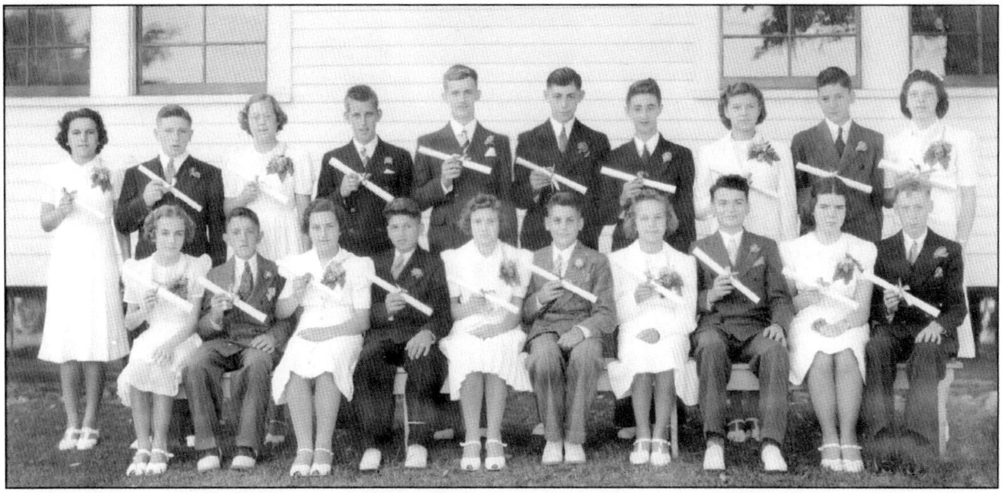

TOWPATH SCHOOL GRADUATES, 1939. Eighth-graders, from left to right, are as follows: (front row) Eleanor Bogino, Fred Brunoli, Elizabeth Smith, Lawrence Lattazori, Benny Battistoni, John Pellegrini, Irene Aliski, David Stuart, Mary O'Neill, and Justin Johnson; (back row) Anne Desimoni, Hugo Gaioni, Dolores Kulpick, Arthur Anderson, Paul Kruse, Lothar Candels, Albert Simonelli, Jane Plona, Emilio Guarnieri, and Lydia Turchi. (Dr. Lothar Candels Collection.)

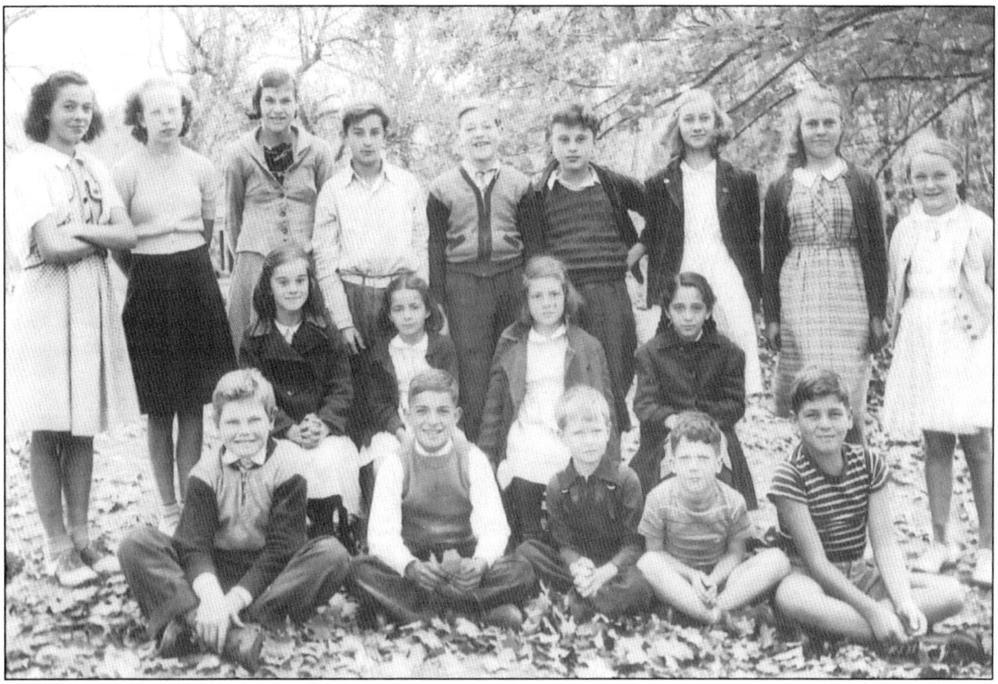

SCHOOL DISTRICT 4, LOVELY STREET, 1940. The schoolhouse at the corner of Lovely Street and Country Club Road was built in 1831 and operated until 1949. A student there in 1890 wrote that the teachers taught "well midst great handicaps." Pictured from left to right are the following: (front row) Clarence Jensen, Roger Labbe, Richard Haberan?, Ralph Rexinger, and George Andretta; (middle row) Dorothy Lomnicky?, Joan Mulligan, and Felicia Mulligan; (back row) Jeanette Labbe, Irene Distin, Alice Manning, Albert Lomnicky, Elton Buel, John Hoffman, Florence Keeney, Gladys Grunewald, and Patricia Parker. (Patricia Parker Vibert Collection.)

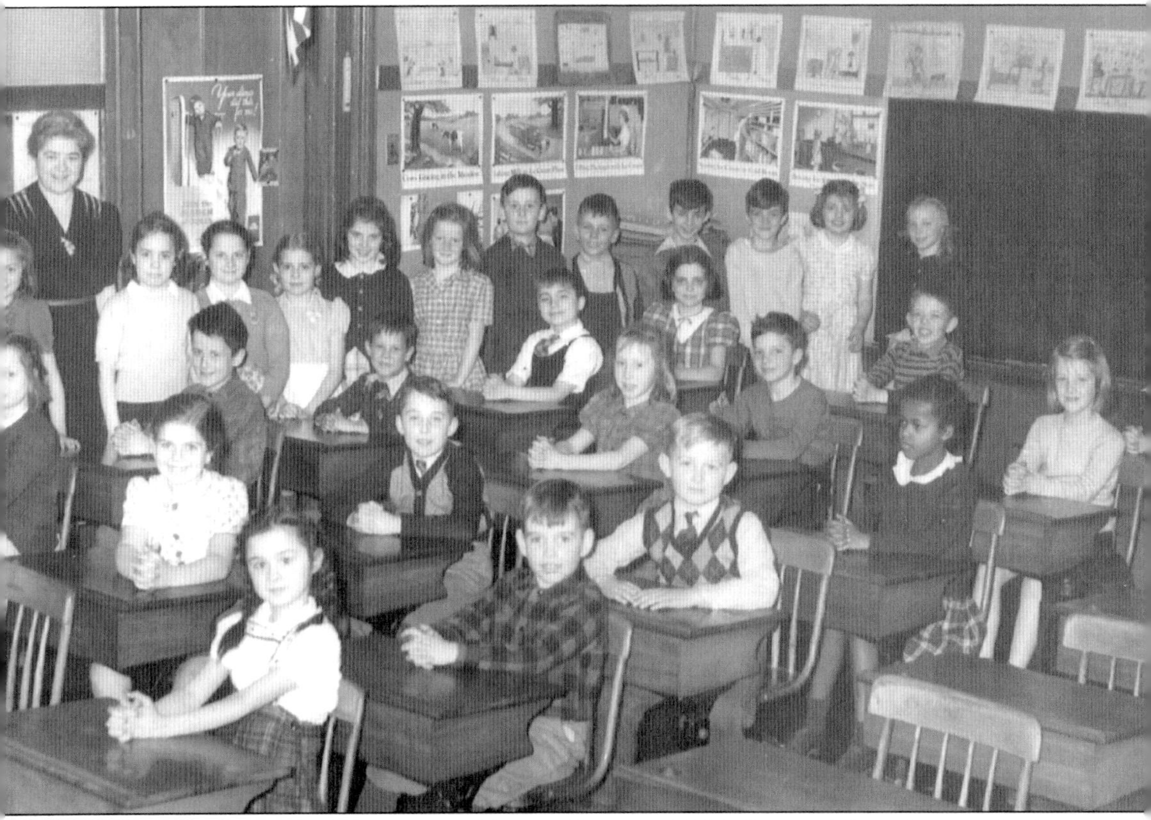

TOWPATH SCHOOL, SECOND AND THIRD GRADES, 1946. Pictured from front to back are the following: (front row) Regina Castellani, Robert Hopkins, Tommy Nettelbladt, Nancy Spivey, Priscilla Woodford, and Paul Webster; (middle row) Mary Calcagni, Ron Plude, Caroline Wilcox, Jim Emilio, and Russell Hunter; (back row) Sybella Maskell, John Pellegrini, Peter Bussolini, Donald Pearsall, and Eleanor Read. Standing with teacher Kathleen O'Neill Leonard, from left to right, are Alice Brunoli, Jane Andrews, Carla Benea, Nancy Evanyo, Joan Milliken, Lois Wilcox, James Mutch, Robert Vail, Jimmy Manzi, Tom Dimock, Janet Read, and Regina Scheidel. (Janet Carville Collection.)

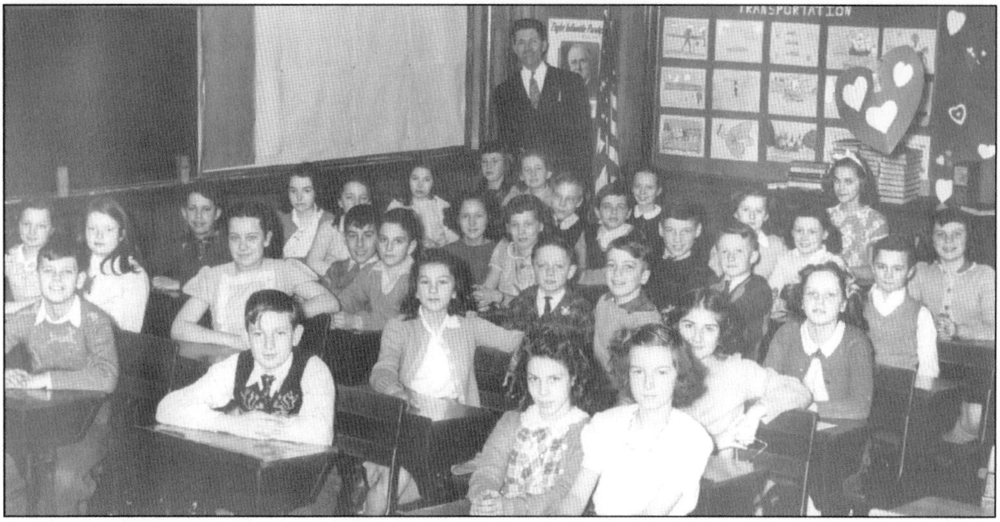

TOWPATH SCHOOL, FIFTH AND SIXTH GRADES, FEBRUARY 1946. Pictured from front to back with teacher John Carrol are the following: (first row) Marian Zaugg sitting with Frances Dimock, Janet Bogino, Vivian Burger, Bernard Castellani, and Martha Eddy; (second row) Frank Panulaitis, Mary Nascimbeni, David Marshall with Dwight Eakin, Ray Aramini with John Dalbon, Anita Tarca, Betty Pelligrini, and Jerry Kruse; (third row) Paul Bussolini, Marilyn Bussolini, Philip Rotondo with Frank Zacchera, Rosemary Goralski with Shirley Morelli, Robert Scheidel with Clarence King, and Mildred Prowe; (fourth row) Norma Brunoli, Mary Pearsall, Robert Gold, Martha Sisson, Carolyn Durphey, Irene Gaioni, Beverly Woodford, and Darcy Deveraux. (Marilyn Dumas Collection.)

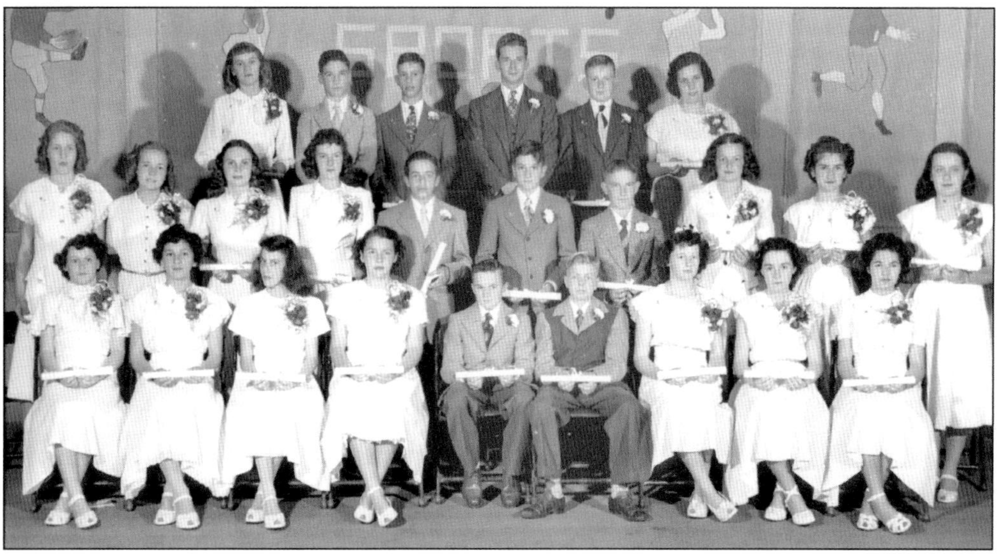

TOWPATH SCHOOL GRADUATES, 1948. Eighth-graders, from left to right, are as follows: (front row) Betty Pellegrini, Mary Nascimbeni, Marian Zaugg, Carolyn Durphey, Bernard Castellani, Frank Leavitt, Lorraine Case, Martha Sisson, and Irene Gaioni; (middle row) Shirley Morelli, Darcy Devereaux, Martha Eddy, Francis Dimrock, Clarence King, Frank Zacchera, George Kyle, Norma Brunoli, Janet Bogino, and Marilyn Bussolini; (back row) Geraldine Kruse, Ray Aramini, Robert Gold, teacher George Kincade, Frank Panilaitis, and Marian Holloway. (Marvin Deming photograph, Marilyn Dumas Collection.)

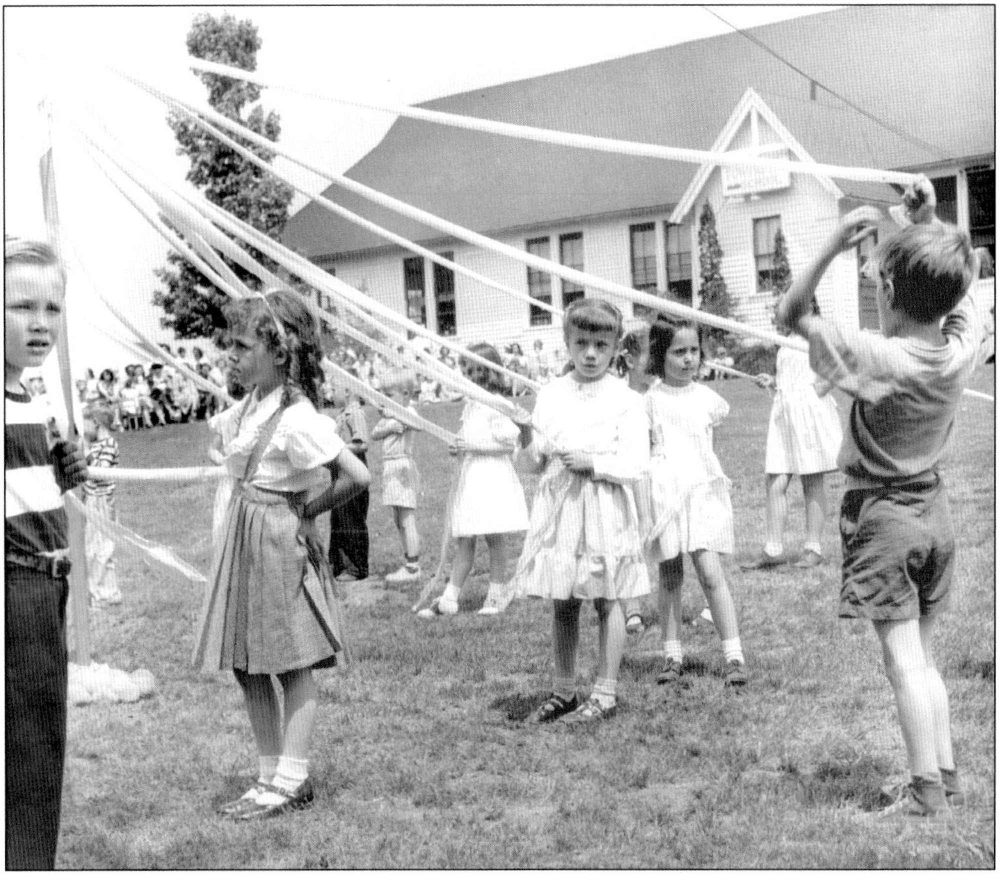

TOWPATH SCHOOL, MAY FESTIVAL, JUNE 1949. Girls and boys perform the maypole dance at the annual May Day festival. At the left are Tommy Safcak and Inez Aramini. (Marvin Deming photograph, Avon Collection.)

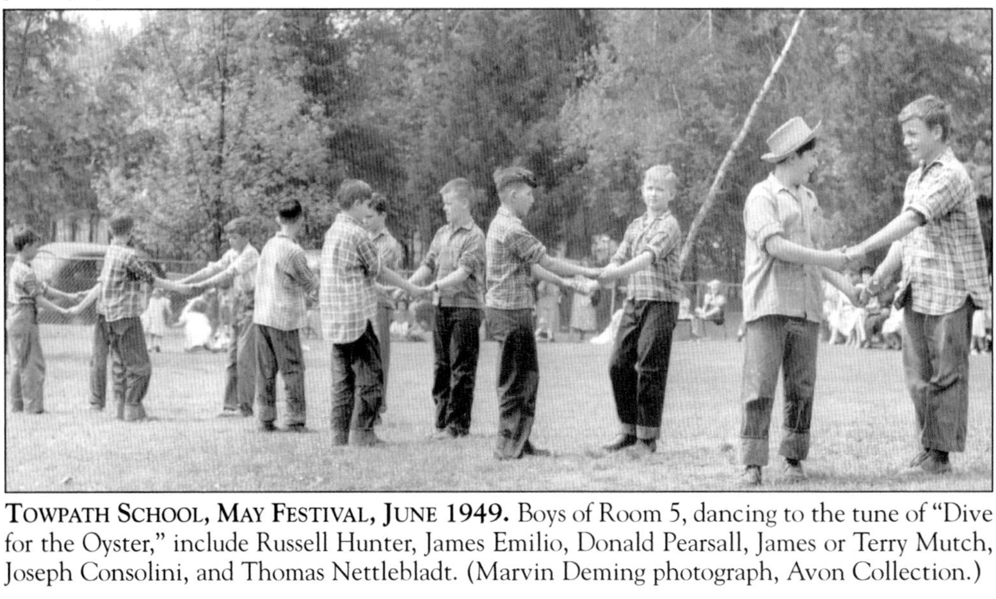

TOWPATH SCHOOL, MAY FESTIVAL, JUNE 1949. Boys of Room 5, dancing to the tune of "Dive for the Oyster," include Russell Hunter, James Emilio, Donald Pearsall, James or Terry Mutch, Joseph Consolini, and Thomas Nettlebladt. (Marvin Deming photograph, Avon Collection.)

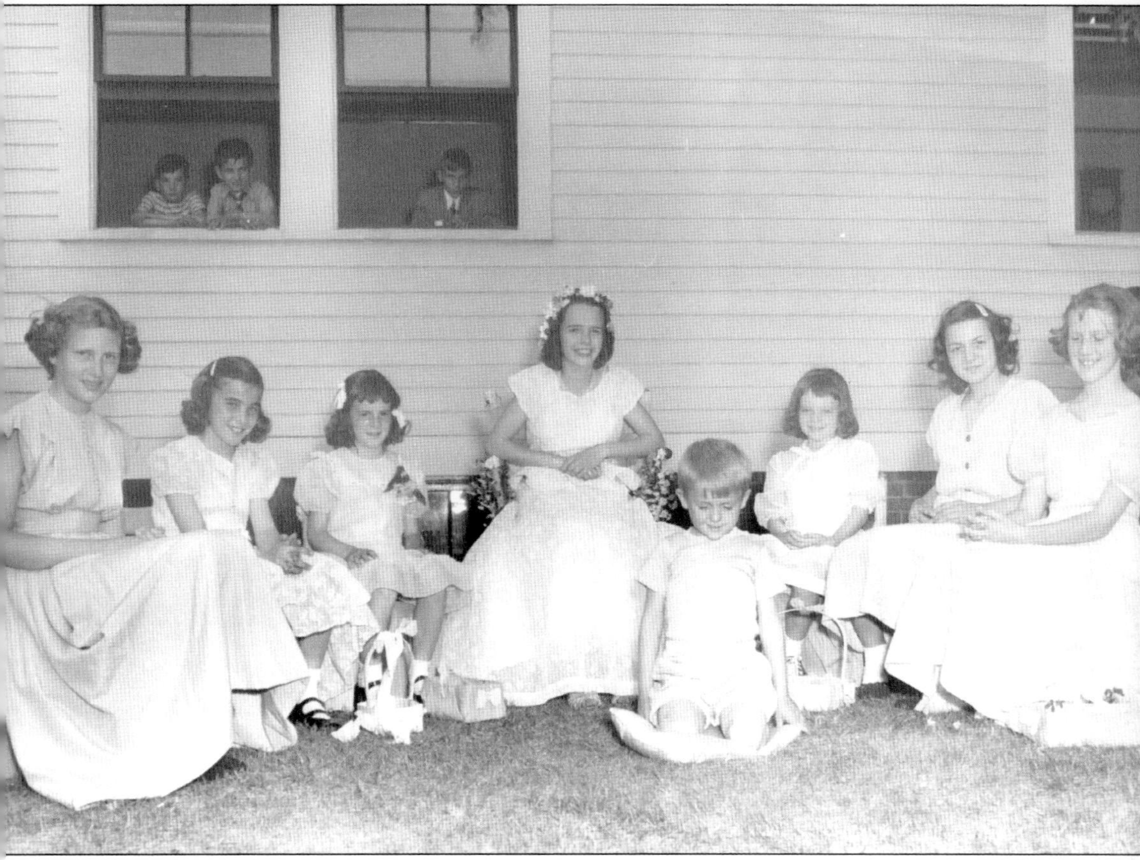

TOWPATH SCHOOL MAY FESTIVAL, JUNE 1949. Pictured from left to right are Honora Hopp, Betty Bogino, Judy Harkins, eighth-grade May queen Mildred Prowe, crown bearer Jonathan Sewall, unidentified, Alice Brunoli, and Diana Hartwick. (Marvin Deming photograph, Avon Collection.)

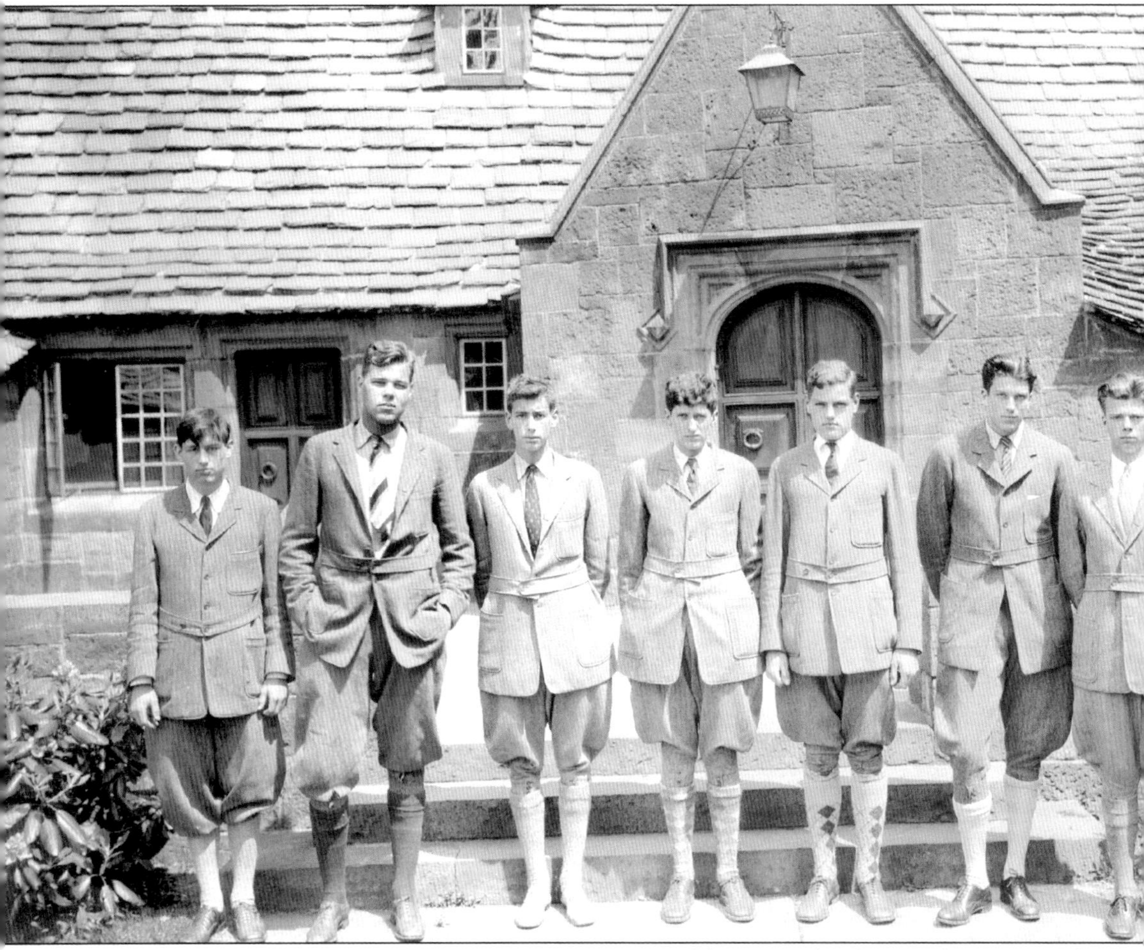

AVON OLD FARMS STUDENT COUNCIL, 1929. Avon Old Farms School opened in 1927 with 48 boys. The 3,000-acre school was designed and founded by architect Theodate Pope Riddle (1868–1946), who called it "my life." Mrs. Riddle, a survivor of the sinking of the *Lusitania*, recalled that nearly drowning in the water, she had "counted the buildings I had designed—the ones built and building, and hoped I had made good." Pictured from left to right are Philip Schenck '30, Larz Holloway '31, C.B. Fraley Jr. '30, John Burlig '30, Samuel Colgate '31, Isaac Jeanes II '31, and Halford Jay '31. The 1929 Student Handbook, written in part by Schenck, noted that "this council is empowered to pass ordinances regulating the citizens' [students'] conduct and to perform any other legislative duty." (Avon Old Farms School Collection, courtesy of Carol Ketcham.)

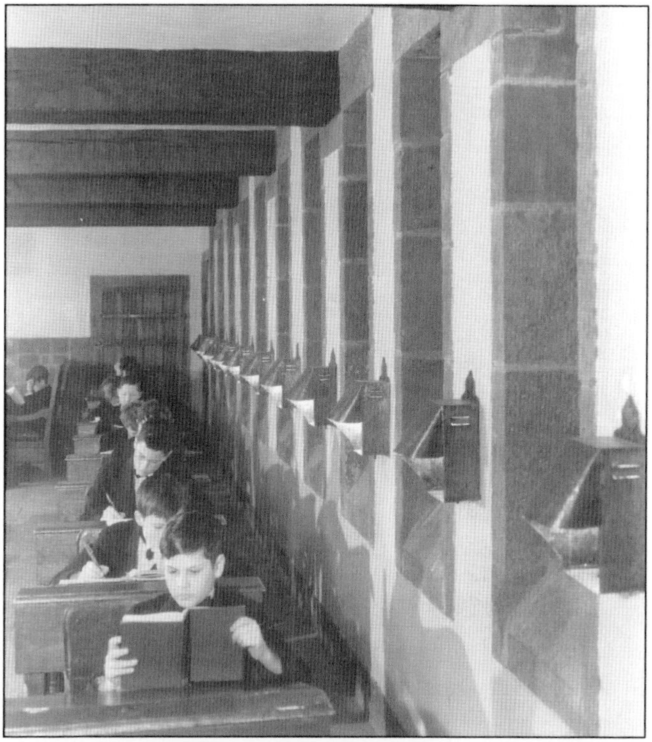

Avon Old Farms School Study Hall. First- and second-form students, the middle school students of today, work in a study hall on the first floor in one of the quadrangle buildings. (Avon Old Farms School Collection, courtesy of Carol Ketcham.)

Avon Old Farms School, Christmas Vespers. Students are shown by candlelight in the Chapel of Jesus the Carpenter, the original carpenters' shop during the school's construction. (Avon Old Farms School Collection, courtesy of Carol Ketcham.)

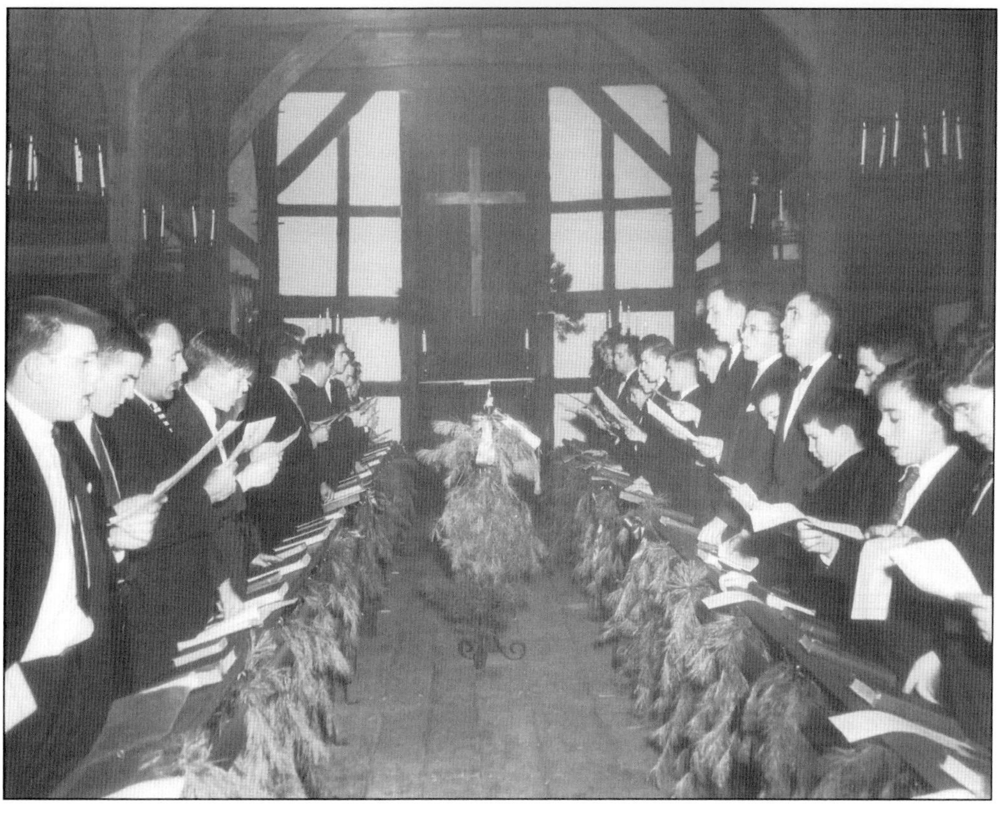

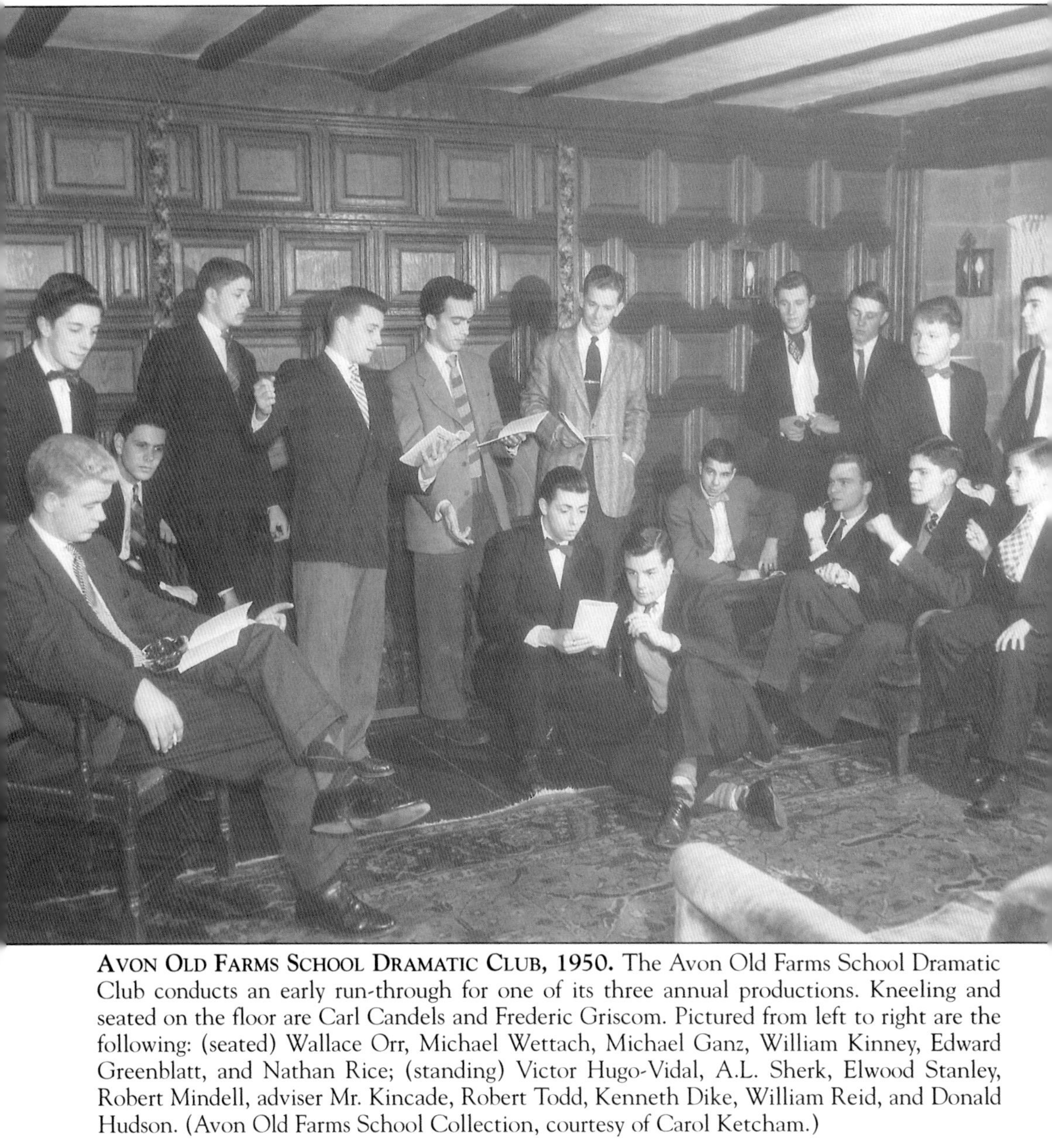

AVON OLD FARMS SCHOOL DRAMATIC CLUB, 1950. The Avon Old Farms School Dramatic Club conducts an early run-through for one of its three annual productions. Kneeling and seated on the floor are Carl Candels and Frederic Griscom. Pictured from left to right are the following: (seated) Wallace Orr, Michael Wettach, Michael Ganz, William Kinney, Edward Greenblatt, and Nathan Rice; (standing) Victor Hugo-Vidal, A.L. Sherk, Elwood Stanley, Robert Mindell, adviser Mr. Kincade, Robert Todd, Kenneth Dike, William Reid, and Donald Hudson. (Avon Old Farms School Collection, courtesy of Carol Ketcham.)

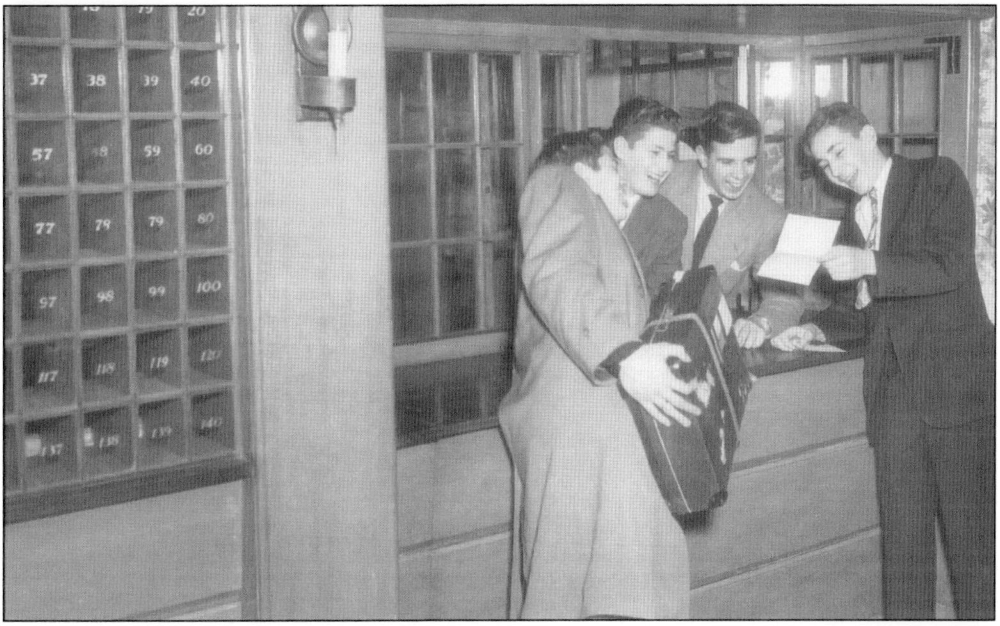

AVON OLD FARMS SCHOOL POST OFFICE. The largely self-sufficient school village ran its own water and waste systems, generated electricity, and operated a bank, tack shop, and post office. (Avon Old Farms School Collection, courtesy of Carol Ketcham.)

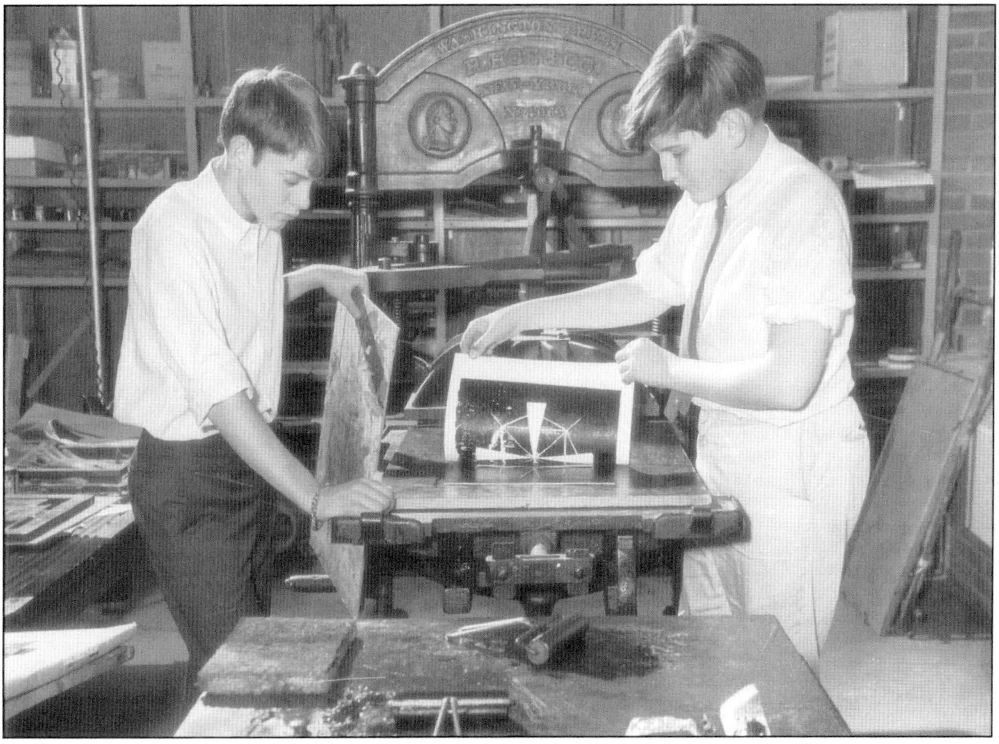

AVON OLD FARMS SCHOOL PRINT SHOP. All the school publications, as well as many student projects, were printed on this Washington Press. (Avon Old Farms School Collection, courtesy of Carol Ketcham.)

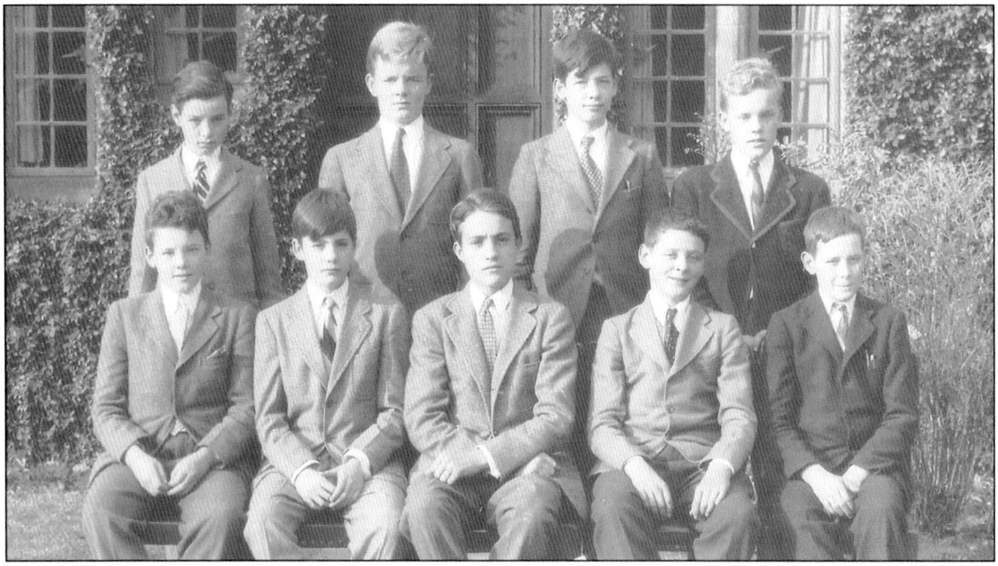

AVON OLD FARMS SCHOOL, FIRST AND SECOND FORMS, 1943. The school once included seventh and eighth grades. Pictured from left to right are the following: (front row) William Wysong, Henry Larom, Morgan Rogers Jr., William Bartlett, and Eldred Steinmann; (back row) Robert Keedy, Alexander Zabriskie Jr., Gavin Konstam, and James Wysong. All the students had to leave when the school closed to operate as the Old Farms Convalescent Hospital for blinded veterans from 1944 to 1947. (Avon Old Farms School Collection, courtesy of Carol Ketcham.)

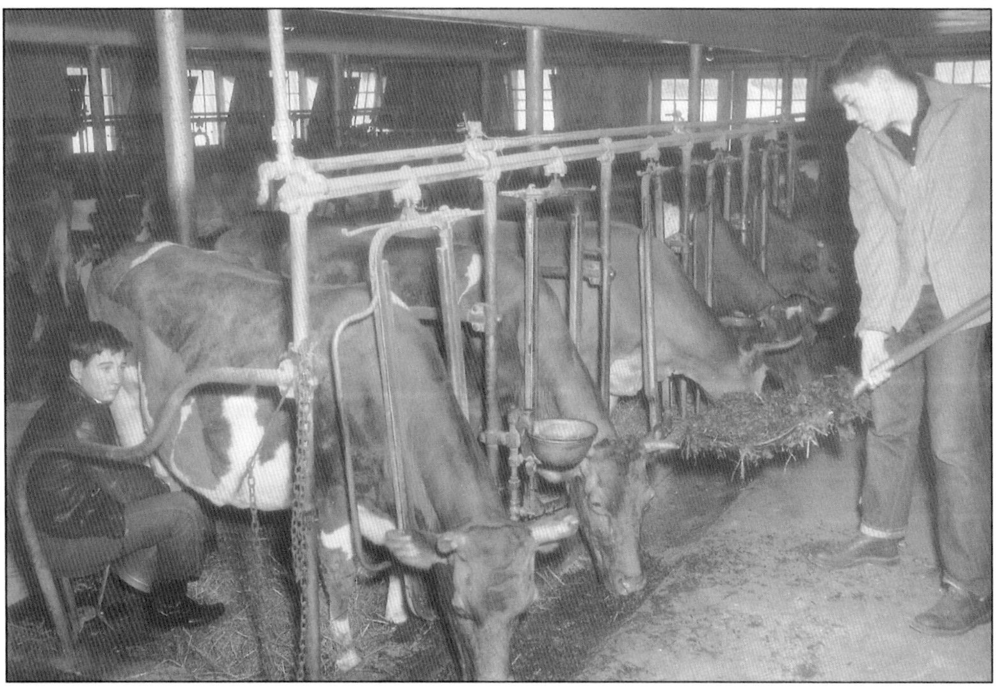

AVON OLD FARMS SCHOOL STUDENTS, FARM CHORES. Students spent two weeks a year doing farm chores at Hill-Stead, the Farmington estate of the school's founder. John Iverson Jr., Class of 1936, reminisced that "Avon taught me a lot more than how to milk a cow and how to tie a bow tie." (Avon Old Farms School Collection, courtesy of Carol Ketcham.)

Five

RELIGION
"HAVING REASON TO HOPE"

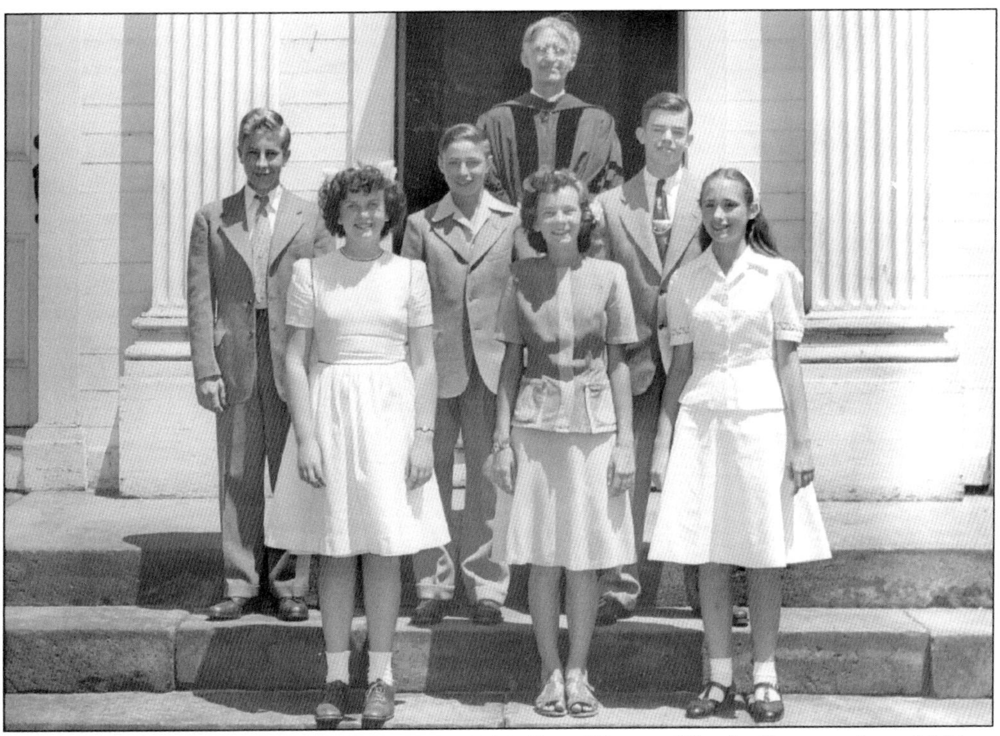

THE AVON CONGREGATIONAL CHURCH, 1946. Rev. Watson Woodruff, pastor from 1944 to 1949, is pictured on the front steps with the following, from left to right: (front row) Edwina Jarvis, Dorothy Plude, and Martha Pearsall; (back row) Robert Quick, Marcello Brighenti, and Lionel Turner. (Avon Congregational Church Collection.)

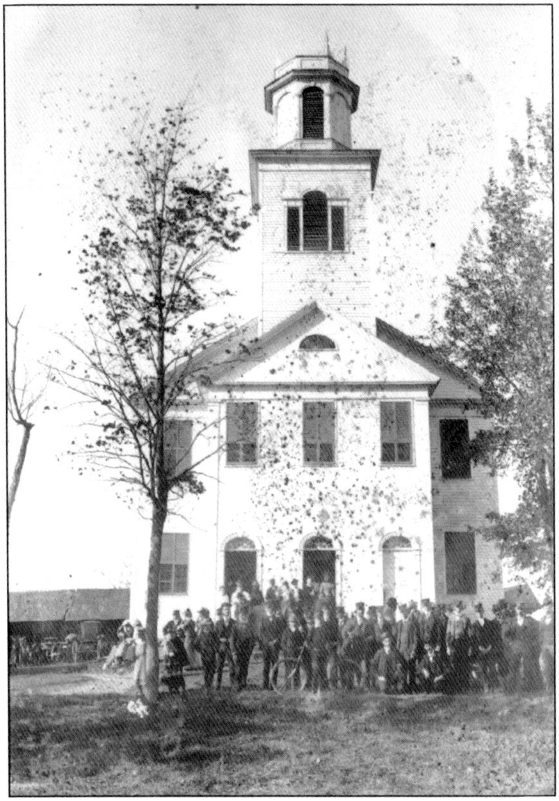

"West Avon Church (Fair Day), October 11, 1900." Pictured is the West Avon Congregational Church and carriage shed. The meetinghouse was built in 1818, after the majority from the original Avon church voted "to build a meeting-house by subscription, at the Center School House." At the church's centennial in 1851, Rev. Joel Grant said that the church had "fought the good fight [and] kept the faith." In 1969, the church was moved from its original location across Burnham Road. (Clinton Hadsell photograph, Avon Collection, courtesy of Seth Stewart.)

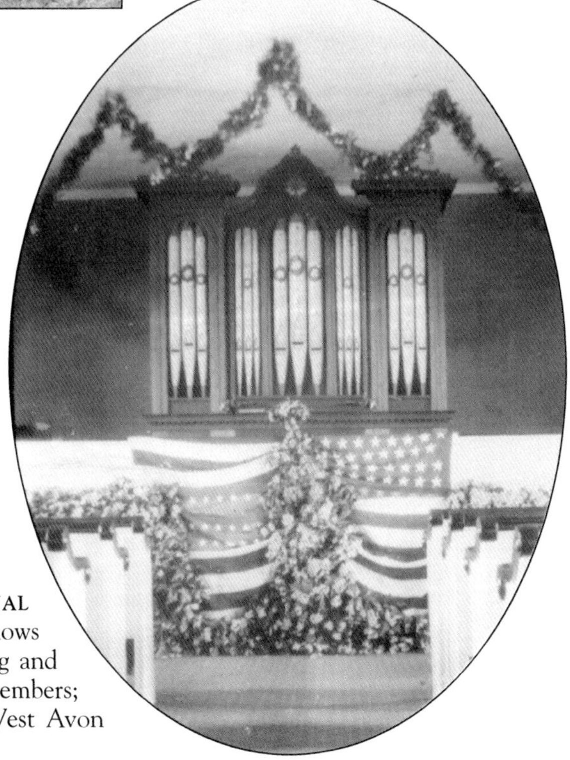

The West Avon Congregational Church, Early 1900s. This postcard shows the altar patriotically draped in bunting and flowers. In 1900, the church had 86 members; 34 were men and 52 were women. (West Avon Congregational Church Collection.)

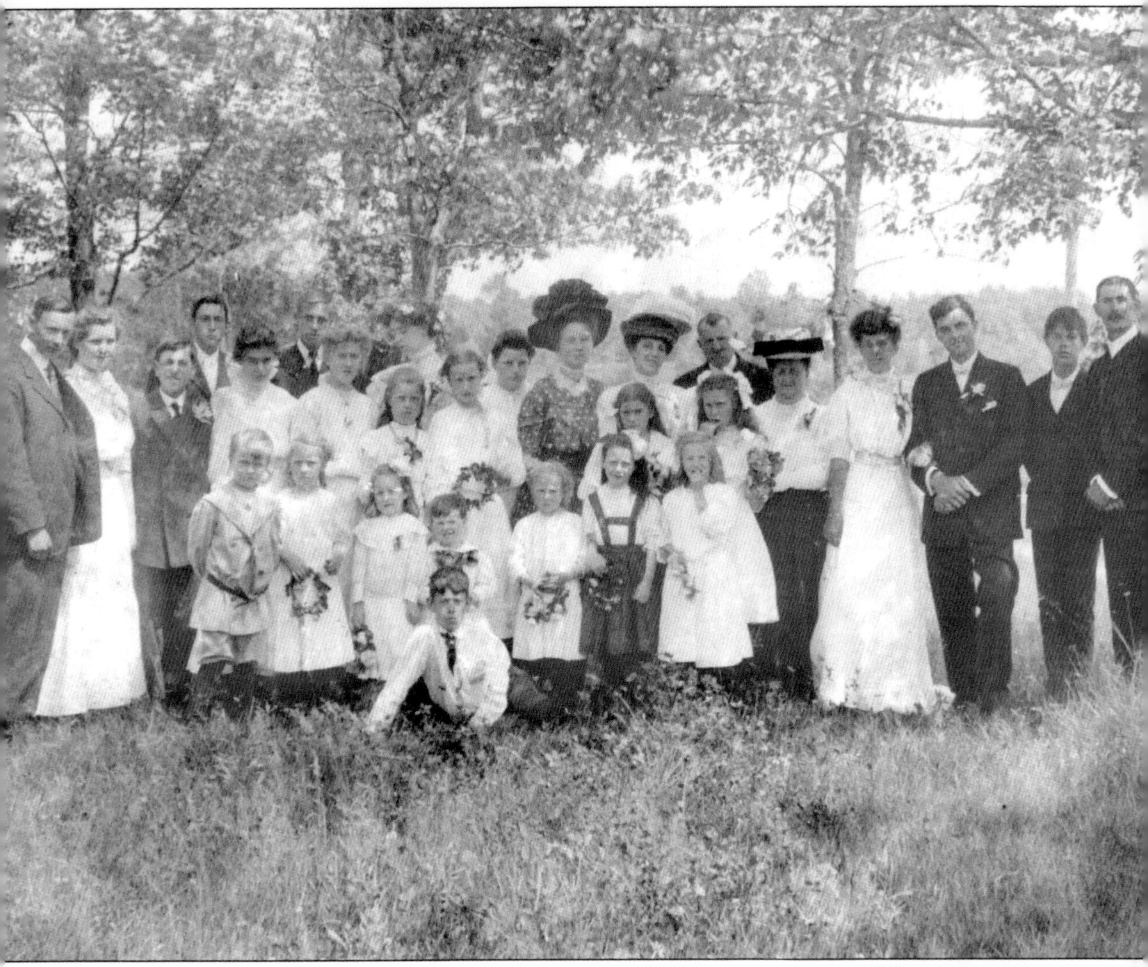

A WEDDING PARTY, 1910. Muriel Stilwell married Ithiel Hart on January 18, 1910, at the West Avon Congregational Church. This photograph is perhaps their wedding reception later that year. On July 10, 1918, the *Farmington Valley Herald* reported that the couple was "picking some very fine red and black raspberries." The Hart family was the first English family to settle in Avon, coming here in 1643. The original Hart farmhouse, built by 1674, stands at 72 Cider Brook Road. (Sunrise Farm Collection.)

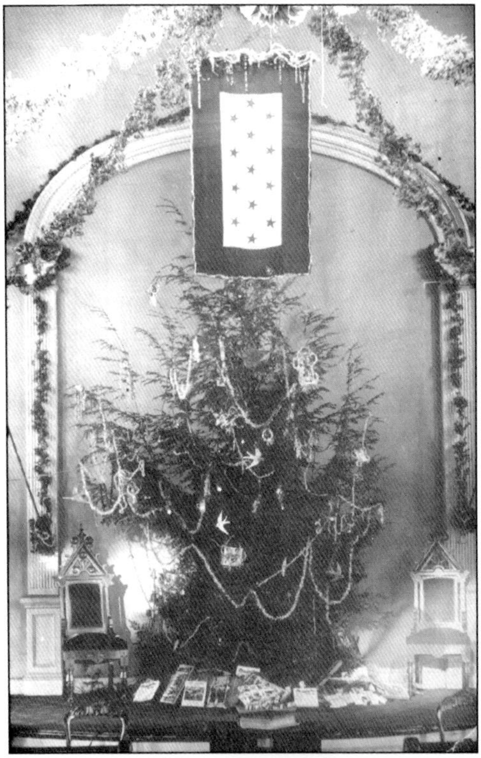

THE AVON CONGREGATIONAL CHURCH, 1918. This postcard shows a Christmas tree decorated with garlands, doves, and a paper bell hanging above the flag. An American flag is at left. The two chairs beside the tree were purchased in 1896 with funds from the Ladies' Aid Society. (Avon Congregational Church Collection.)

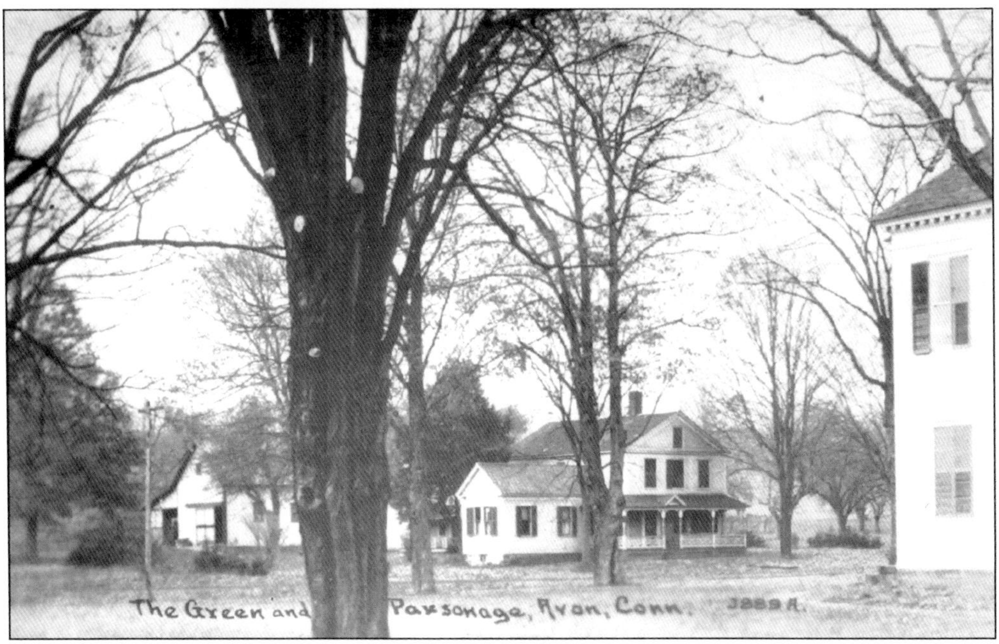

THE AVON CONGREGATIONAL CHURCH AND PARSONAGE, EARLY 1900S. In this postcard view, the church stands at the right with Simsbury Road in the foreground. Across West Main Street is the church's fourth parsonage. The church purchased the house and 3 acres from Dr. J.L. North in 1906 for $3,000. In 1941, John H. O'Neill purchased the parsonage, barn, and about 2 acres for $8,000. (Carl Candels and James Hardy Collections.)

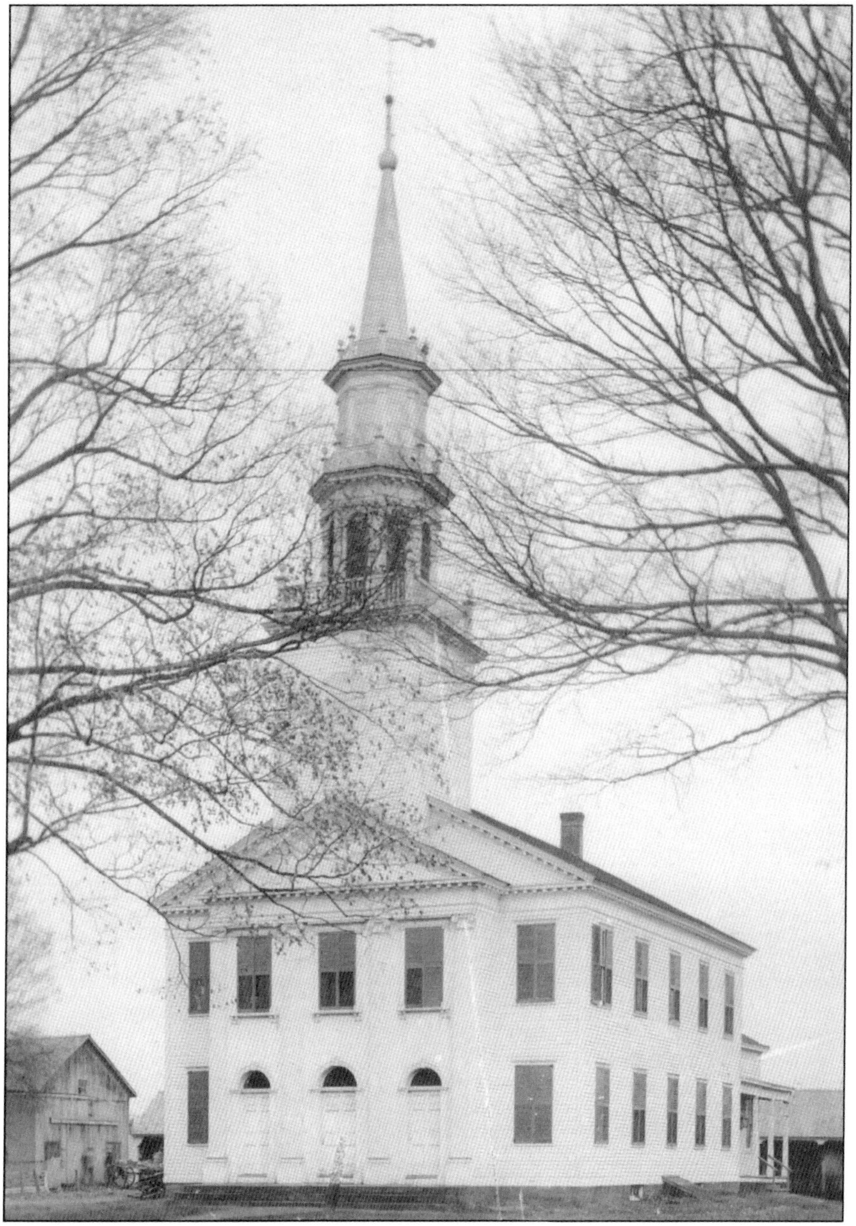

THE AVON CONGREGATIONAL CHURCH, EARLY 1900S. Established in 1751, the Congregational church in Avon split in two about 65 years later. The Avon Congregational Church at 6 West Main Street was built in 1819 under the direction of Building Committee members Amos Wheeler, Thomas Bishop, and Francis Woodford. Costing $2,150, the church was designed by architect David Hoadley. J. Frederick Kelly stated in *Early Connecticut Meetinghouses* that "the projecting front entrance bay is remarkable for the beauty of its proportions and the perfection of its delicate scale . . . . This is one of the few instances in Connecticut where regular Roman Ionic capitals were employed . . . . Hoadley's skill in design is apparent in the beautifully proportioned steeple . . . . Fortunately, the interior of this fine structure has been little changed." Shown at right rear is the church's horse-and-wagon shed. (Avon Congregational Church Collection.)

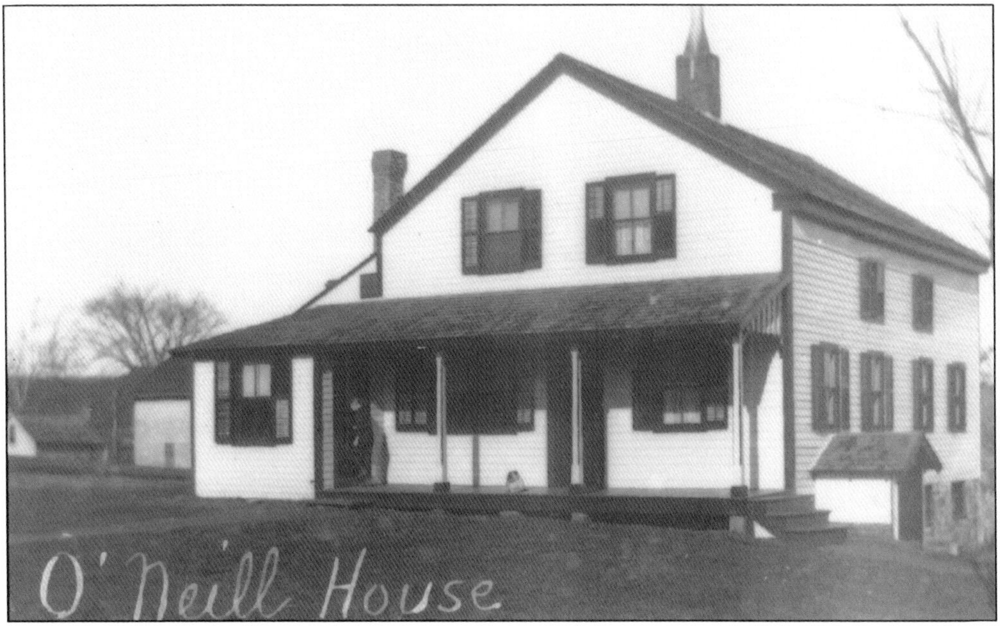

THE HOME OF PATRICK AND BRIDGET O'NEIL, EARLY 1900S. Located at 25 Simsbury Road, this house was adjacent to O'Neil's blacksmith shop and is today the home of Patrick O'Neil's grandson John Anthony O'Neill. Before St. Ann's Church was built, Father Kennedy conducted Catholic Masses in this house. (Avon Collection.)

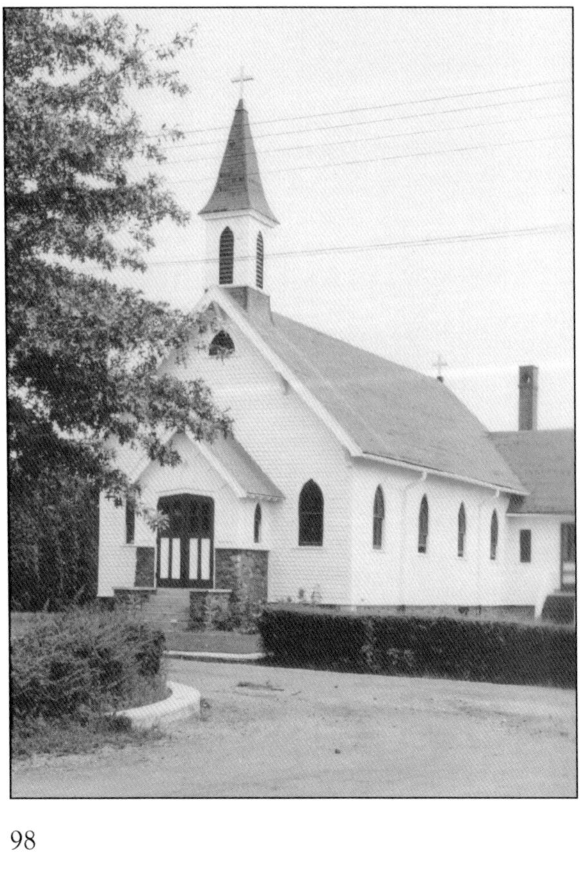

ST. ANN'S CHURCH, EARLY 1920S. At the church's dedication on December 14, 1919, Father Wilson of Farmington said, "May this little chapel long remain a monument to your faith and generosity." The chapel seated 150 and still stands at 32 Mountain View Avenue. The new St. Ann's Church on West Avon Road opened in 1957. (Lee Paulman photograph, Marilyn Dumas Collection.)

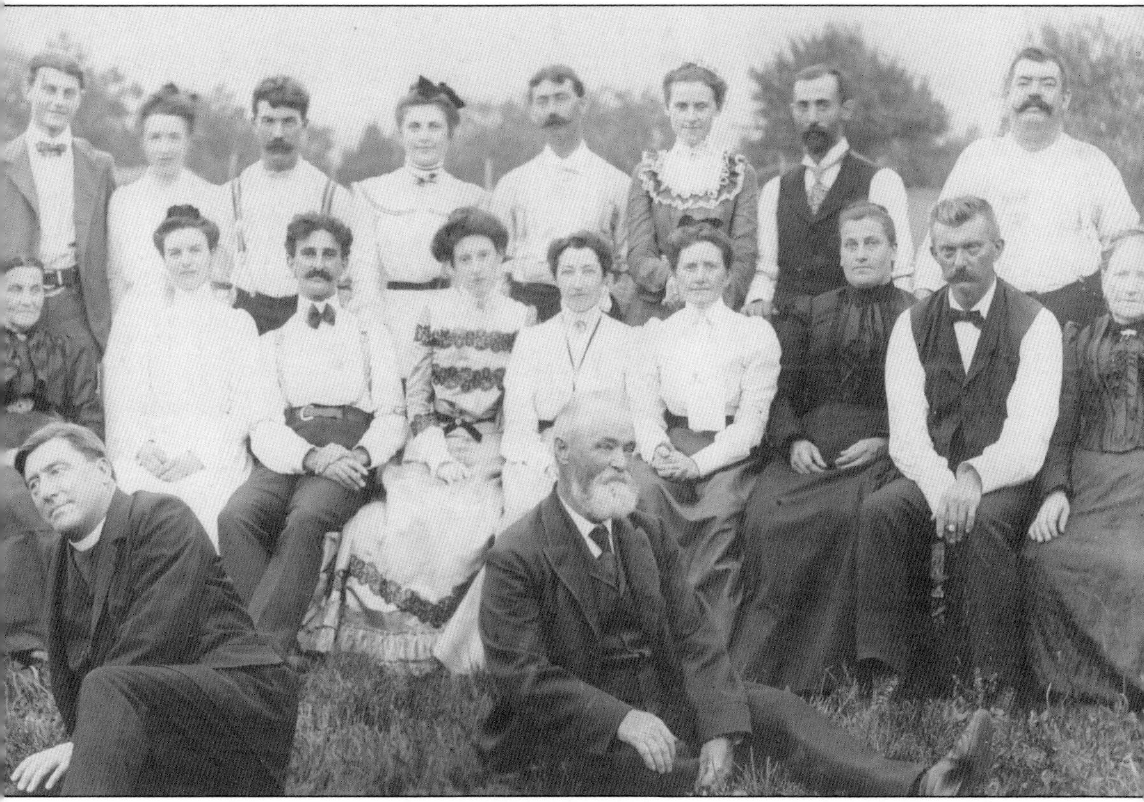

ST. ANN'S CHURCH GROUP, EARLY 1900S. Rev. William F. Kennedy, seated in the front on the left, was born c. 1871 in Putnam, was educated at St. Mary's Seminary in Baltimore, and was ordained in 1897. He was the first pastor of St. Ann's Church on Mountain View Avenue. He began serving Avon, an out-mission from Collinsville, c. 1912, conducting Mass for parishioners in the homes of Patrick O'Neil, Patrick McDonald, John Joyce, and John Sheridan and in Towpath School. He worked with architect George Zunner of Hartford and builder James P. Murphy of West Hartford to design the $7,000 church. The *Hartford Courant* reported in 1919 that "the task of erecting a Catholic Church in Avon seemed at first almost too great to be undertaken, and the fact that it has been pushed to completion speaks volumes for the generosity of the people of Avon, Catholic and Protestants contributing alike generously." (Avon Collection.)

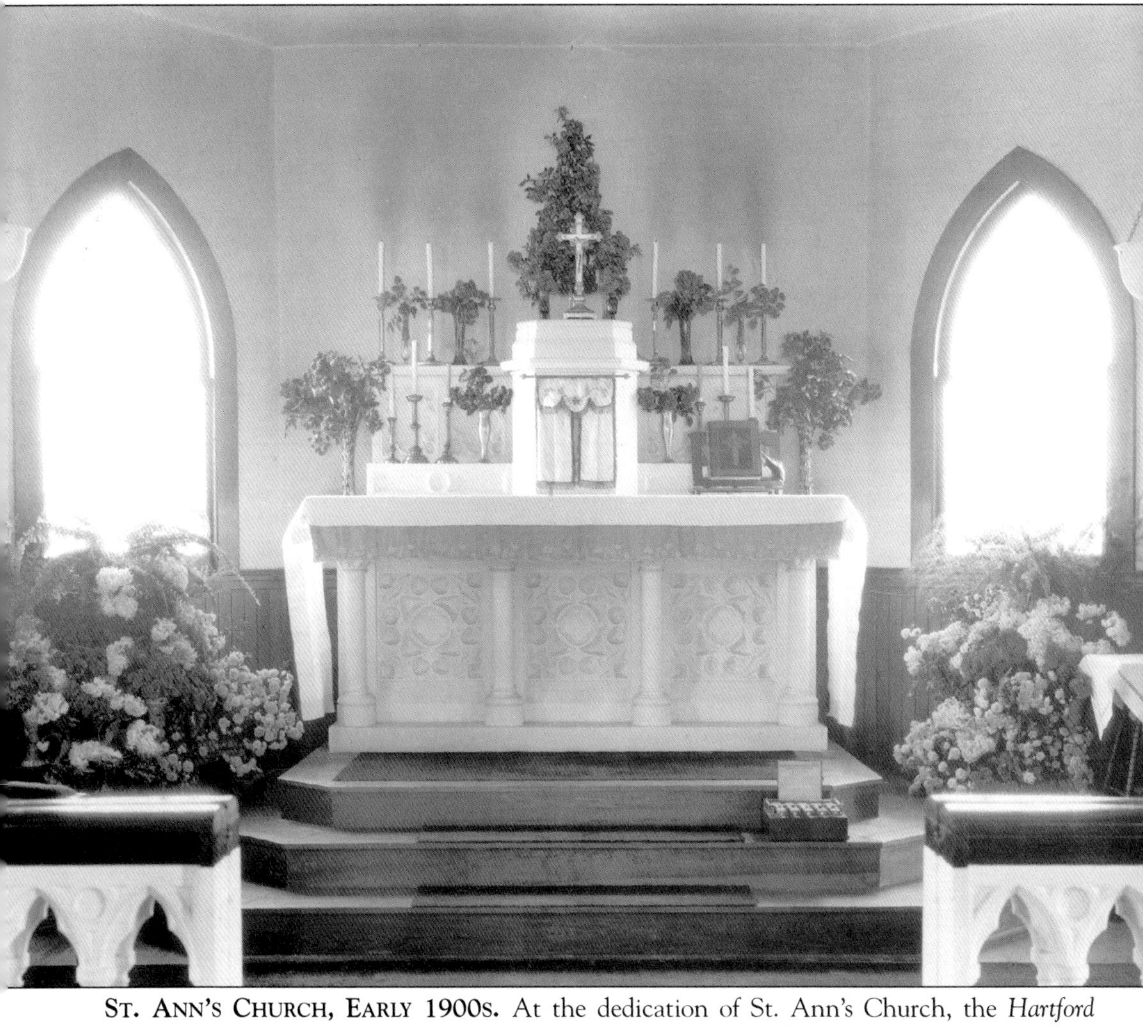

St. Ann's Church, Early 1900s. At the dedication of St. Ann's Church, the *Hartford Courant* reported that the "interior has been planned to give an effect of spaciousness, the walls of cream stucco, windows of amber tinted glass and altar of white hand-carved wood relieved with gold . . . . The pews are of mahogany, woodwork of cypress. The Stations of the Cross are represented by a series of handsome paintings in simple frames of gilded wood, especially suited to the rich simplicity of the whole interior." To the left of the altar stood a statue of St. Joseph, given to the church in memory of Mr. and Mrs. Patrick McDonald by their daughters, Mrs. Thomas Hanifan and Nellie McDonald. At the right stood a Blessed Virgin statue, given by Fred Neville in honor of his parents, Mr. and Mrs. Joseph Neville. At the dedication, Father Wilson of Farmington said, "May the instructions which you receive here give you comfort in times of sorrow, and hope when the clouds of doubt gather." (Anthony O'Neill Collection.)

Seven

AGRICULTURE "THE LAND ATT NOD"

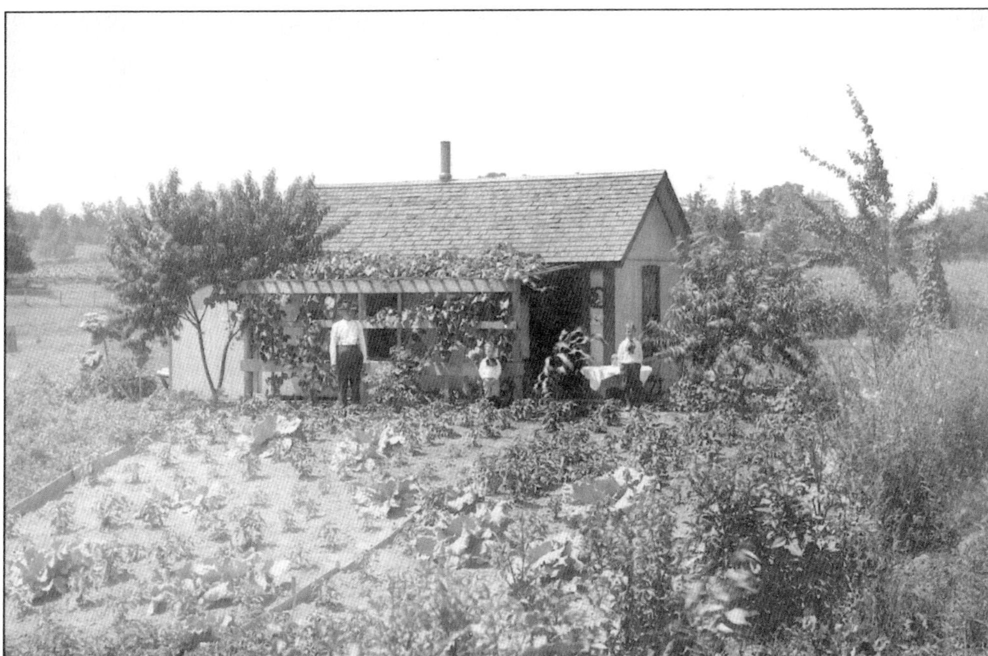

THE ANTONIO DELISSIO HOME, C. 1917. The two-room farmhouse still stands at 185 Thompson Road. It was built by Joseph Thompson of Sunrise Farm for farmhand Antonio Delissio (d. 1925), who came to the United States in the late 1800s and worked for Thompson at the farm. Pictured from left to right are Antonio Delissio, Oliver Thompson, and an unidentified child. Avon farmers raised tobacco, corn, potatoes, rye, oats, buckwheat, and hay and produced large quantities of butter for the Hartford market. (Sunrise Farm Collection.)

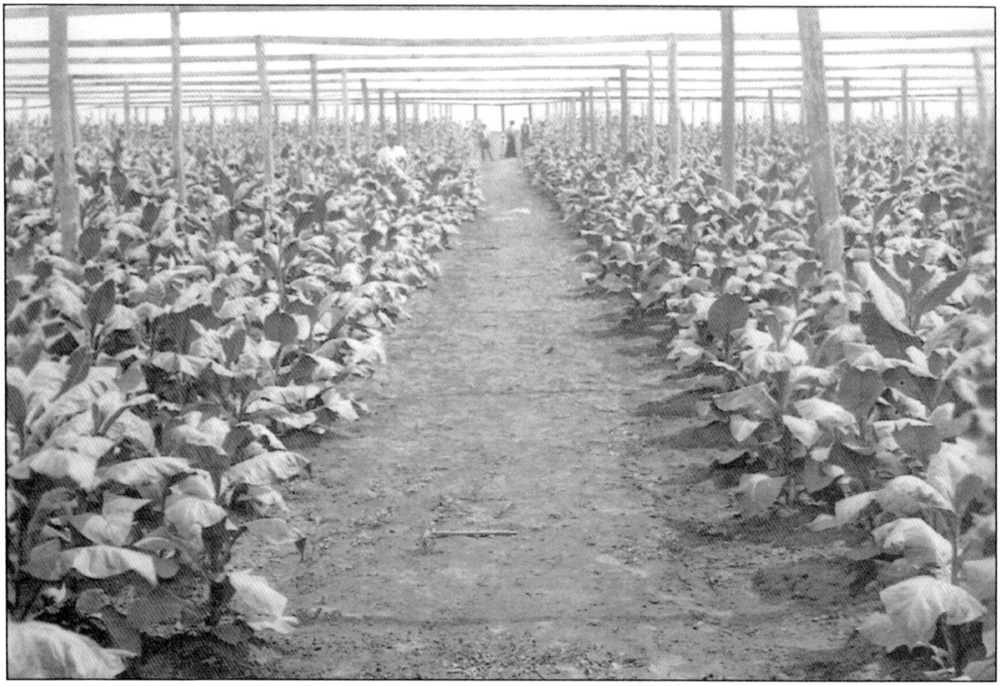

An Avon Tobacco Farm, c. 1901. In this rare view of a shade tobacco farm, three people stand at the end of the path. Shade-grown tobacco produced an excellent leaf for cigar wrappers. This photograph was important enough for the Avon Congregational Church members to include in a small souvenir photograph album that they gave to their pastor, Rev. Samuel Fisk, on February 9, 1902. (Avon Congregational Church Collection.)

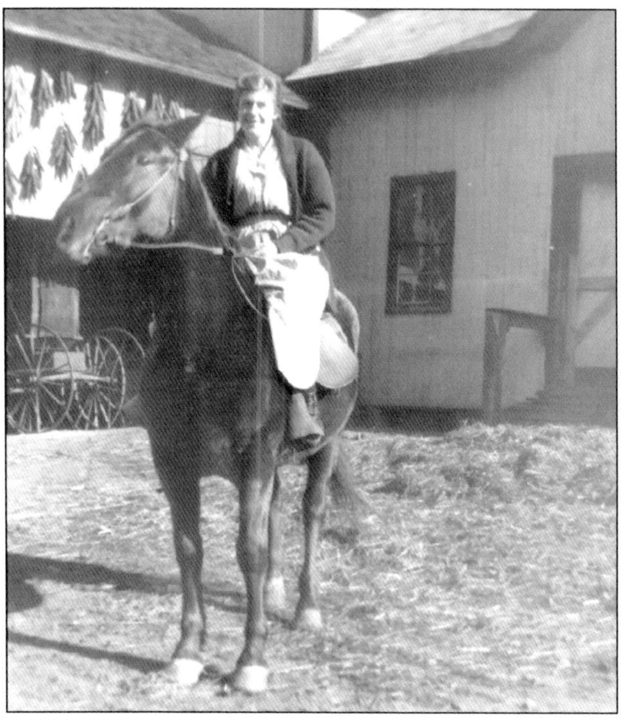

Sunrise Farm, c. 1918. Vesta Lourie grew up at Sunrise Farm on West Avon Road, the niece of owner Joseph Thompson. She is shown at the farm, with a carriage in the barn behind her and corn set out to dry. After her marriage to Albert Thompson, she lived across the street at Cold Spring Farm. (Audrey Thompson Collection.)

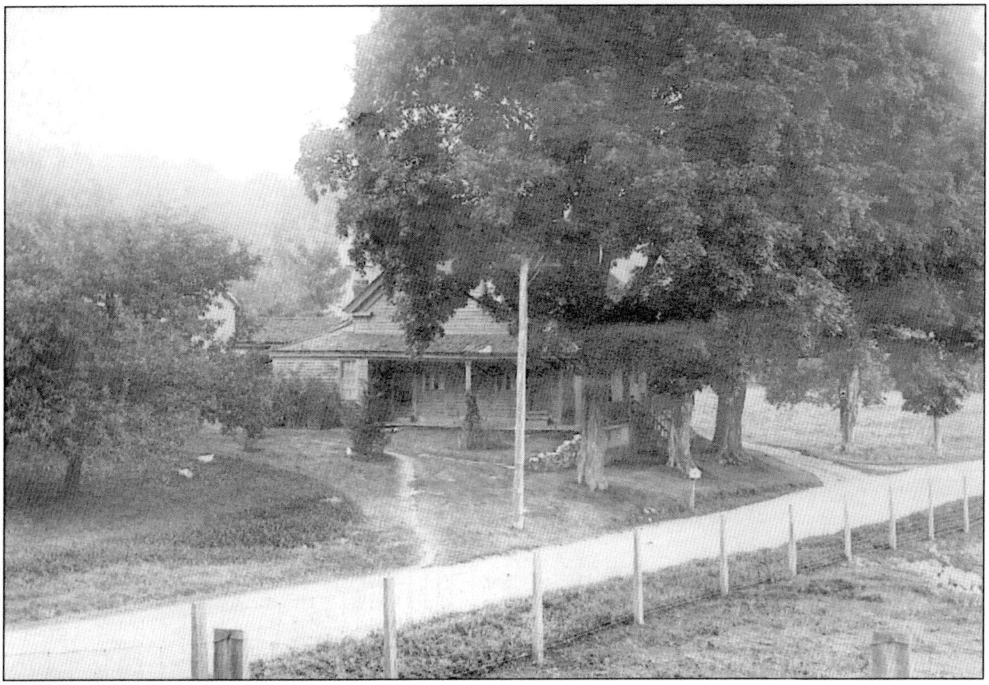

MAPLE ROCK FARM, EARLY 1920S. The barn's sign reads, "Maple Rock Farm, West Avon, C. Keeney, Conn." Still standing at 335 Lovely Street, the dairy farm was owned by Charles Keeney from *c.* 1918 to 1927, by William J. Hickmont from 1927 to 1934, and by Frank and Helen Parker from 1934 to 1979. In later years, the Parkers operated a dog kennel on the property. (Patricia Parker Vibert Collection.)

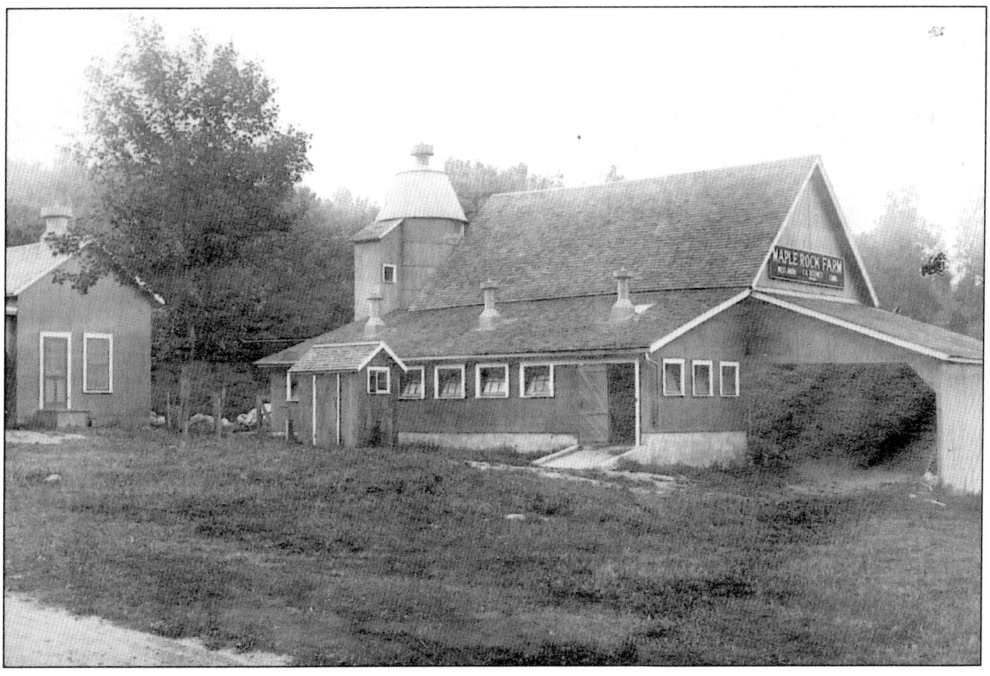

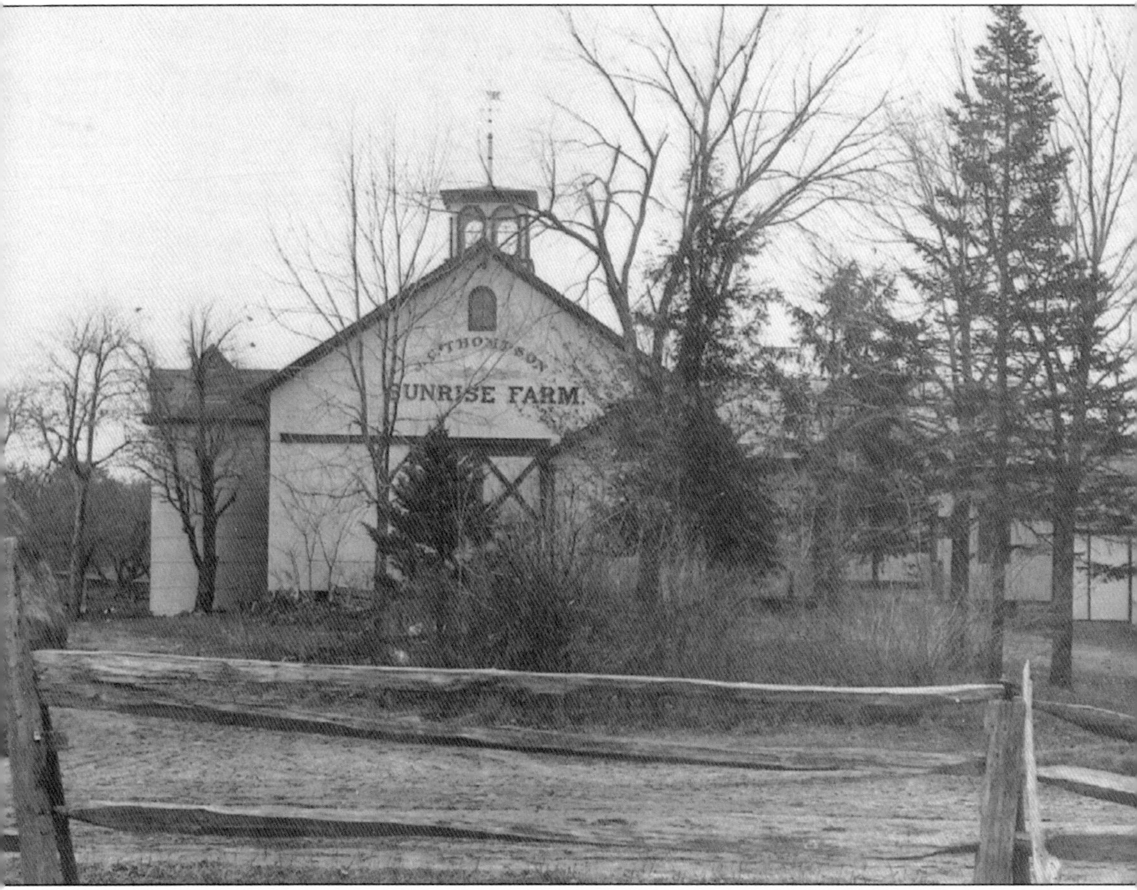

Sunrise Farm, Early 1900s. Mrs. Joseph C. Thompson and another person are in a wagon at the Thompson's Sunrise Farm. Among the farm's products was Havana Seed Tobacco, which was raised there from the late 1800s until 1955. This high-quality tobacco was used to bind the lesser quality broadleaf tobacco together in a cigar. "Sunrise Farm" was painted on the barn sometime between 1895 and 1903. West Avon Road, shown here, was paved in 1933. Farming was Avon's way of life. In 1851, Rev. Joel Grant, pastor of the West Avon Congregational

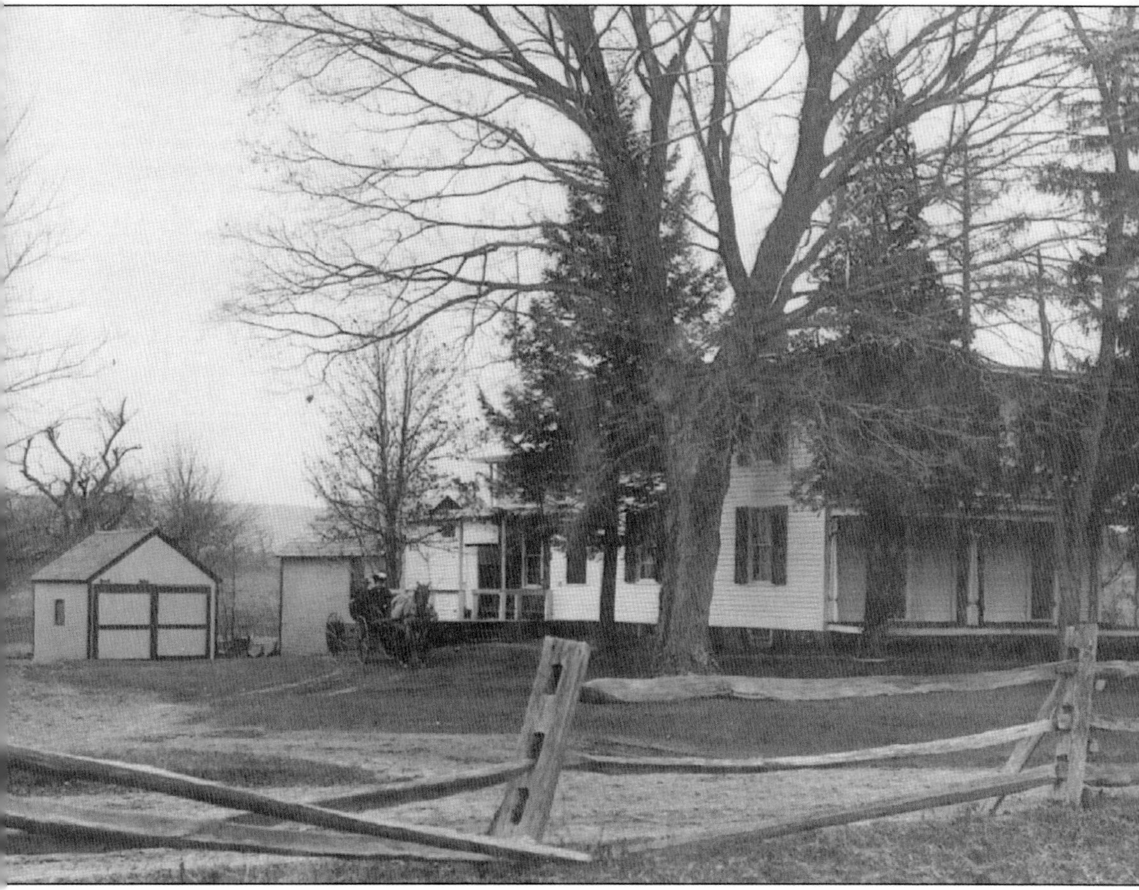

Church, wrote that "agriculture must, in all probability, be *the* employment of the people residing here for the next century, it becomes most desirable that it should be pursued wisely and efficiently . . . . Few places are more inviting as a residence. A moral and pious community, a soil not rich but yet exceedingly grateful for the kind culture; a convenient market; pure water, and healthful breezes." (Sunrise Farm Collection.)

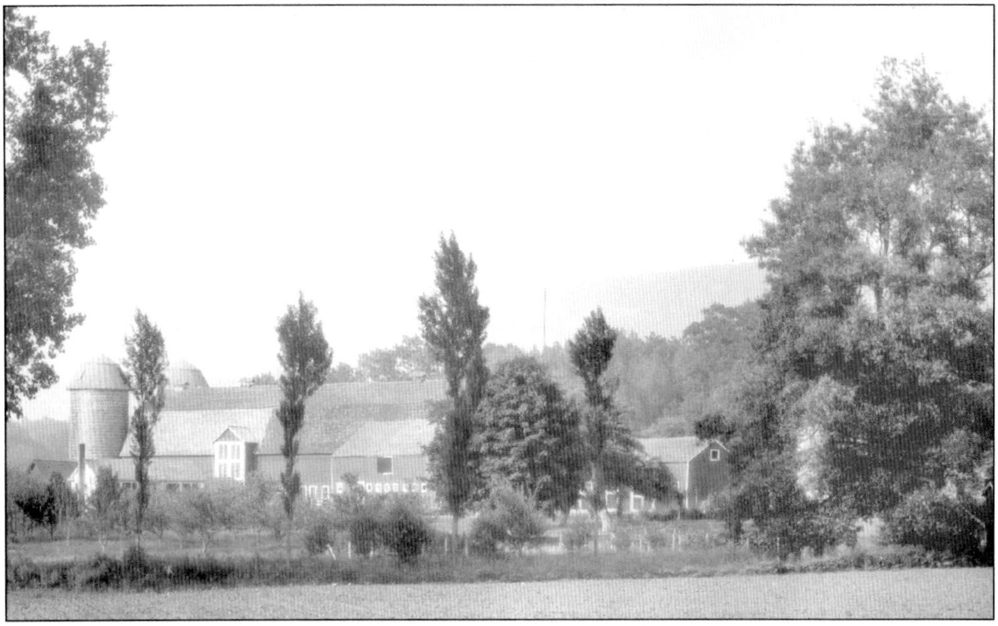

WOOD FORD FARM. In 1902, Joseph Wright Alsop (1876–1953) of Middletown purchased what became a 700-acre farm in what he called "the finest" small town in Connecticut. Alsop ran a dairy, grew tobacco, was an insurance executive, served in the state legislature, and was first selectman in Avon (1920–53). His wife, Corinne Robinson Alsop (1886–1971), Pres. Theodore Roosevelt's niece, also served in the state legislature and was Avon's Republican party chairman for 22 years. (Avon Collection.)

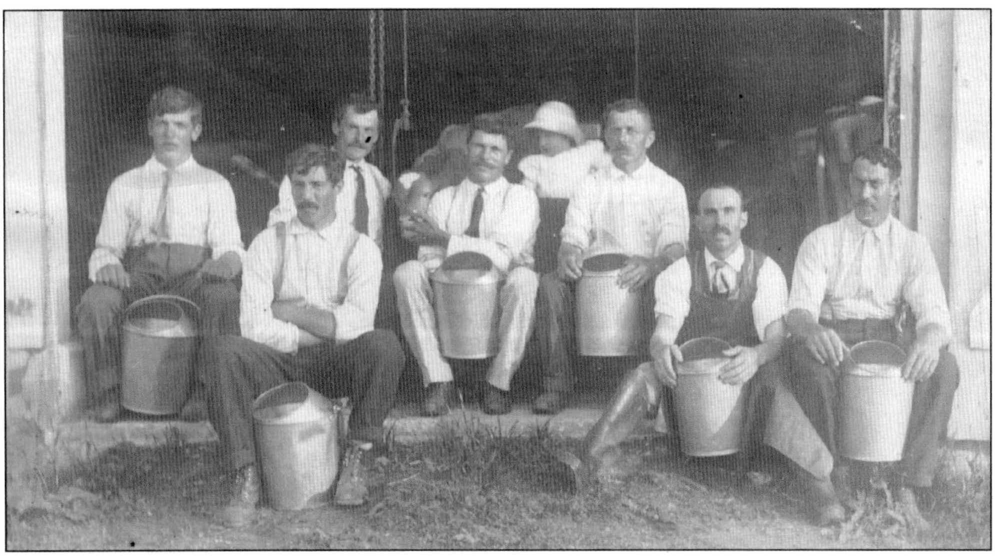

WOOD FORD FARM, MAY 1912. Honeymooning in 1909, Joseph and Corinne Alsop traveled to Italy and hired 30 or so farmhands for Wood Ford Farm. Pictured from left to right at the dairy barn are Carlo Simonelli, Antonio Nascimbeni, Domanico Gaioni, Francesco Zamperini, Joseph Wright Alsop V (the boy in the hat), Antonio Veronesi, Luigi DalBon, and Domenico Kena. (Clinton Hadsell photograph, Avon Collection.)

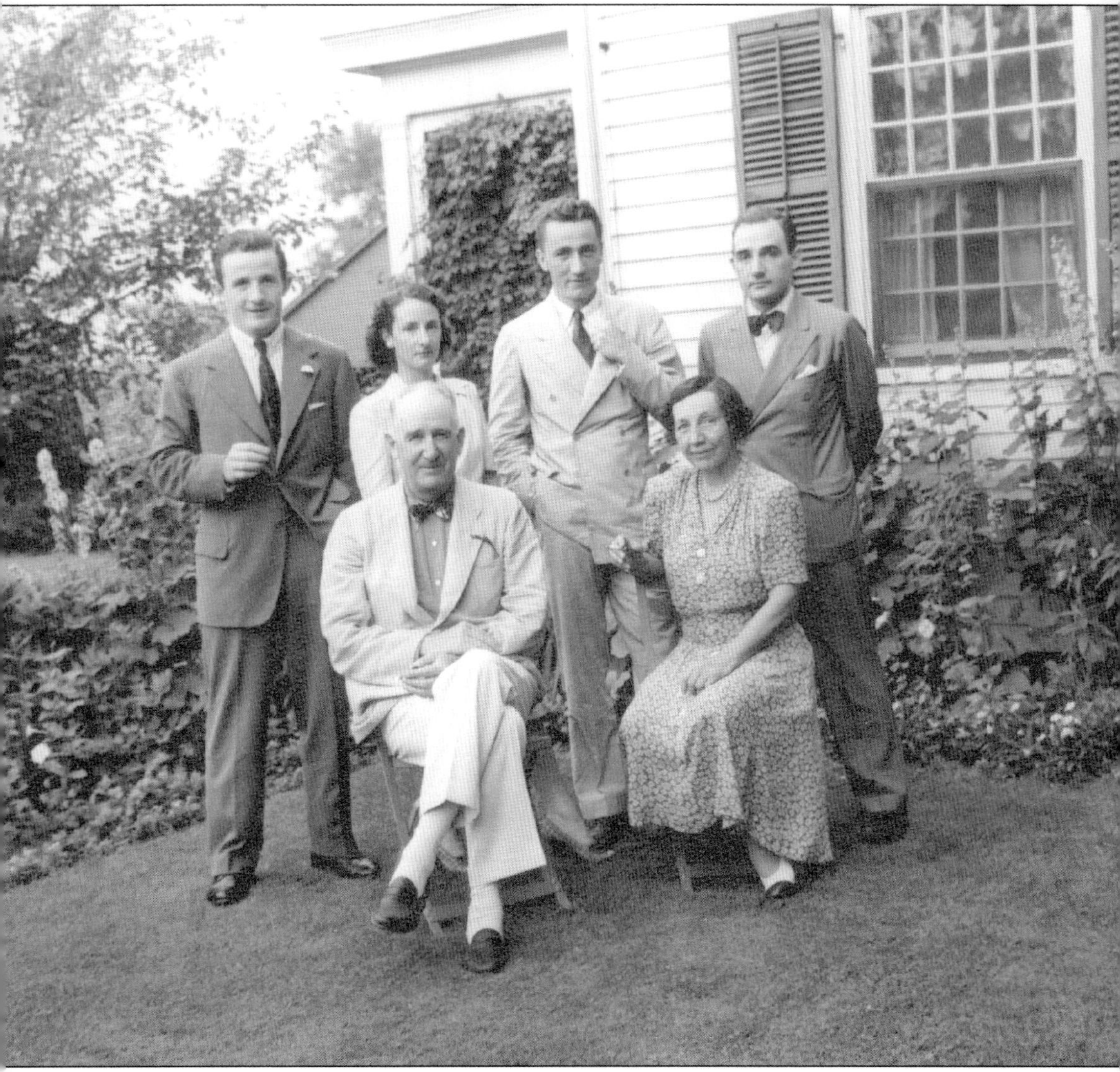

THE ALSOP FAMILY, 1941. This photograph was taken at Wood Ford Farm the weekend before Joseph Alsop Jr. left for World War II. Shown at 27 Nod Road are Joseph and Corinne Alsop and their children. Pictured from left to right are John (1915–2000), Corinne (b. 1912) Stewart (1914–74), and Joseph (1910–89) Alsop. Stewart and Joseph Alsop became nationally known political writers. Stewart Alsop worked for the *Saturday Evening Post*; Joseph became a syndicated columnist working out of Washington, D.C. John Alsop, who remained in Avon, was an insurance executive, a state legislator, a Republican candidate for governor in 1962, and a member of the Republican National Committee from 1968 to 1984. Upon his death a *Hartford Courant* editorial noted that he "was one of Connecticut's finest sons." (Anthony O'Neill Collection.)

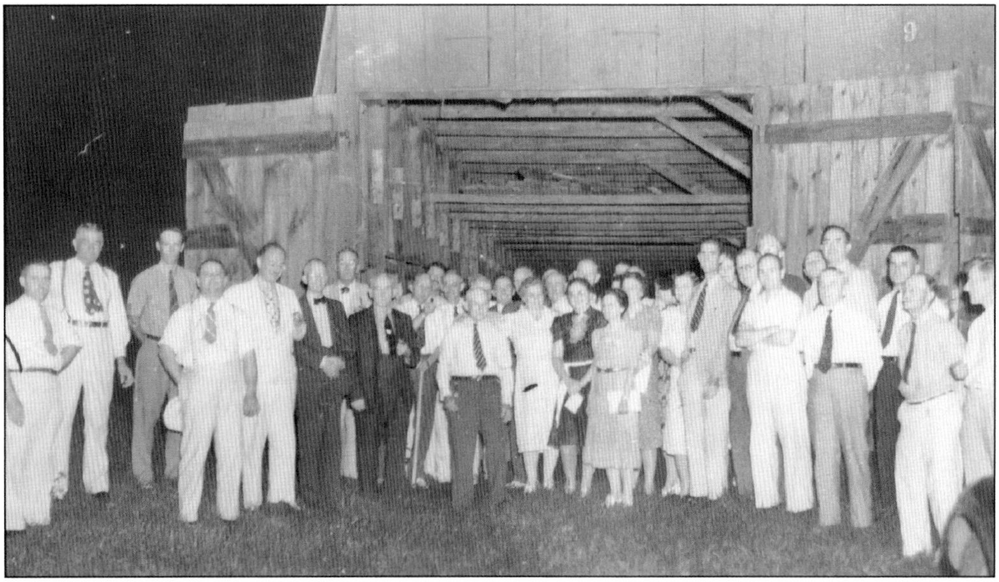

The Republican Town Committee Picnic, July 29, 1940. Joseph Alsop, first selectman, and Corinne Alsop, Republican party chair, entertain town officials in their tobacco shed. At each table serving was a glass bottle of Wood Ford Farm milk. Guests included Willis Chidsey, C. Fred Woodford, John O'Neill, Ted Manion, Lavinia Hadsell, Frank Holloway, Primo Viti, Parker Young, Ben Miller, and Joseph Thompson. A film of the picnic is at the Avon Free Public Library. (Avon Collection.)

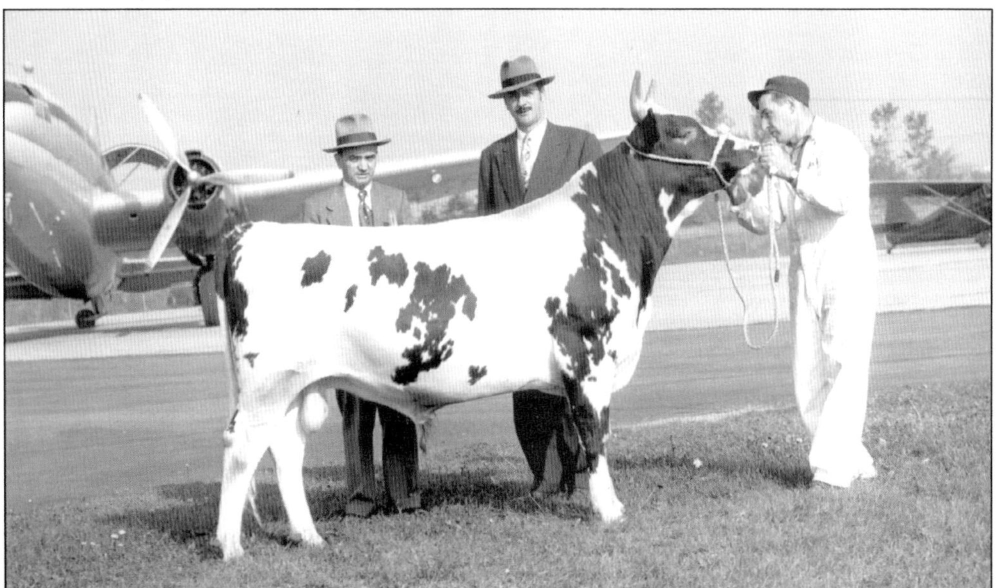

A Wood Ford Farm Ayshire Bull, c. 1950. Buyers from Columbia, South America, pose with their prize bull before departing from Brainard Field. Pictured at the right is farm herdsman Frank Gaioni. Beginning in the 1930s, under farm manager Jesse Anderson, Wood Ford Farm became nationally known for milk production. In 1950, it had the highest-producing Ayshire herd in America. The farm sold Ayshires and frozen semen worldwide to improve herds. (Russell S. Anderson photograph, Avon Collection.)

Eight

Getting from Here to There

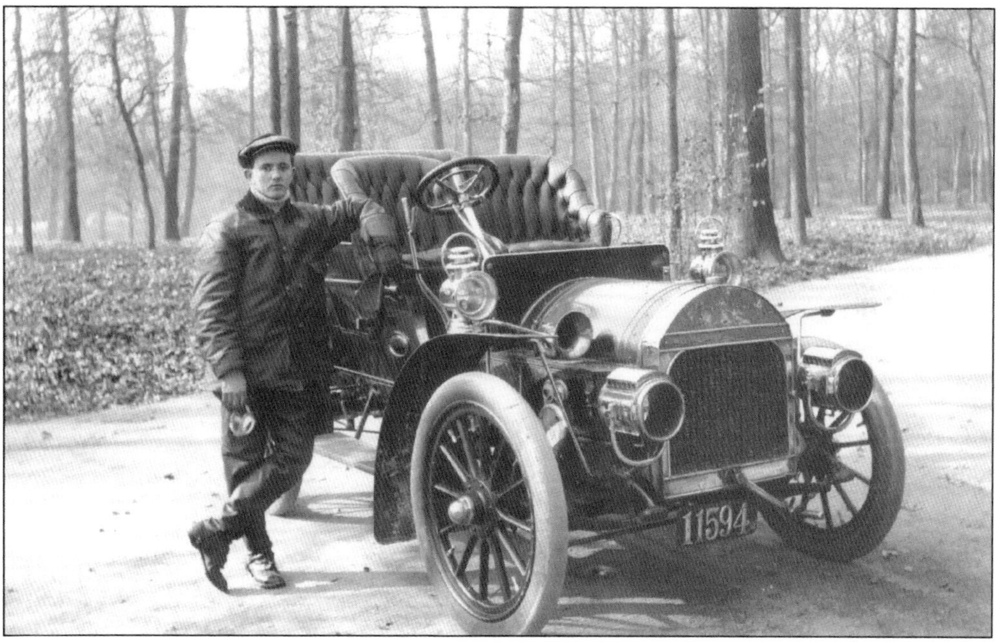

Howard Stowe, c. 1905. Howard Stowe was raised in Avon, the son of a traveling sewing machine salesman. A chauffeur and photographer, Stowe poses—probably not in Avon—with a $3,000 Haynes automobile of 1905. Designed by Elwood Haynes, the inventor of stainless steel, this automobile was one of 243 produced by the Haynes Automobile Company of Kokomo, Indiana. The license plate number is too high to have been on a Connecticut vehicle at this time. Avon's most prominent family, the Alsops, did not even own a car until 1914. In 1933, Stowe was living in Florida, harvesting thousands of gallons of honey for the Miami market. (Anthony O'Neill Collection).

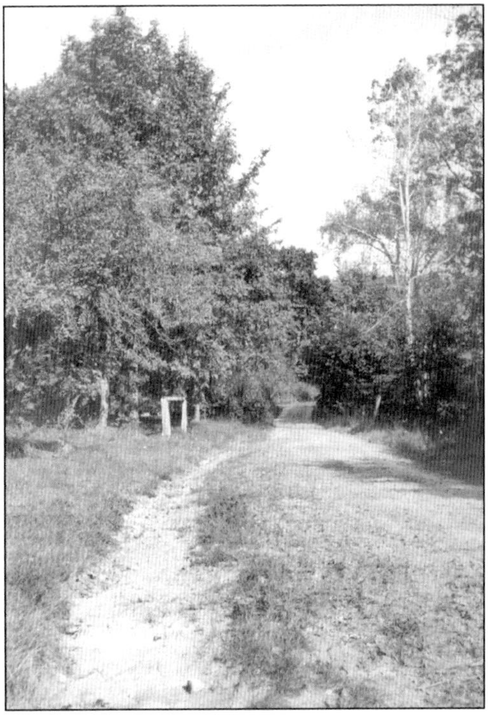

Country Club Road near Lovely Street. Originally called Pleasant Street, the road in 1869 boasted a sawmill at the west end), a few homes, a tavern on the southwest corner of West Avon Road and Country Club, the West Avon Congregational Church and parsonage, the post office for West Avon in Corydon Woodford's dry goods and grocery store on the southwest corner of Country Club and Burnham Roads, and the District 3 schoolhouse. (Avon Collection.)

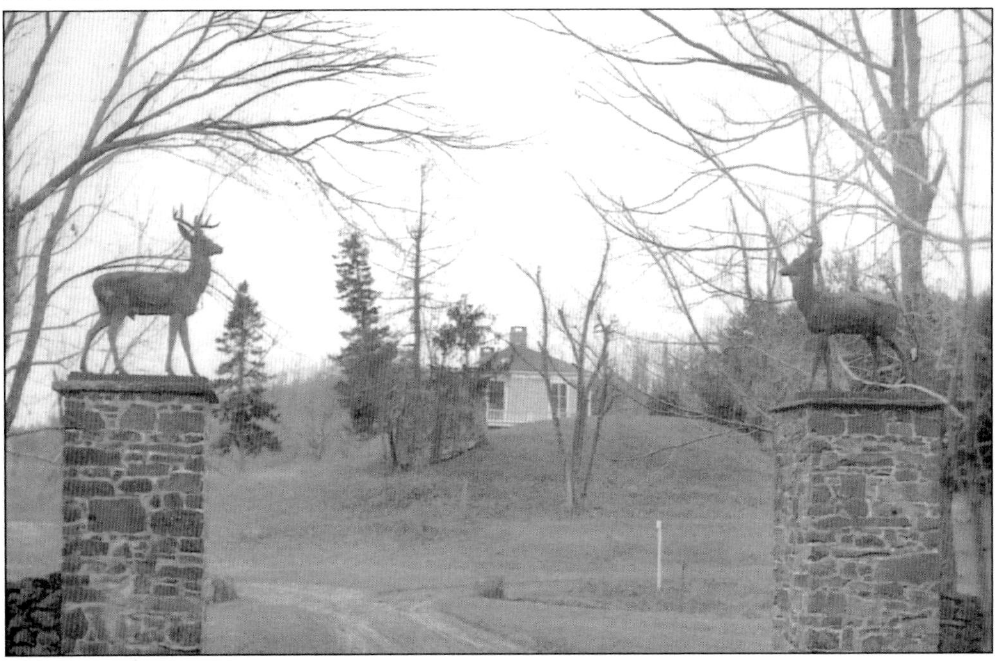

Deercliff Farm, c. 1901. In 1835, Richard Ely of New York purchased Deercliff Farm, just off Albany Turnpike, for a summer residence and dairy farm with Jersey cattle. *The Memorial History of Hartford County* described it as "one of the most picturesque sites" in Connecticut. Tradition states that it was a refuge for slaves traveling the Underground Railroad to freedom. Ely's daughter Maud Ely Gibbons was a benefactor of Avon's public library, dedicated in 1932. (Avon Congregational Church)

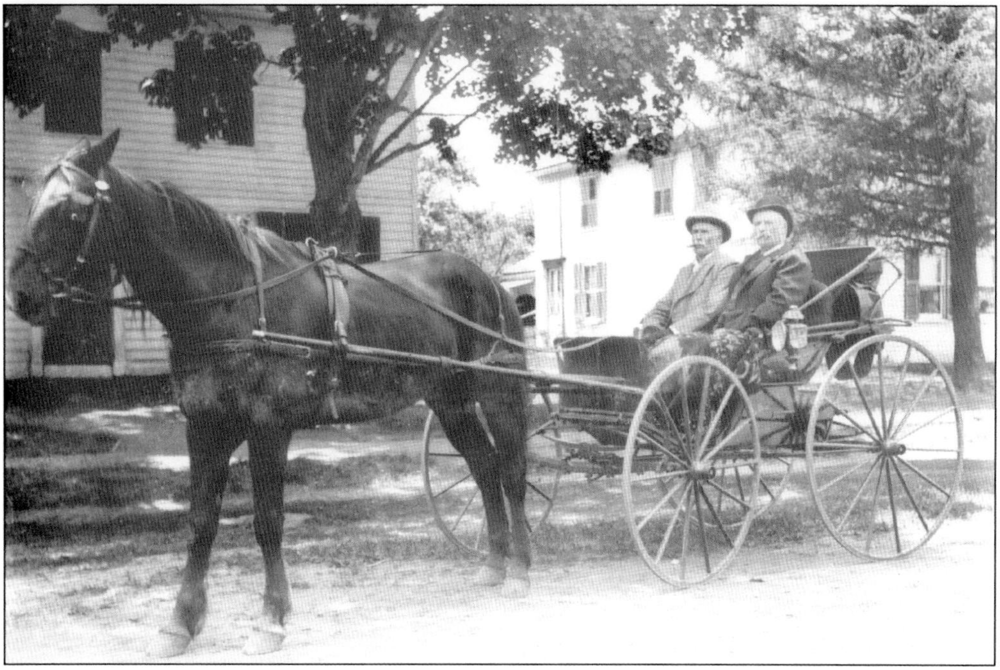

"JOHN MALONE AND BROTHER WITH TEAM, MAY 27, 1900." The brothers pose on West Main Street in front of the former Farmington Canal Administration Building. At the right is the Avon Congregational Church. (Clinton Hadsell photograph, Avon Collection, courtesy of Doris Miller.)

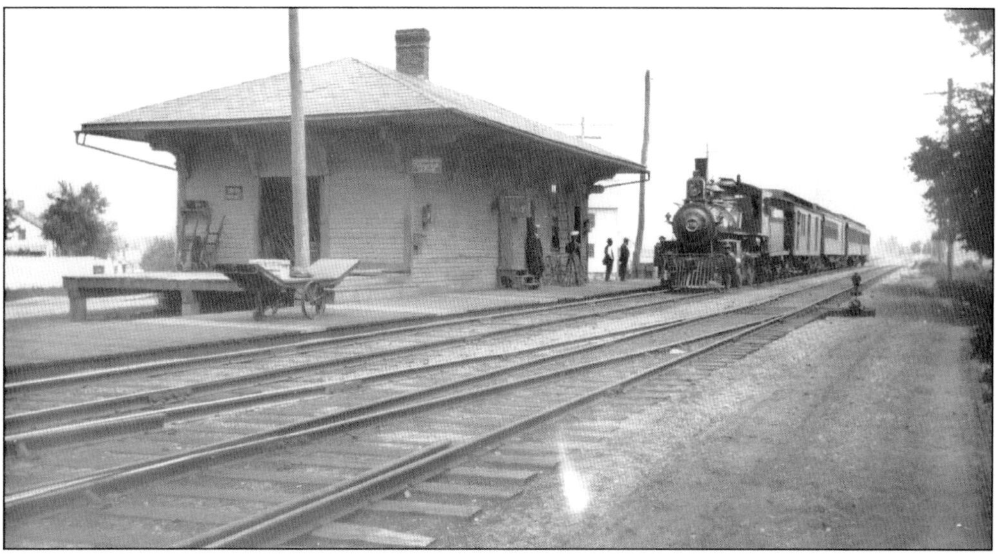

THE 1880 RAILROAD STATION, EARLY 1900S. The Farmington Canal Railroad was chartered in 1847, and the route from New Haven to Avon opened in 1850. The line to Northampton opened in 1856. Passenger service ended in the 1940s, freight service in 1991. The station, built by the New Haven & Northampton Railroad Company, was moved in 1955 to Holloway's sand and gravel business, now Riverdale Farms. In 1992, Lino Viti said, "The locomotive ringing bells and smoke coming out and the whistle blowing—those steam engines were quite a sight. Those days are gone." (Anthony O'Neill Collection.)

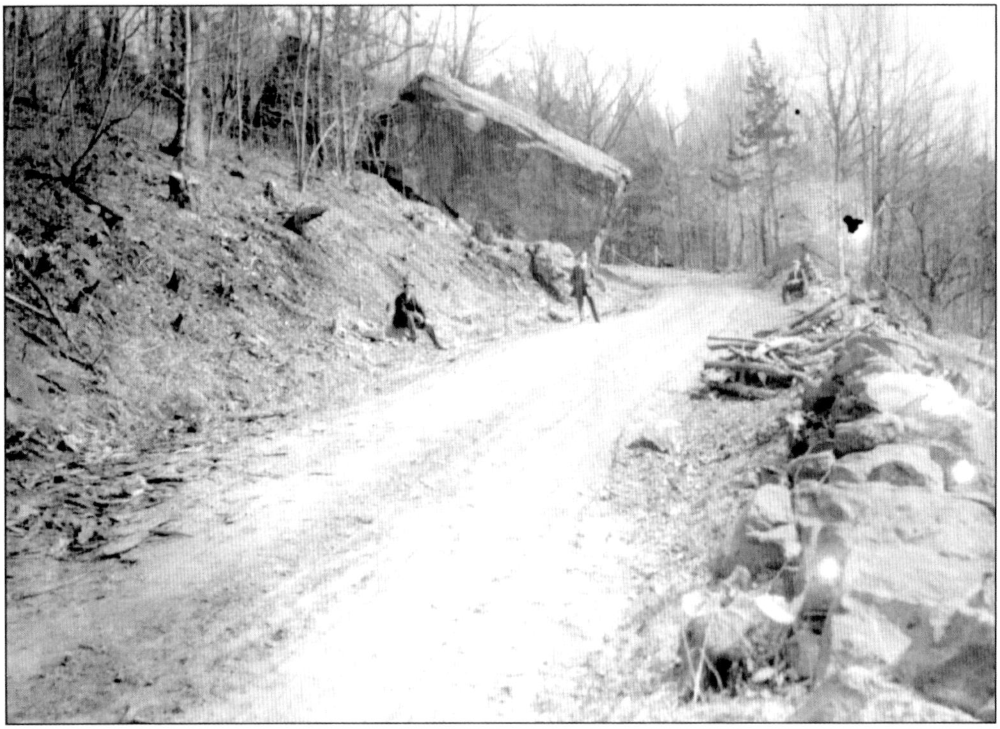

THE ALBANY TURNPIKE OVER TALCOTT MOUNTAIN, MAY 1911. The Connecticut General Assembly chartered the Talcott Mountain Turnpike Company in 1798. It completed the road through Avon, between Hartford and New Hartford, in 1799. The turnpike connected Avon to Hartford and Albany, New York, and was one of New England's busiest highways. One month after this photograph was taken, Harrison Rock was blasted to pieces. (Clinton Hadsell photograph, Avon Collection, courtesy of Doris Miller.)

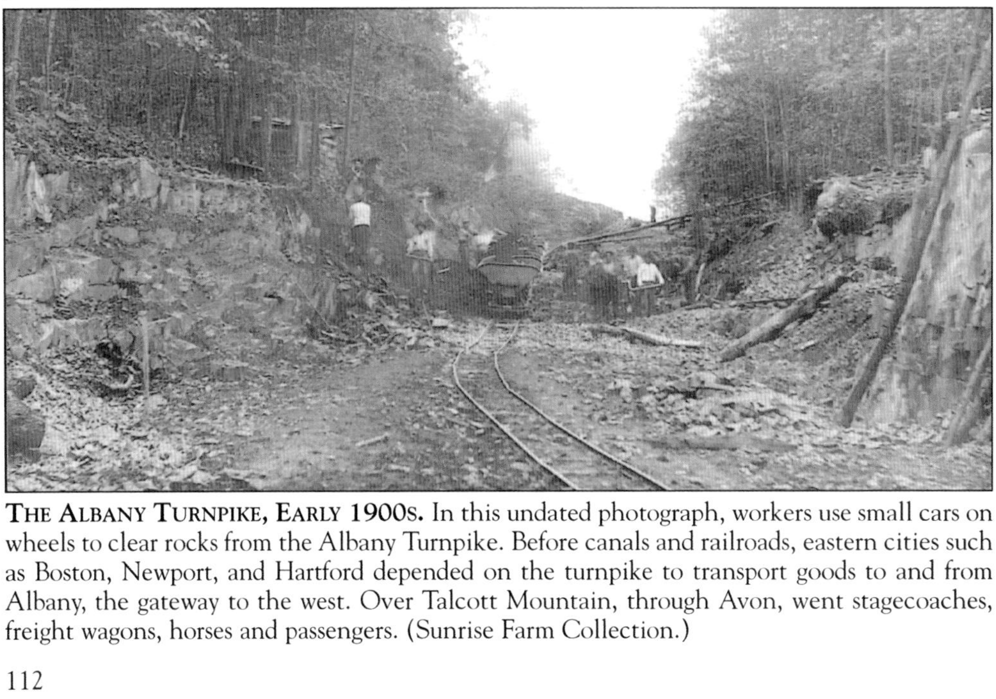

THE ALBANY TURNPIKE, EARLY 1900S. In this undated photograph, workers use small cars on wheels to clear rocks from the Albany Turnpike. Before canals and railroads, eastern cities such as Boston, Newport, and Hartford depended on the turnpike to transport goods to and from Albany, the gateway to the west. Over Talcott Mountain, through Avon, went stagecoaches, freight wagons, horses and passengers. (Sunrise Farm Collection.)

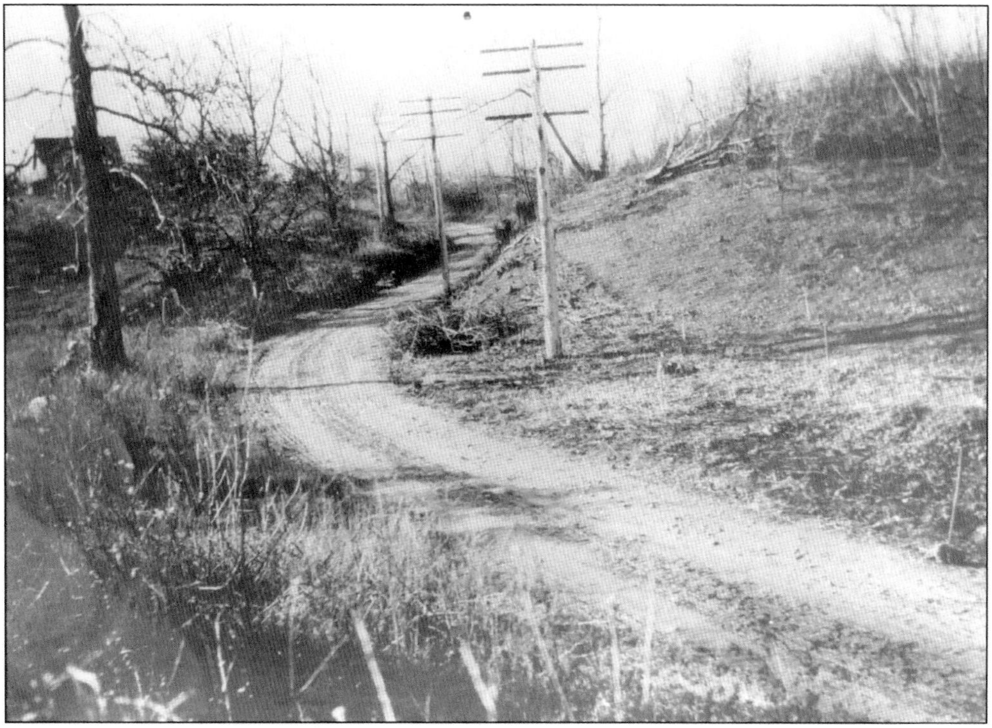

The Albany Turnpike, Looking East up Talcott Mountain, 1915. Improvements to the Albany Turnpike cut the two-hour ride to Hartford to half an hour. By 1920, the turnpike was paved; by 1929, it had four lanes. The Alsop family had two cars in 1914, a Pierce Arrow and a Ford Model T. Son Joseph Alsop wrote, "Our ritual isolation began to fade." Avon's dairy farmers had an easier time transporting milk and cream to Hartford schools and hospitals. (Department of Transportation photograph, Anthony O'Neill Collection.)

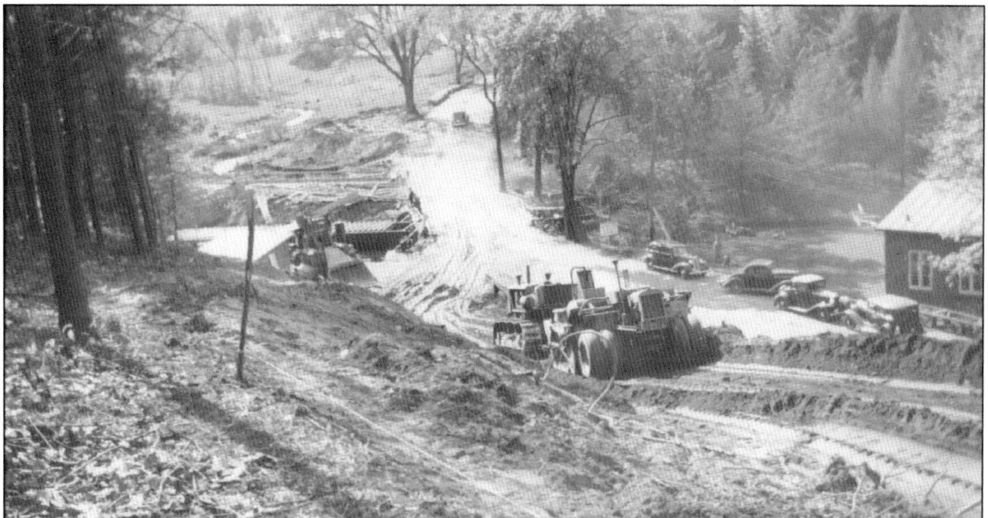

West Main Street, 1937. In this view looking west, a bulldozer and other machinery make improvements to Route 44. At right is a portion of the present police station. (Anthony O'Neill Collection, courtesy of Bruce Wiepert.)

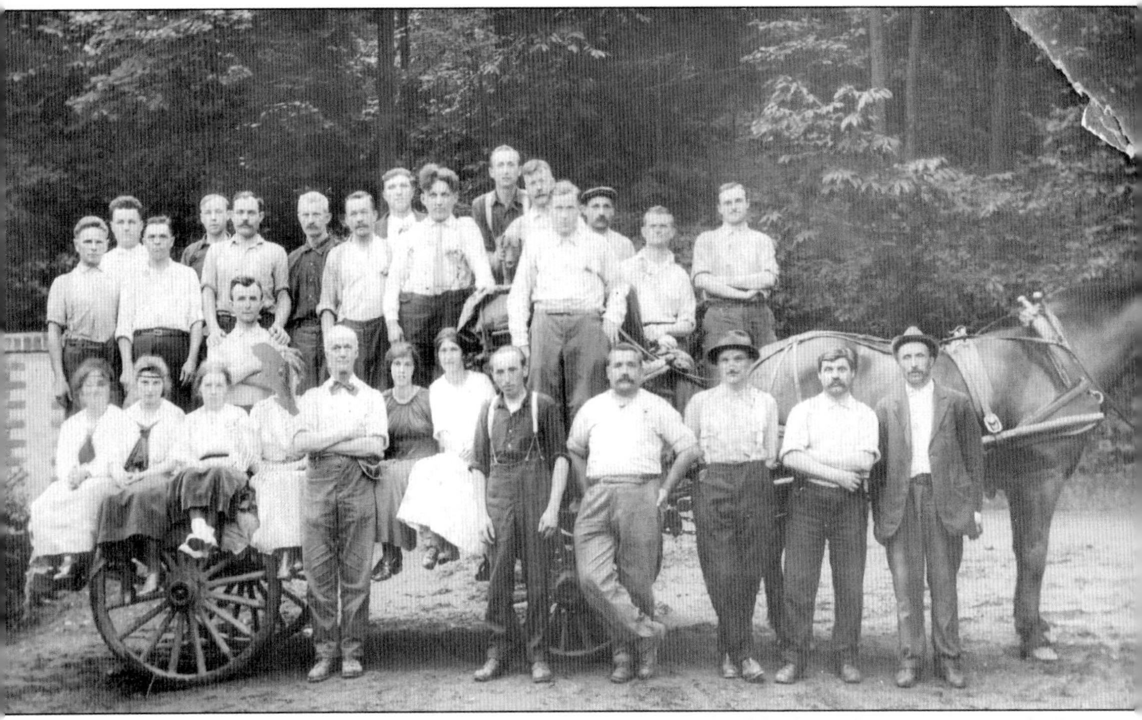

THE ENSIGN-BICKFORD COMPANY, LATE 1920S. Ensign-Bickford employees go to work. In the front row at the far right is Paulo Bussolini. Emigrating here from Italy to escape the World War I, Bussolini worked for Joseph Alsop clearing land and then for Ensign-Bickford. Pictured in the second row at the far left is John Kulikowski Sr. (Marilyn Dumas Collection.)

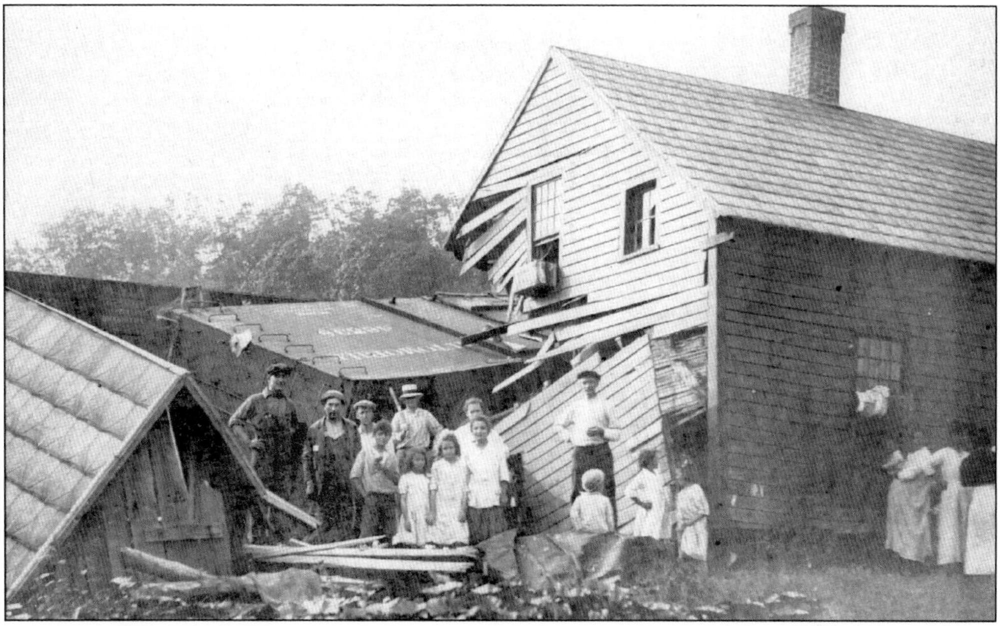

A Train Wreck, August 1918. On August 2, 1918, nine overloaded freight cars speeding north crashed one-quarter mile south of the station. The train tore out 1,000 feet of track and tumbled down the embankment. One car carrying cement crashed into an unoccupied house owned by Ensign-Bickford. According to the *New Hartford Tribune*, it was Avon's worst accident since 1901. (Anthony O'Neill Collection.)

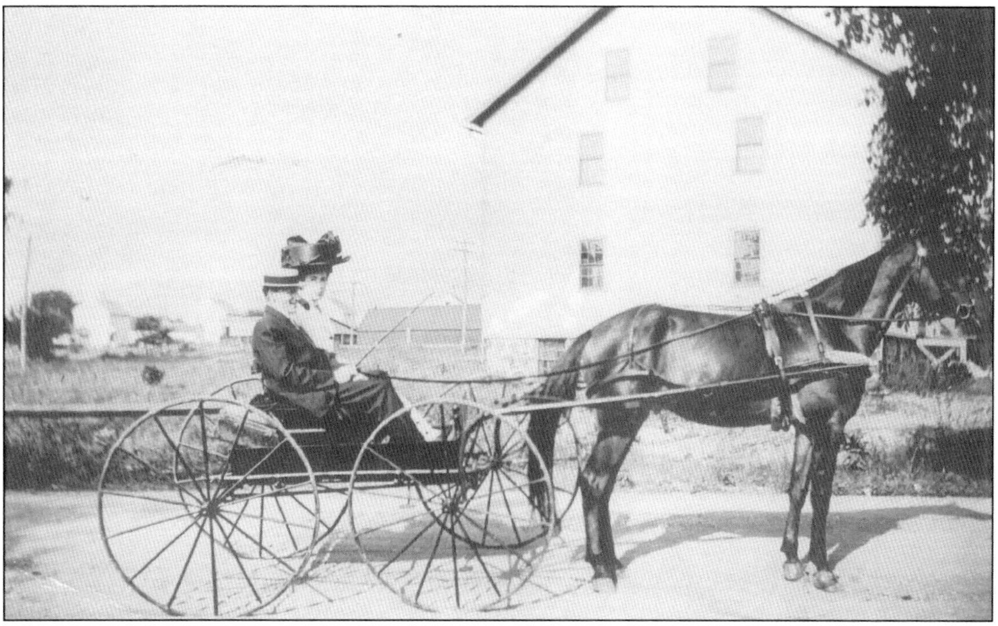

Simsbury Road, 1910. Mary O'Neil poses with a friend opposite 25 Simsbury Road. The building is the Avon Tobacco Company warehouse, purchased two years later by American Sumatra Tobacco. At this time, carriages and automobiles were coming into conflict. After a series of accidents in 1908, the *Farmington Valley Herald* wrote that "horses have not been afraid of automobiles before." (Anthony O'Neill Collection.)

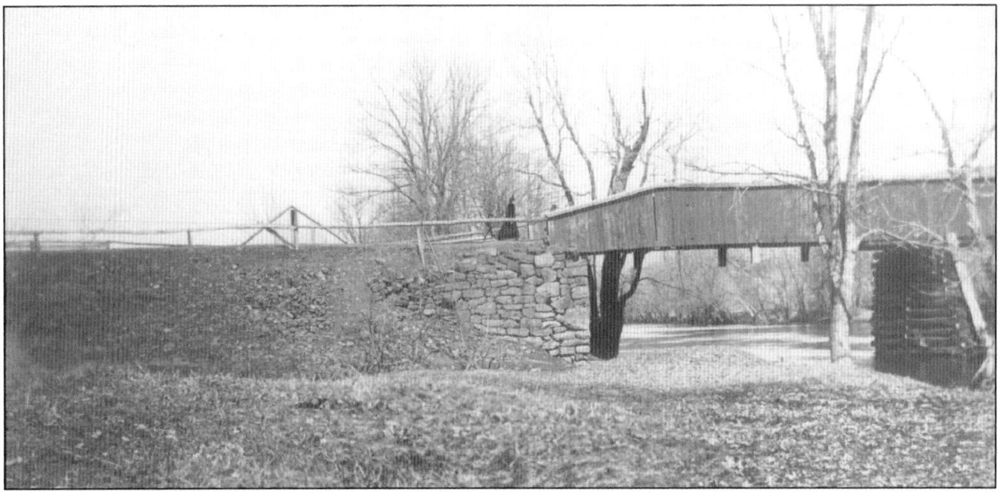

THE FARMINGTON RIVER BRIDGE, BEFORE 1896. This bridge carried traffic on the Albany Turnpike (Route 44), cost less than $1,000 to build, and stood from 1878 to 1896. Describing the 1896 flood that destroyed the bridge but spared the life of a man who was on it at the time, Frank Hadsell wrote that "[Jimmy] Joyce floated under some trees . . . caught a limb, drew himself up, and a little later a boatman found him comfortably perched, smoking a cigar." (Avon Collection.)

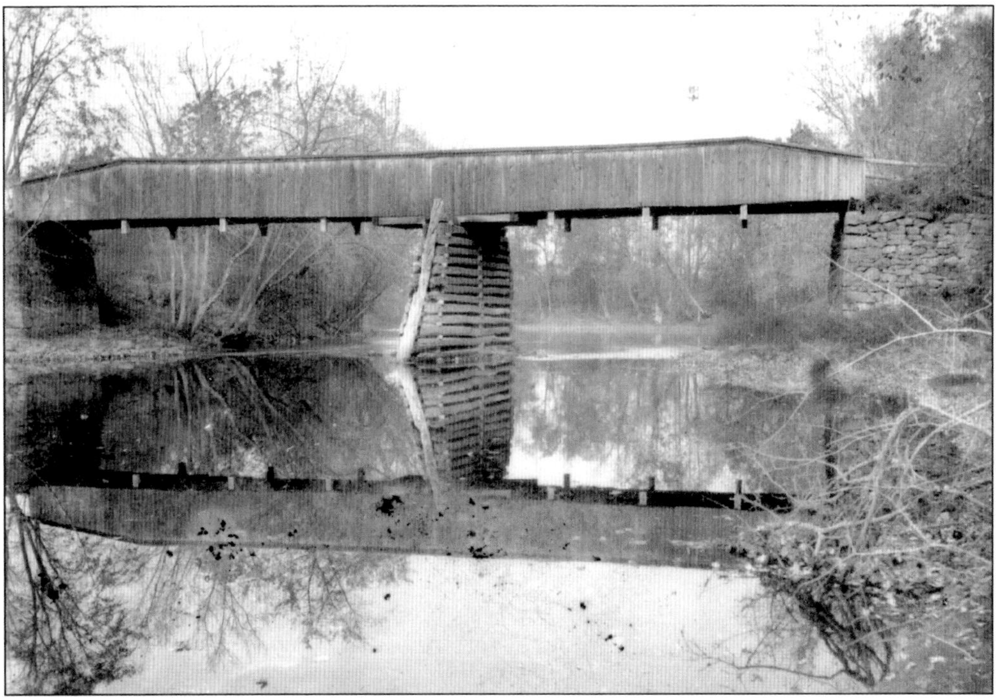

"CIDER BROOK BRIDGE, OCTOBER 15, 1899." The bridge was built in 1883 for $1,400. Avon struggled to maintain its bridges, ravaged by floods, ice, and time. Rev. Rufus Hawley wrote in 1797 of visiting Captain Norman, "hurt by the falling of Nod Bridge which all broke down . . . . The bridge was new & just finished." In January 1798, Hawley "spent most of the day at the bridge, with others, clearing away the ice." (Clinton Hadsell photograph, Avon Collection, courtesy of Doris Miller.)

Nine

SPARE TIME PLEASURES

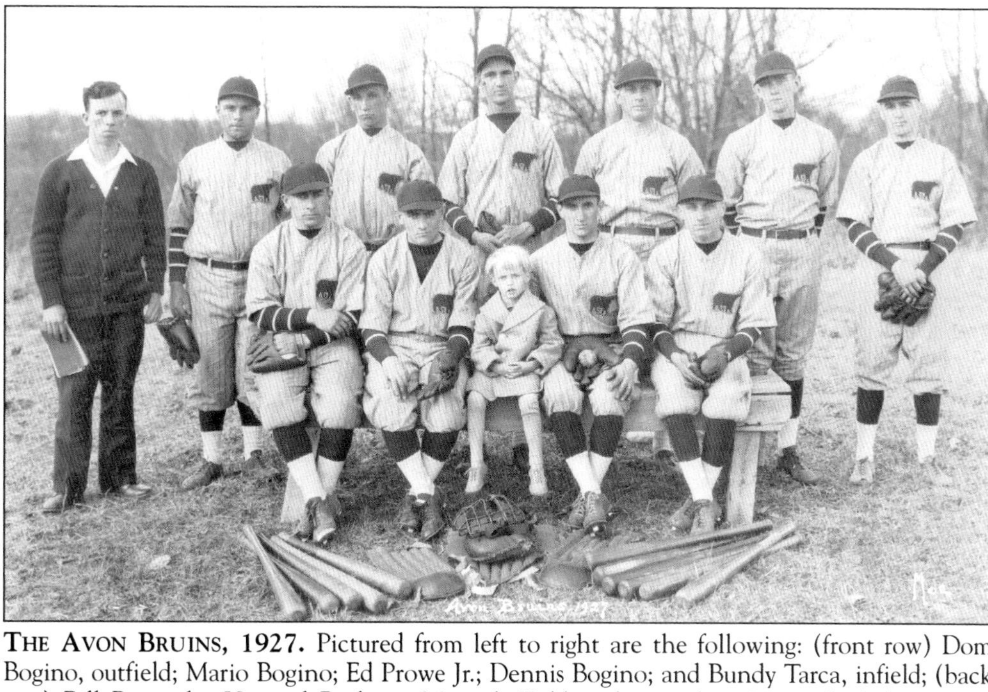

THE AVON BRUINS, 1927. Pictured from left to right are the following: (front row) Dom Bogino, outfield; Mario Bogino; Ed Prowe Jr.; Dennis Bogino; and Bundy Tarca, infield; (back row) Bill Borawski; Howard Rodgers; Maneck Kulikowski, catcher; Howard Plude, infield; Arnold Miller; Ernest Plude, pitcher; and Ed Prowe. In 1904, Franklin Sperry gave permission to use his land near his sawmill and cider mill for a ball park. Avon's first uniformed team was formed the following year. Sperry died in 1934, and bequeathed the park to the town. Sperry Park, with an additional 2 acres donated by the Ensign-Bickford Company, was dedicated that year. (Avon Collection.)

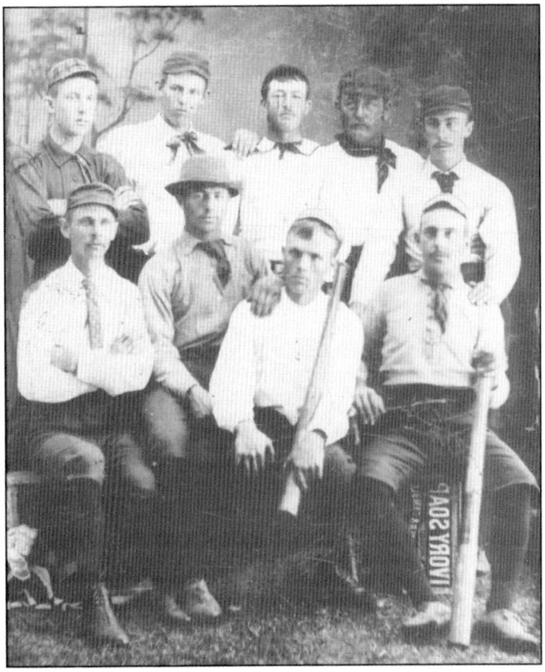

BASEBALL, C. 1890. This tintype shows the team, wearing neckties and knee-length pants, sitting on wooden boxes, one of which reads, "Ivory Soap, Proctor & Gamble." The group presumably includes men from Avon and perhaps from surrounding towns. Observers of American life at this time called baseball the "national pastime." The National League of Professional Ball Clubs had been formed in 1876. (Anthony O'Neill Collection.)

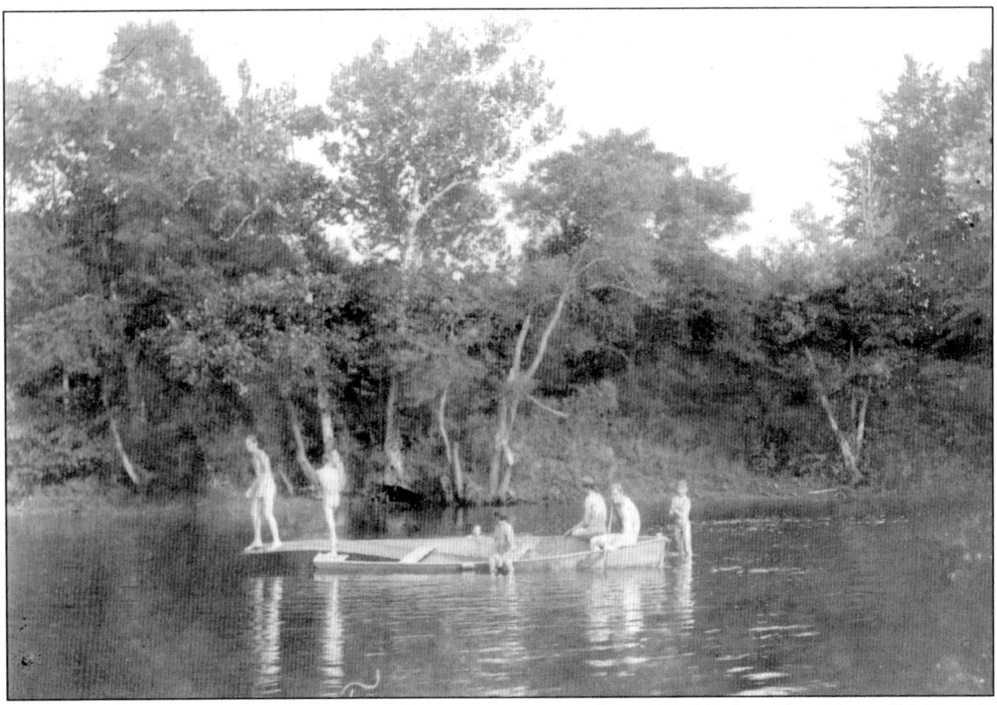

"BOYS IN SWIMMING FARMINGTON RIVER, AUGUST 26, 1900." Joseph Alsop (1910–89) wrote of his childhood that "Avon had a particularly fine men's swimming hole about a hundred yards above the bridge across the river, where all went in naked without regard to age . . . . Throughout the hot weather . . . most of the male population went to the swimming hole every fine evening when the day's work was done . . . . There might be three score of them on a good evening." (Clinton Hadsell photograph, Avon Collection, courtesy of Doris Miller.)

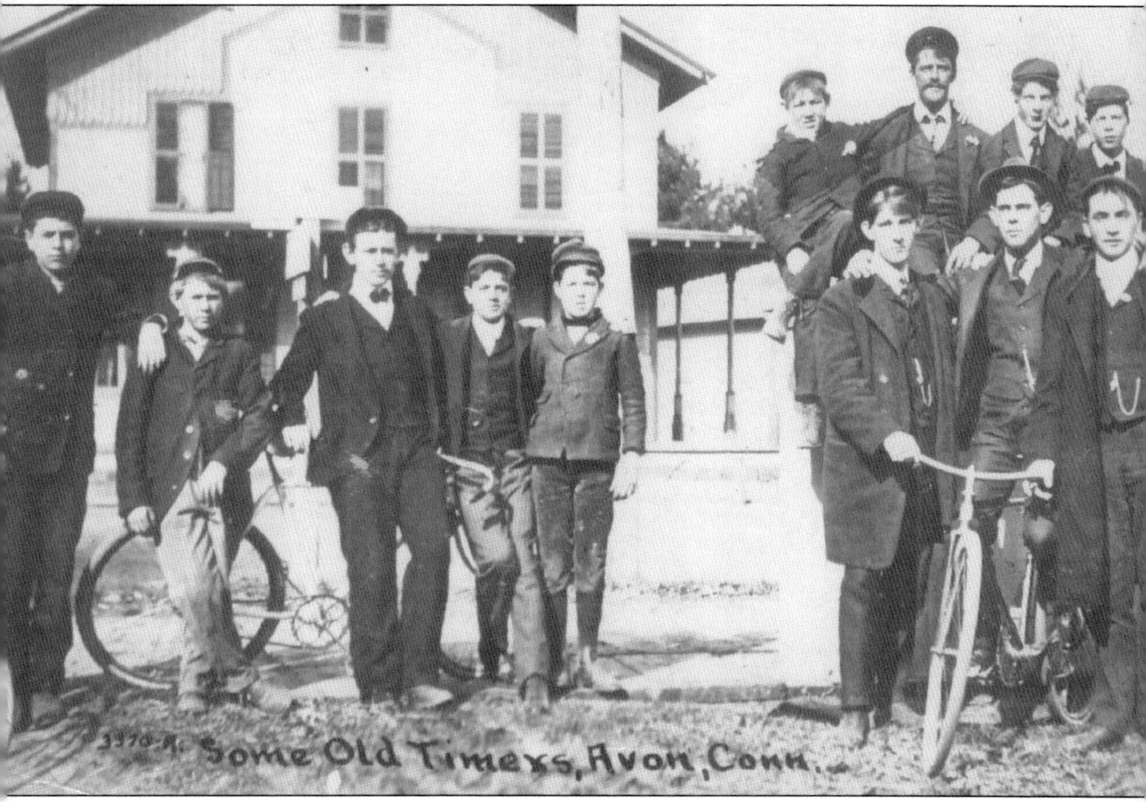

"BOYS ON SCALES, MAY 1903." This was one of many Avon views that Frank Hadsell made into a postcard to sell at his store. Some of the men shown here, in front of the former Baptist church building, worked for the Climax Fuse Company. Pictured fourth and fifth from the left are Horace Morran and John H. O'Neill. Pictured at the far right, with the watch fob, is Leon Edgerton. (Clinton Hadsell photograph, Anthony O'Neill Collection.)

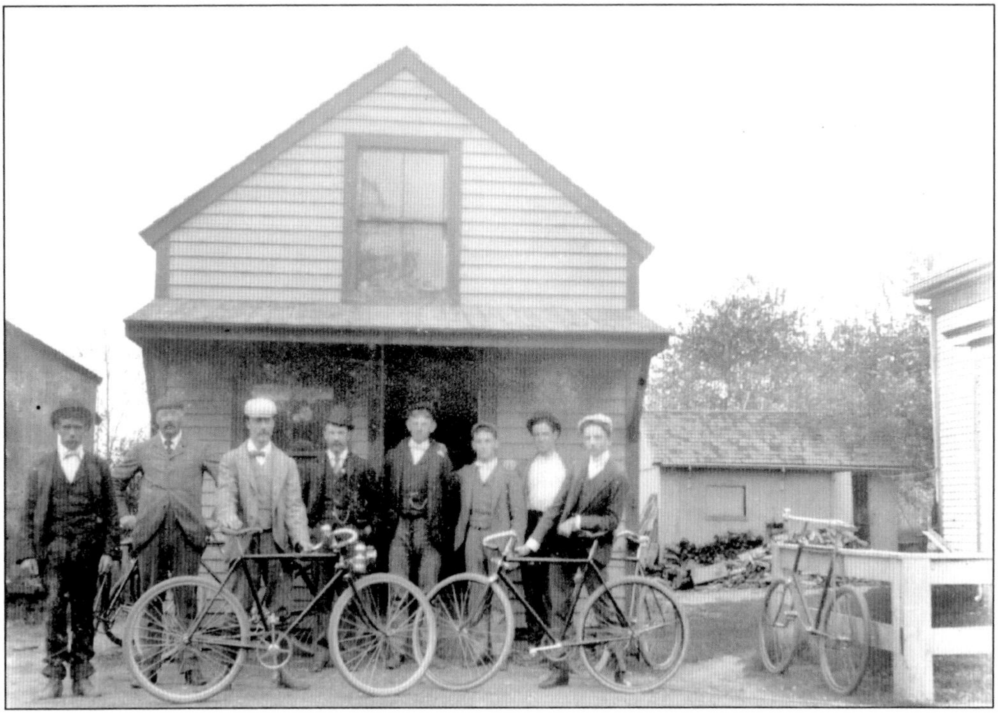

"NEWS OFFICE WITH BOYS, MAY 20, 1900." Flanked by Frank Hadsell's home on the right and a woodpile to the rear, a crowd with bicycles gathers outside Hadsell's variety shop. Today the building is the barbershop at 12 East Main Street. In 1898, Hadsell wrote about his new bicycle, "There was a riding school in Hartford . . . and I took my first lesson . . . . I was continually buying something for it—bell, saddle, handle oiler." (Clinton Hadsell photograph, Avon Collection, Courtesy of Seth Stewart.)

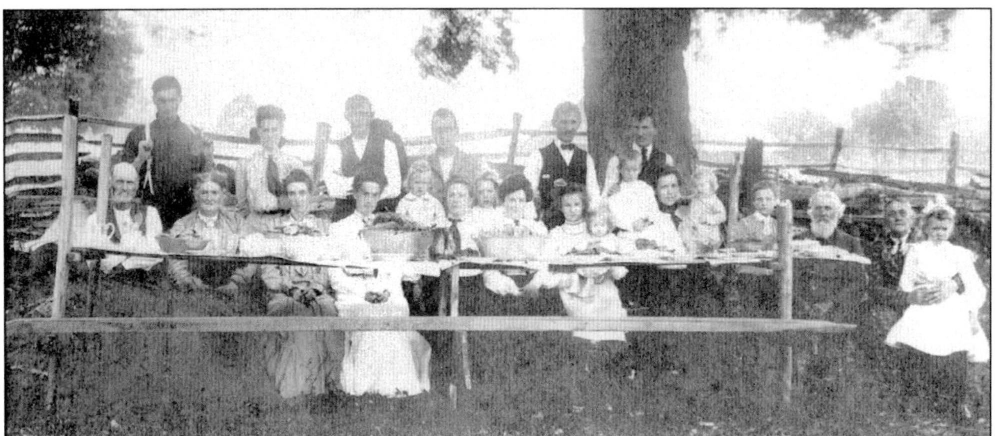

AN OYSTER BAKE, 1905. Members of the Stuart S. Bishop family and others enjoy an oyster bake outside the Bishop home at 56 Talcott Notch Road. Pictured from left to right are the following: (front row) Stuart Bishop (1851–1932), his wife, Frances Bishop (1846–1931), Florence Bishop, Stella Bishop, Millie LeGeyt with children Ralph and Frances LeGeyt, Bennet family members, and Mr. and Mrs. Burt holding Winifred Burt; (back row) Frank L. Bishop, Viola Bishop, Fred Burt, hired hand George Swarte, and the Bennet brothers. (The Cider Brook Miller & Bishop Families' Collection.)

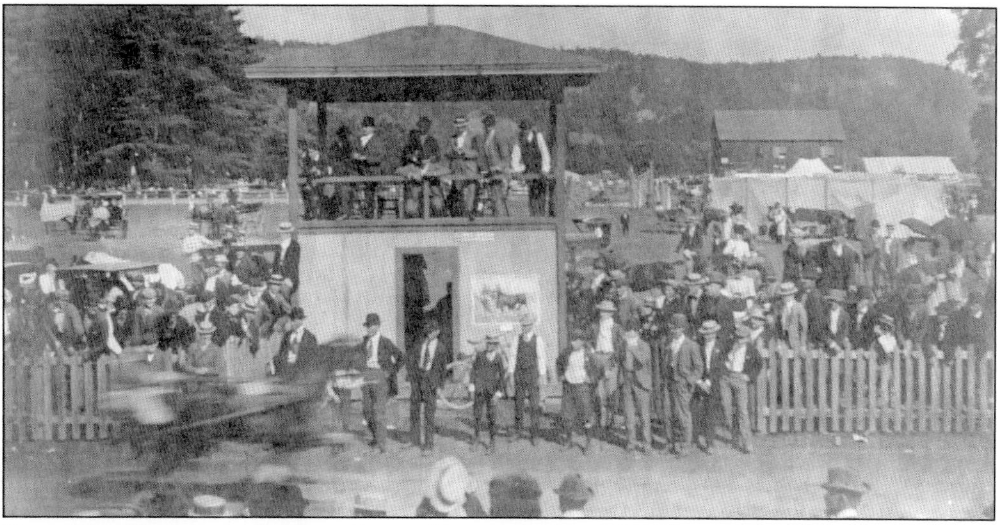

TROTTING RACES AT CHERRY PARK, EARLY 1900S. The Farmington Valley Agricultural Corporation, organized in 1882, operated the fair from 1883 to 1911. Schools closed and attendance at the fair reached 10,000. The fair included a grandstand, animal and farm produce displays, oxen pulls, balloon ascensions, and a race track for trotting, pacing, and bicycle races. The corporation stopped operating this particular fair in 1911 because it was impossible "to keep up a fair so far from a railroad and trolley." (Avon Collection.)

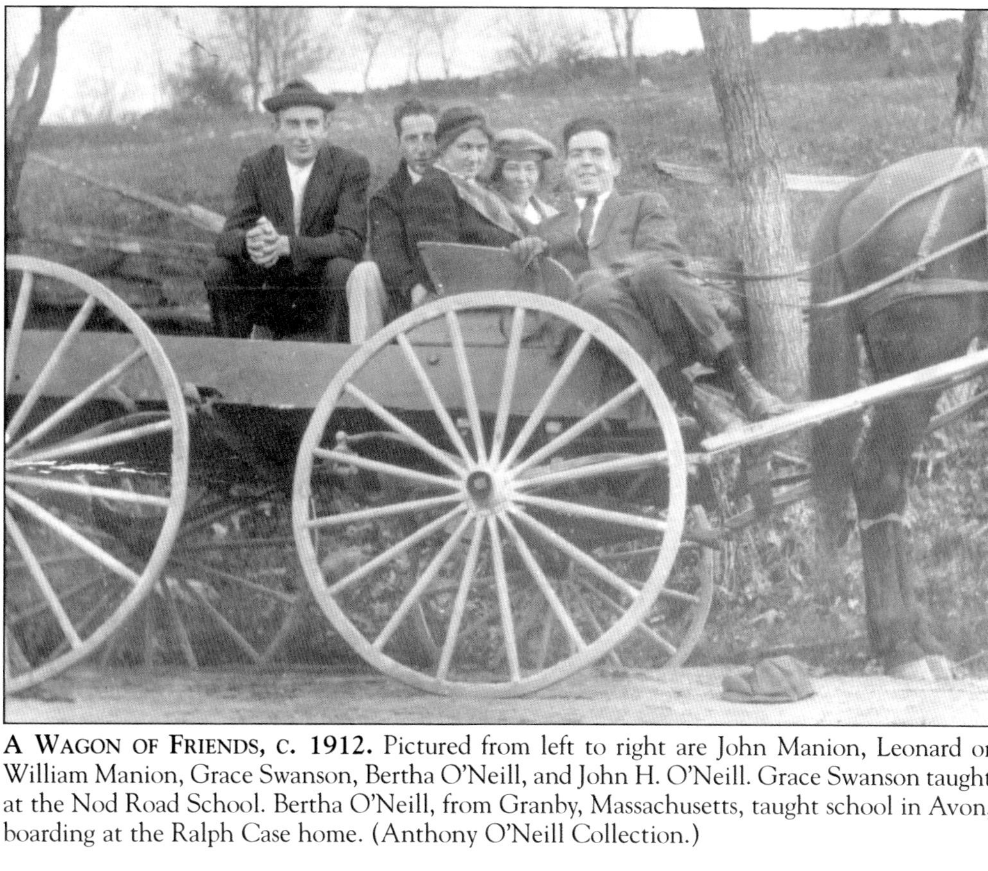

A WAGON OF FRIENDS, C. 1912. Pictured from left to right are John Manion, Leonard or William Manion, Grace Swanson, Bertha O'Neill, and John H. O'Neill. Grace Swanson taught at the Nod Road School. Bertha O'Neill, from Granby, Massachusetts, taught school in Avon, boarding at the Ralph Case home. (Anthony O'Neill Collection.)

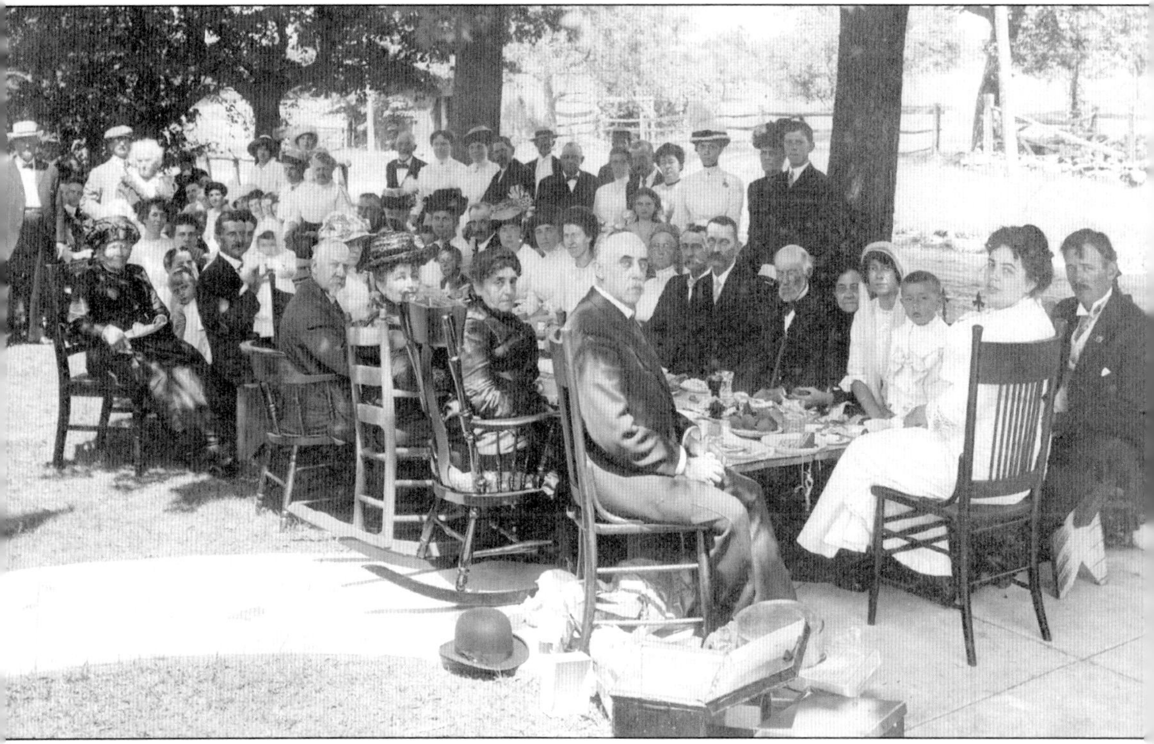

The Miller Reunion, 1913. The Miller farm still stands at 331 Waterville Road. The ladies seated in the clearly visible chairs at the left side of the table are, from left to right, Ida Miller Hodge, Eugenia Curtiss Mills, and Ella Mills. To Ella Mills's right is William Mills. Mrs. Robert Lane is at the head of the table, beside her husband. To Robert Lane's right are Mills Lane, Emily Mills, Fanny Mills, and Washburn Mills. (Anthony O'Neill Collection.)

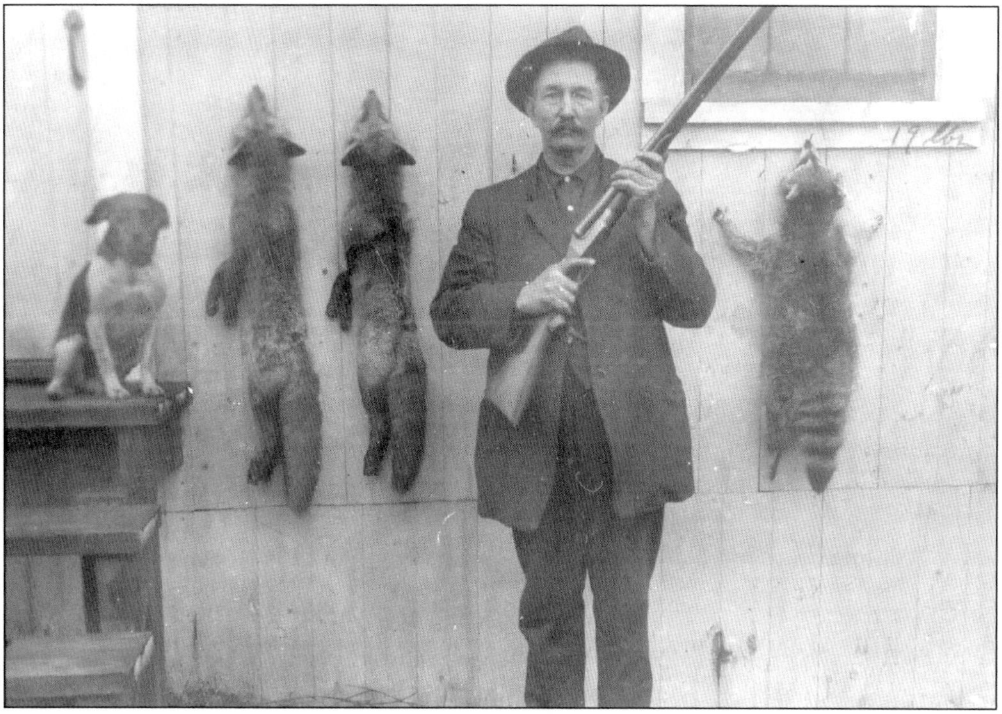

LEWIS J. GARRETT, DECEMBER 23, 1913. Lewis Garrett poses with two foxes, one 19-pound raccoon, and a dog. Garrett may have belonged to the Avon Fish and Game Club, founded in 1908, which leased fishing and hunting properties in or near Avon for use by members. (Clinton Hadsell photograph, Anthony O'Neill Collection.)

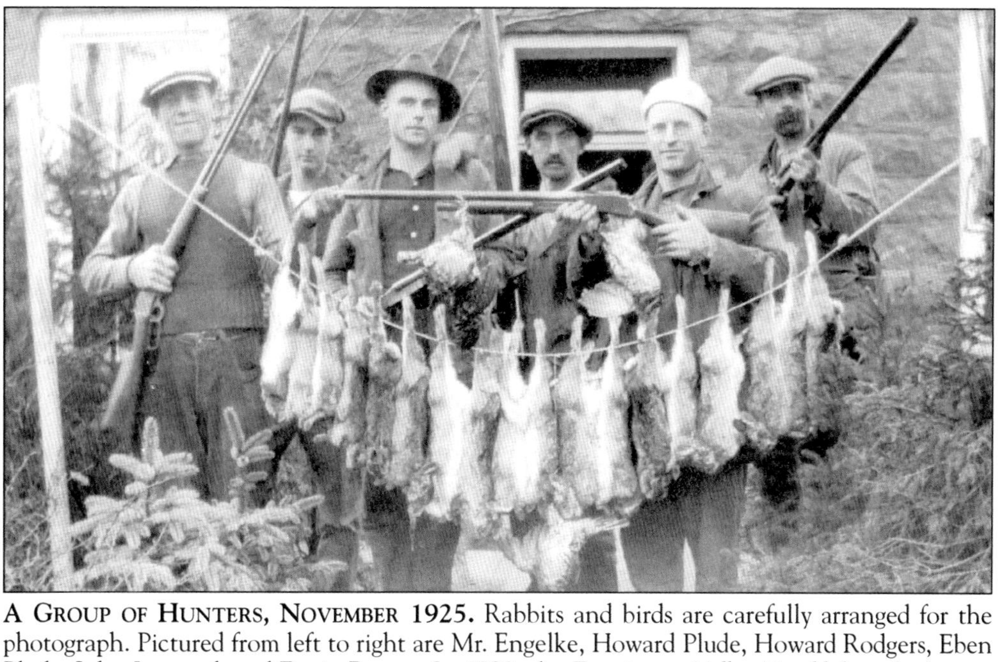

A GROUP OF HUNTERS, NOVEMBER 1925. Rabbits and birds are carefully arranged for the photograph. Pictured from left to right are Mr. Engelke, Howard Plude, Howard Rodgers, Eben Plude, John Leonard, and Erwin Rogers. In 1932, the *Farmington Valley Herald* described some of the group as "sportsmen of note." (Barbara Plude Thomas Collection.)

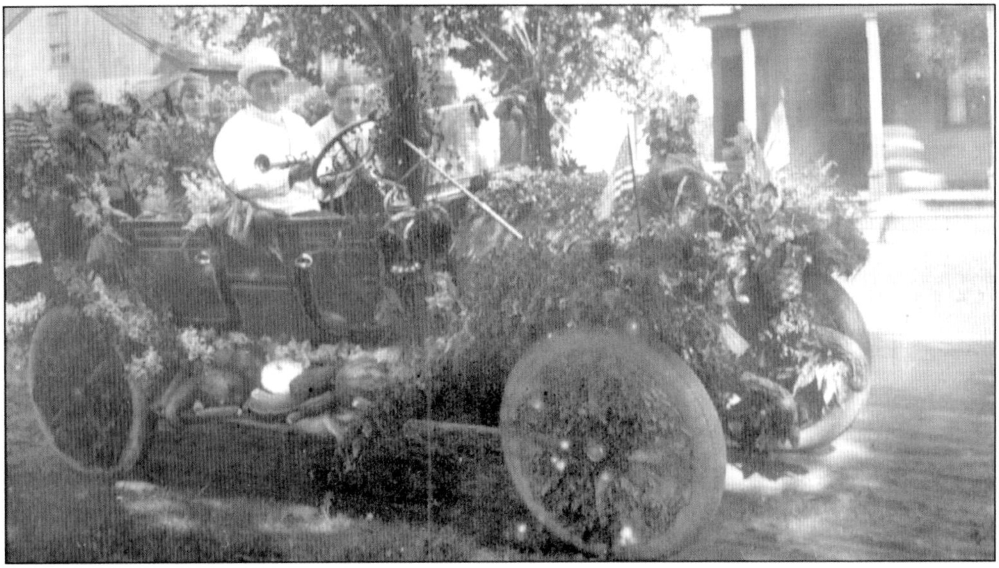

"EDDIE'S CAR TRIMMED FOR FAIR SEPT. 1914." Sherman Eddy poses in his car, decorated with agricultural products and American flags. Eddy was an accomplished gardener and town booster. In the early 1900s, he held the annual Avon Fish and Game Club dinner at his home, Tow Path Lodge on Old Farms Road. Members dined on oysters, venison, bear stew, and coon pie. (Clinton Hadsell photograph, Avon Collection, courtesy of Doris Miller.)

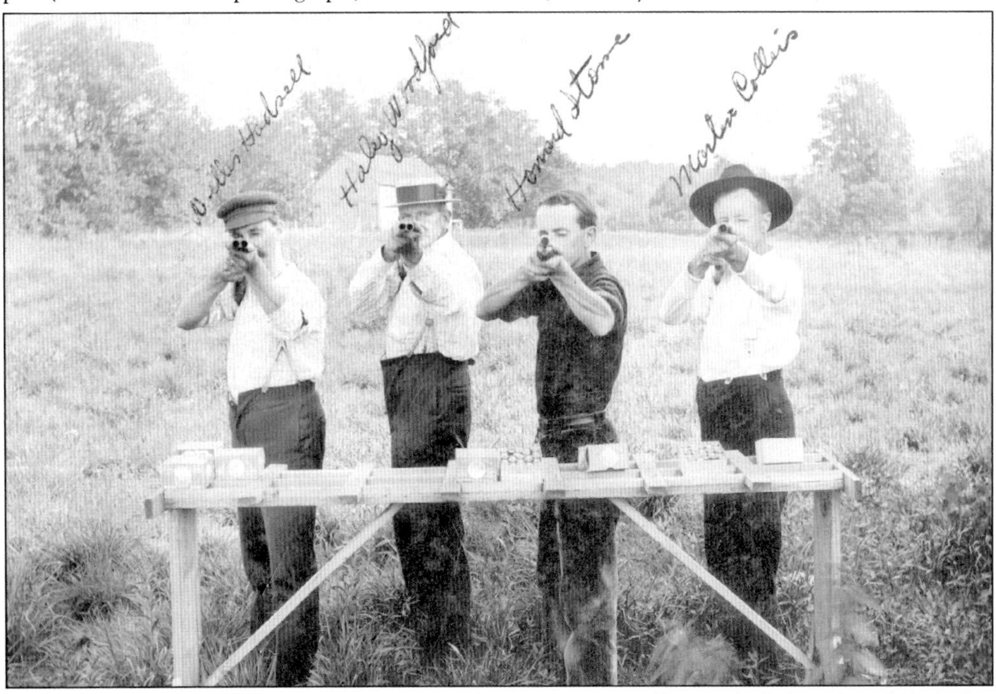

THE RIFLE CLUB, C. 1920. Pictured from left to right are Willys Hadsell (1875–1953), Haley Woodford (1855–1936), Howard Stone, and Martin Collins. Hadsell was a shipping clerk at the Ensign-Bickford Company. Woodford was a farmer and, as noted in *The Lure of the Litchfield Hills*, "a live wire. He kept Avon people guessing as to what he was going to do next." (Avon Collection.)

VISITING, c. 1940. Walter and Celia Legutko and their daughter Betty Legutko visit the Larry Piwnicki family at 237 Huckleberry Hill Road. A Woody station wagon is at the rear. (Regina Pilitowski Collection.)

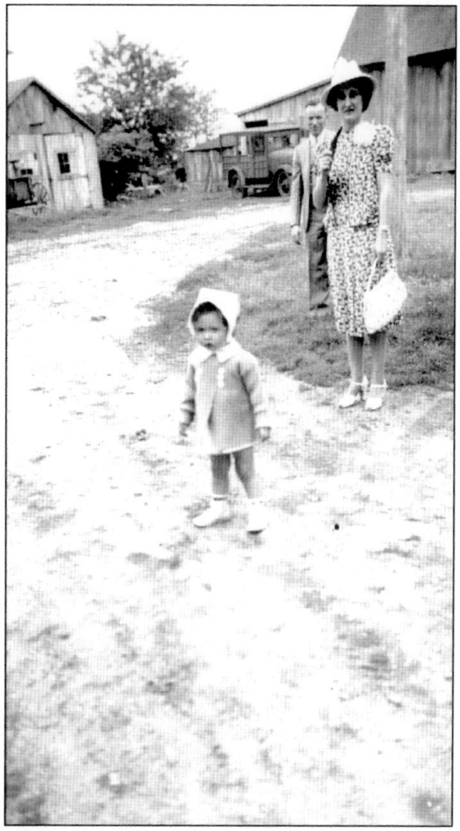

THE OLD TOWN GRILL, 1947. Veterans gather after a VFW meeting at 5 East Main Street. To the rear is the bandstand for Saturday night dances. The bar, located in an adjacent room, was restricted to men. Pictured clockwise from the front are Ted Stafford, John Gaioni, Abbot Rhodes, Clayton Bergeron, Harold Bonesio, Doris Bonesio, Augusta Robinson, and John Alsop. (Anthony O'Neill Collection.)

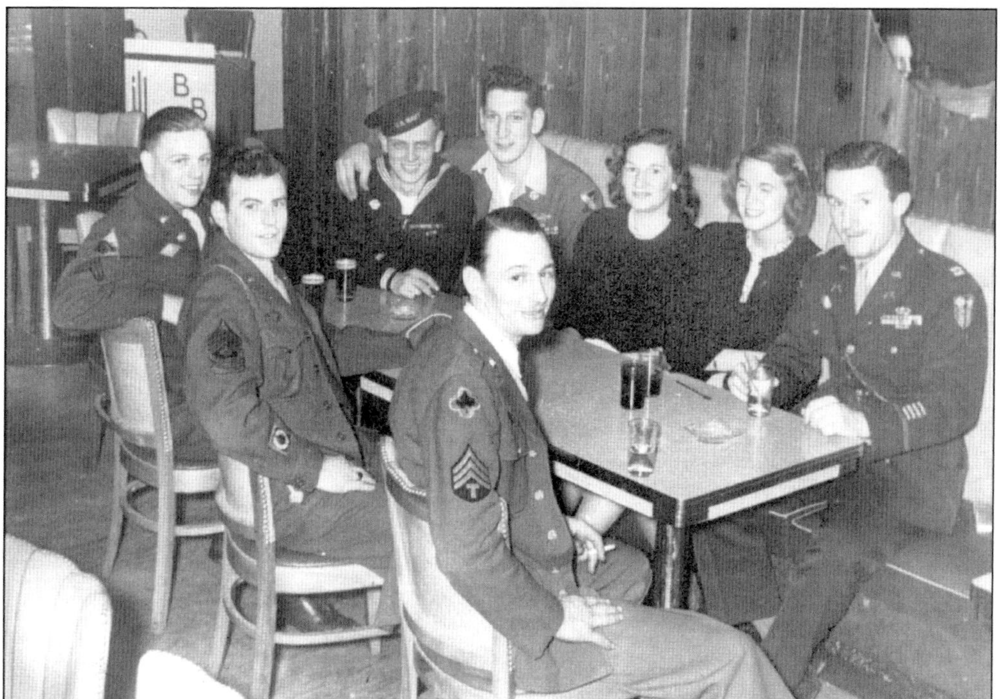

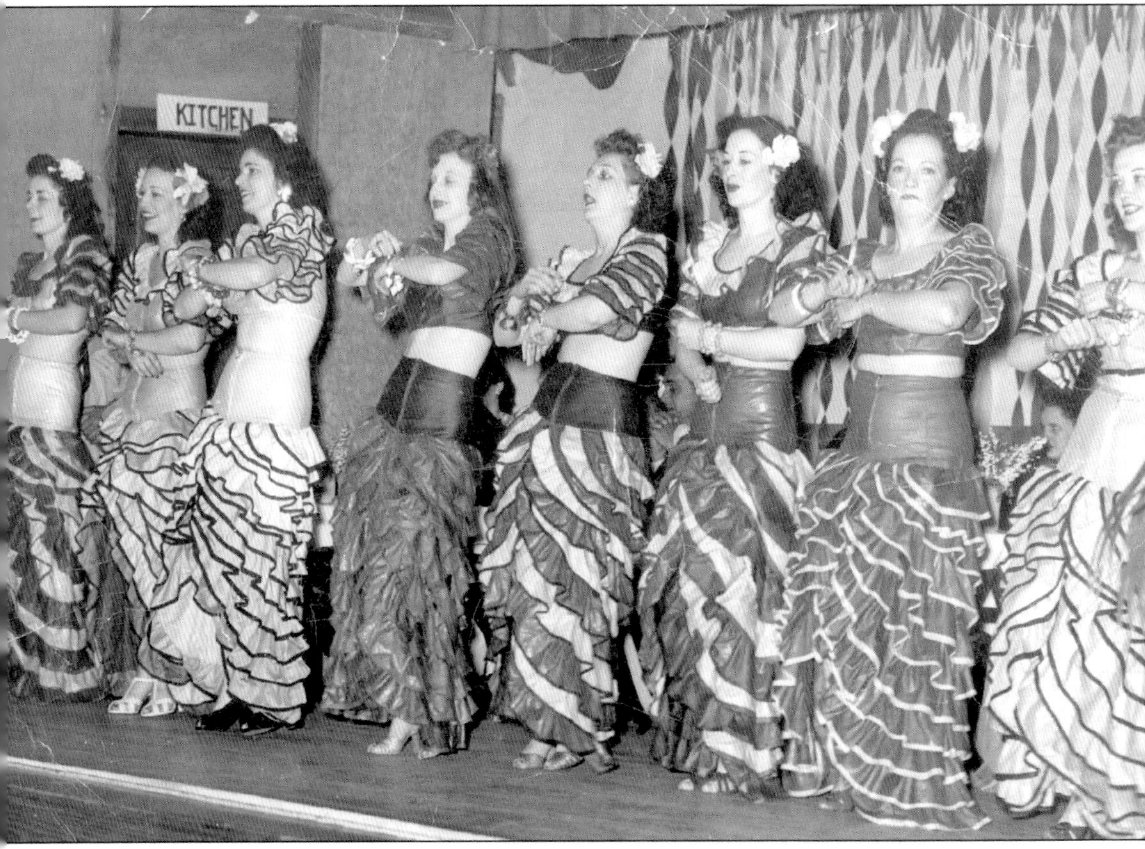

SECRET LAKE SHOW TIME, 1940S. Marion Pease taught dancing and produced many of the Secret Lake shows. Pictured from left to right are Bobbie Stoner, Bobbie Johnson, four unidentified dancers, Doris Coreau, and Irene LaChance. (Avon Collection.)

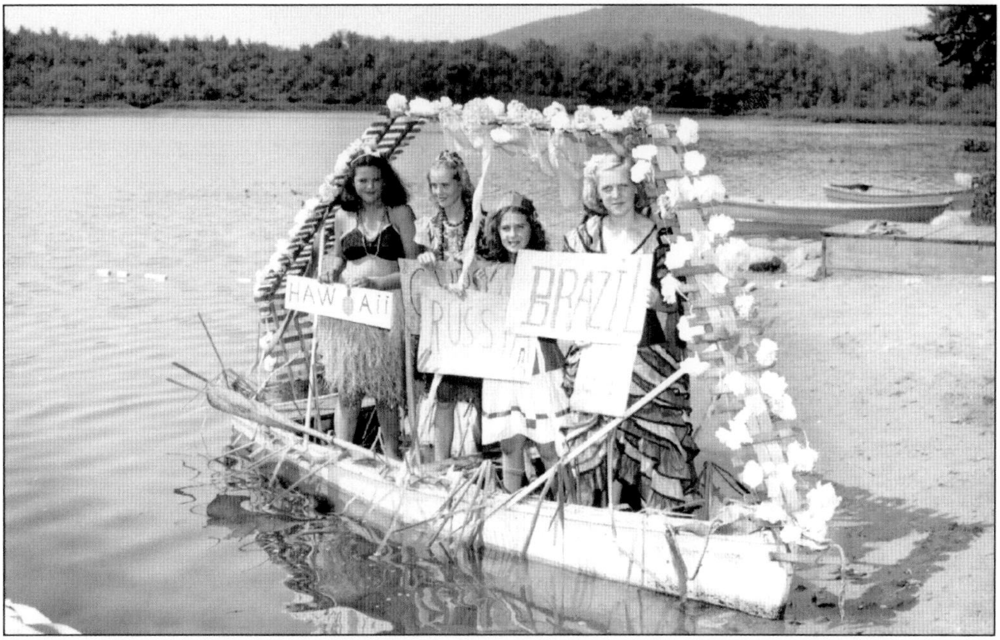

SECRET LAKE, 1940S. Paper garlands decorate a boat of costumed Secret Lake girls. Second from the left is Jackie Frechette. In 1928, developers renamed Cherry Pond, calling it Secret Lake and selling cottages and campsites. Advertisements read, "being only an hour's drive from Hartford, the business man can give his family the benefits of a summer in the country, and still be within reach of his office." (Avon Collection.)

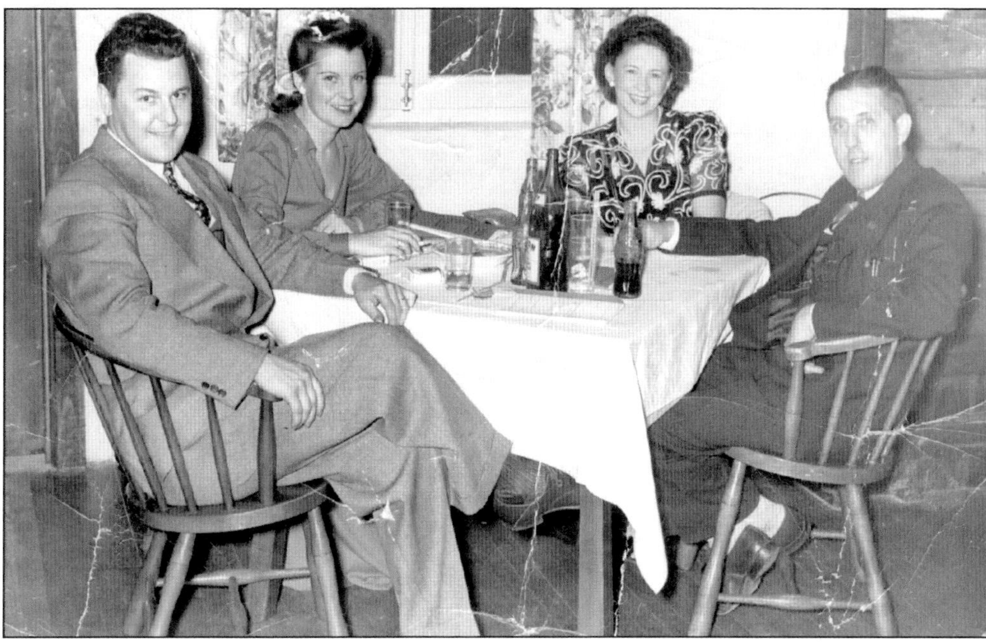

SECRET LAKE, 1940S. The Secret Lake Association was incorporated in 1931; after World War II, many lake cottages were converted to year-round homes. Residents took part in family activities, including suppers and card playing. Pictured from left to right are George and Marion Pease, and Mary and Dick Larson. (Avon Collection.)

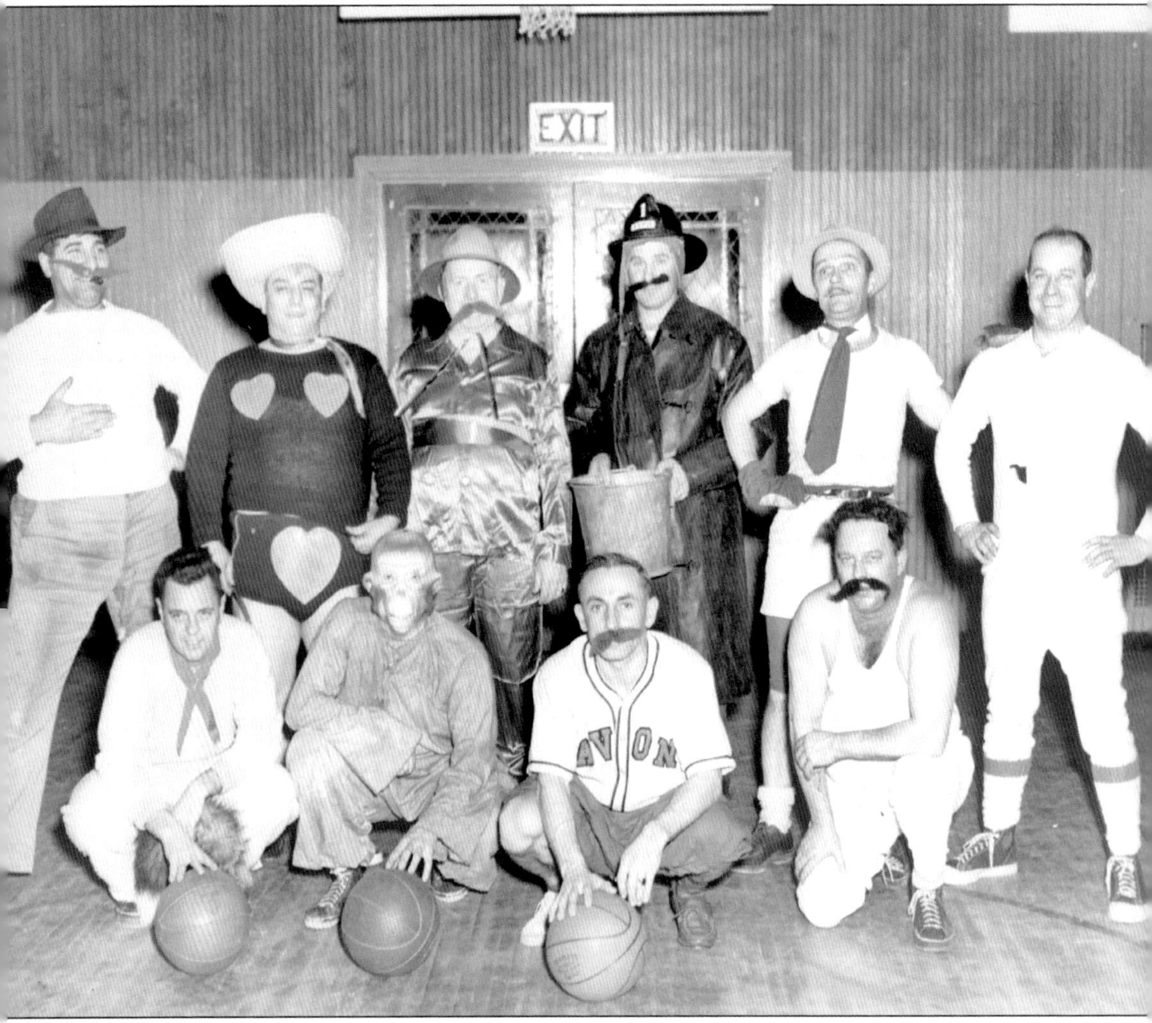

BASKETBALL, 1950. After Avon's "old-timers" played Simsbury to benefit the March of Dimes, the *Farmington Valley Herald* wrote that Avon was "not playing in the strictest sense of the word," and that Simsbury was "all stars, or seeing same." Pictured from left to right are the following: (front row) Ed Donohue, Albert Rubenstahl, Dominick Bogino, and Wilbur Plude; (back row) William Gold, Primo Viti, Ted Manion, George Gold, Ben Deming, and Rene Ruez. (Marvin Deming photograph, Anthony O'Neill Collection.)